The War for Palestine
Rewriting the History of 1948

The 1948 Palestine War was one of the most momentous events in the history of the contemporary Middle East. It was the last and most dramatic phase in the struggle for Palestine and it ended in triumph and tragedy: triumph for the Israelis and tragedy for the Arabs. The subsequent history of the Middle East was punctuated by six Arab–Israeli wars, although none of them had such far-reaching consequences and none generated so much controversy.

Israelis call the 1948 War "The War of Independence", while the Arabs call it *al-Nakba* or "the disaster." The conventional Israeli version portrays 1948 as an unequal struggle between a Jewish David and an Arab Goliath, as a desperate, heroic and ultimately successful battle for survival against overwhelming odds. In this version, all the surrounding Arab states sent their armies into Palestine to strangle the Jewish state at birth, and the Palestinians left the country on orders from their own leaders and in the expectation of a triumphal return. Since the late 1980s, however, a group of "new historians" or revisionist Israeli historians have challenged many of the claims surrounding the birth of the state of Israel and the first Arab–Israeli war.

The present volume was conceived as a contribution to the ongoing debate about 1948. It re-examines the role of all the participants in the Palestine War on the basis of archival sources where they exist, contemporary reports, memoirs, and other primary sources. The collection brings together leading Israeli new historians with prominent Arab and Western scholars of the Middle East who revisit 1948 from the perspective of the countries involved in the war. The result is a volume which is rich in new material and new insights and which enhances considerably our understanding of the historical roots of the Arab–Israeli conflict.

Eugene L. Rogan is University Lecturer in the Modern History of the Middle East at the University of Oxford and Fellow of St Antony's College, Oxford. His publications include *Frontiers of the State in the Late Ottoman Empire* (1999). Avi Shlaim is Professor of International Relations, University of Oxford, and Fellow of St Antony's College, Oxford. His publications include *War and Peace in the Middle East* (1995) and *The Iron Wall: Israel and the Arab World* (2000).

Cambridge Middle East Studies 15

Editorial Board
Charles Tripp (general editor)

Julia A. Clancy-Smith   Israel Gershoni   Roger Owen
Yezid Sayigh   Judith E. Tucker

Cambridge Middle East Studies has been established to publish books on the nineteenth- and twentieth-century Middle East and North Africa. The aim of the series is to provide new and original interpretations of aspects of Middle Eastern societies and their histories. To achieve disciplinary diversity, books will be solicited from authors writing in a wide range of fields including history, sociology, anthropology, political science and political economy. The emphasis will be on producing books offering an original approach along theoretical and empirical lines. The series is intended for students and academics, but the more accessible and wide-ranging studies will also appeal to the interested general reader.

A list of books in the series can be found after the index

The War for Palestine

Rewriting the History of 1948

Edited by

Eugene L. Rogan
University of Oxford

and

Avi Shlaim
University of Oxford

CAMBRIDGE
UNIVERSITY PRESS

PUBLISHED BY THE PRESS SYNDICATE OF THE UNIVERSITY OF CAMBRIDGE
The Pitt Building, Trumpington Street, Cambridge, United Kingdom

CAMBRIDGE UNIVERSITY PRESS
The Edinburgh Building, Cambridge CB2 2RU, UK
40 West 20th Street, New York, NY 10011-4211, USA
10 Stamford Road, Oakleigh, VIC 3166, Australia
Ruiz de Alarcón 13, 28014 Madrid, Spain
Dock House, The Waterfront, Cape Town 8001, South Africa

http://www.cambridge.org

First published 2001
Reprinted 2001 (twice)

Printed in the United Kingdom at the University Press, Cambridge

Typeface 10/12pt Plantin   *System* 3b2   [CE]

A catalogue record for this book is available from the British Library

ISBN 0 521 79139 1 hardback
ISBN 0 521 79476 5 paperback

Contents

Contributors

FAWAZ A. GERGES holds the Christian A. Johnson Chair in international affairs and Middle East Studies at Sarah Lawrence College, New York.

RASHID KHALIDI is Professor of History and Director of the Center for International Studies at the University of Chicago.

JOSHUA LANDIS is Assistant Professor of Middle East History at the University of Oklahoma.

BENNY MORRIS is Associate Professor of Middle East History at the Ben-Gurion University of the Negev.

LAILA PARSONS is Associate Director of the Center for Middle Eastern Studies and lectures in the history of the Middle East at Harvard University.

EUGENE ROGAN is a Fellow of St Antony's College and lectures in the modern history of the Middle East at the University of Oxford.

EDWARD W. SAID is University Professor at Columbia University.

AVI SHLAIM is a Fellow of St Antony's College and Professor of International Relations at the University of Oxford.

CHARLES TRIPP is Senior Lecturer in the Politics of the Middle East at the School of Oriental and African Studies, University of London.

Chronology

29 November 1947	United Nations adopts Palestine partition resolution
30 November 1947	Outbreak of civil war in Palestine
10 March 1948	Plan D adopted by the Haganah for the capture of Arab villages, neighborhoods and towns
19 March 1948	US proposes suspension of partition plan and a trusteeship for Palestine
3–15 April 1948	Operation Nahshon: Jewish military offensive to open the road to Jerusalem
8 April 1948	Abd al-Qadir al-Husayni killed in the battle for Kastel
9 April 1948	The massacre of Deir Yassin
18 April 1948	Tiberias captured by the Haganah
22 April 1948	Haifa captured by Haganah
10 May 1948	Golda Meir meets King ʿAbdullah in Amman
11 May 1948	Safad captured by the Haganah
13 May 1948	Gush Etzion captured by the Arab Legion
13 May 1948	Jaffa surrenders to the Jewish forces
14 May 1948	Termination of the British Mandate over Palestine
15 May 1948	Proclamation of the State of Israel
15 May 1948	Armies of Iraq, Syria, Lebanon, Transjordan and Egypt enter Palestine
20 May 1948	UN appoints Count Folke Bernadotte as mediator for Palestine
28 May 1948	Jewish Quarter in the Old City of Jerusalem falls to Arab Legion
11 June 1948	Four-week truce begins
8 July 1948	Arabs resume fighting; Israel gains on all fronts
11–12 July 1948	IDF captures Lydda and Ramla
18 July 1948	Second truce begins

6 September 1948	Arab League decision to create the All-Palestine Government with a seat in Gaza
17 September 1948	Count Bernadotte assassinated by the Stern Gang; Dr. Ralph Bunche appointed acting mediator
20 September 1948	Bernadotte plan published by the UN
15 October 1948	Israel launches an offensive against the Egyptian army in the Negev
29–31 October 1948	Operation Hiram: IDF expels Arab Liberation Army from the Galilee and crosses the border into Lebanon
16 November 1948	UN Security Council calls for armistice talks
11 December 1948	UN established Palestine Conciliation Commission and calls for repatriation or resettlement of refugees
22 December 1948	Israel launches a second offensive; Egyptian forces driven beyond mandatory borders but retain the Gaza Strip
7 January 1949	End of hostilities
13 January 1949	Israeli and Egyptian delegations meet in Rhodes for armistice talks, chaired by Dr. Bunche
24 February 1949	Israel and Egypt sign Armistice Agreement
23 March 1949	Israel and Lebanon sign Armistice Agreement
3 April 1949	Israel and Transjordan sign Armistice Agreement
20 July 1949	Israel and Syria sign Armistice Agreement

Abbreviations

AACOI	Anglo-American Commission of Inquiry
ALA	Arab Liberation Army
BG Archive	Ben-Gurion Archives, Sede Boker, Israel
CZA	Central Zionist Archives, Jerusalem, Israel
FRUS	*Foreign Relations of the United States*
ICP	Iraqi Communist Party
IDF	Israel Defense Forces
IDFA	Israel Defense Forces Archive, Givatayim, Israel
IEF	Iraqi Expeditionary Force
IJMES	*International Journal of Middle East Studies*
ISA	Israel State Archives, Jerusalem, Israel
ISA, FM	Israel State Archives, Foreign Ministry Papers
IZL	*Irgun Zvai Leumi* or simply "Irgun," lit. National Military Organization
JAE	Jewish Agency Executive
JNF	Jewish National Fund
LHI	*Lohamei Herut Yisrael* or simply "Stern Gang," lit. Freedom Fighters of Israel
PRO	Public Records Office, Kew, UK
PRO, FO	Public Records Office, Foreign Office Papers
USNA	United States National Archives, Suitland MD and Washington DC

Map 1 Mandate Palestine
Source: Avi Shlaim, *Collusion across the Jordan: King Abdullah, the Zionist Movement and the Partition of Palestine* (Oxford: Oxford University Press, 1988), frontispiece

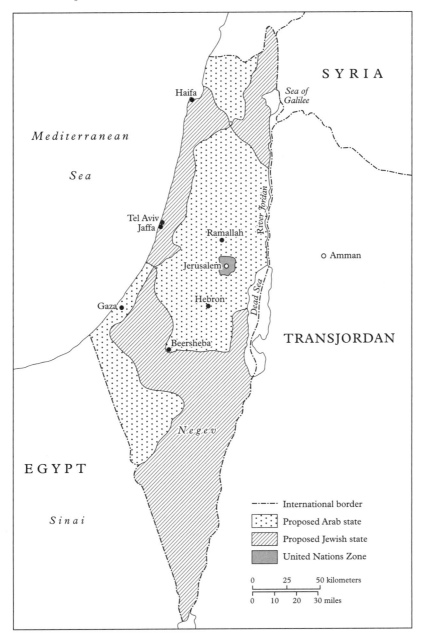

Map 2 The United Nations Partition Plan, 1947
Source: Avi Shlaim, *Collusion across the Jordan: King Abdullah, the Zionist Movement and the Partition of Palestine* (Oxford: Oxford University Press, 1988), p. 118

Invasion Plan   Actual Invasion

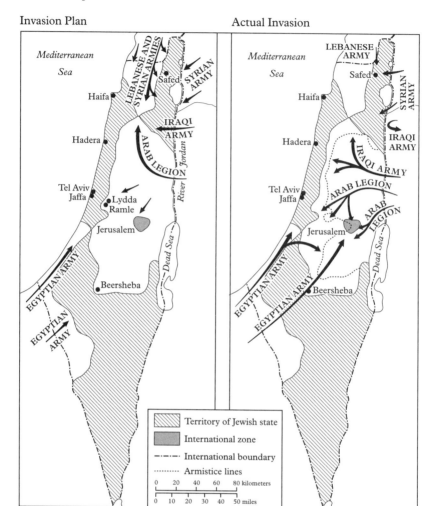

Map 3 The Arab League invasion plan compared with the actual invasion
Source: Simha Flapan, *Zionism and the Palestinians* (London: Croom Helm, 1979), p. 322

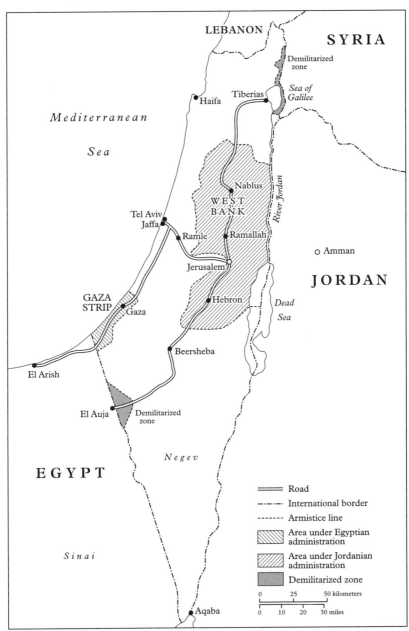

Map 4 Israel following the Arab–Israeli armistices, 1949
Source: Avi Shlaim, *Collusion across the Jordan: King Abdullah, the Zionist Movement and the Partition of Palestine* (Oxford: Oxford University Press, 1988), p. 429

Introduction

The Palestine War lasted less than twenty months, from the United Nations resolution recommending the partition of Palestine in November 1947 to the final armistice agreement signed between Israel and Syria in July 1949. Those twenty months transformed the political landscape of the Middle East forever. Indeed, 1948 may be taken as a defining moment for the region as a whole. Arab Palestine was destroyed and the new state of Israel established. Egypt, Syria and Lebanon suffered outright defeat, Iraq held its lines, and Transjordan won at best a pyrrhic victory. Arab public opinion, unprepared for defeat, let alone a defeat of this magnitude, lost faith in its politicians. Within three years of the end of the Palestine War, the prime ministers of Egypt and Lebanon and the king of Jordan had been assassinated, and the president of Syria and the king of Egypt overthrown by military coups. No event has marked Arab politics in the second half of the twentieth century more profoundly. The Arab–Israeli wars, the Cold War in the Middle East, the rise of the Palestinian armed struggle and the politics of peace making in all of their complexity are a direct consequence of the Palestine War.

The significance of the Palestine War also lies in the fact that it was the first challenge to face the newly independent states of the Middle East. In 1948, the Middle East was only just emerging from colonial rule. Though Israel was the newest state in the region when it declared independence on 15 May 1948, its neighbors were hardly much older. Egypt was still bound to Britain in a semi-colonial relationship by the treaty of 1936. Transjordan's 1946 treaty gave Britain such extensive control over the state's military and finances that the international community would not recognize its "independence" and the terms of the treaty had to be renegotiated in January 1948. Lebanon and Syria had been given their independence from France in 1943 and 1946. Even Iraq, which had enjoyed international recognition as an independent state in the interwar years, entered secret negotiations with Britain in 1947 to renegotiate the 1930 treaty to reduce the British

1

military presence in "independent" Iraq. In the Arab world, the nationalist leaders who oversaw the transition to independence fell at their first hurdle when they failed to live up to their rhetoric and save Palestine from the Zionist threat. This failure provoked a crisis of legitimacy in nearly all the Arab states.

History plays a fundamental role in state formation, in legitimizing the origins of the state and its political system, in the Middle East as elsewhere. Governments in the region enjoy many direct and indirect powers over the writing of history. Elementary and secondary school texts in history are the preserve of the state. Most universities in the Middle East are state-run and their faculty members are state employees. National historical associations and government printing presses serve as filters to weed out unauthorized histories and to disseminate state-sanctioned truths. As promotion within the historical establishment is closely linked to adherence to the official line, historians have had little incentive to engage in critical history writing. Instead, most Arab and Israeli historians have written in an uncritically nationalist vein. In Israel, nationalist historians reflected the collective memory of the Israeli public in depicting the Palestine War as a desperate fight for survival and an almost miraculous victory. In the Arab world, histories of the Palestine War have been marked by apologetics, self-justification, onus-shifting and conspiracy theories. Both the Arab and the Israeli nationalist histories are guided more by a "quest for legitimacy" than by an honest reckoning with the past.[1]

A fabric of myths

The burden of legitimating national actions in the Palestine War, in the halls of politics as well as in the classroom, has conflated history writing and patriotism in the Middle East in what might best be termed "official history."[2] This political invention of history is common to both Israel and the Arab states, though for markedly different reasons. Arab official histories seek to advance state interests by mobilizing citizens disillusioned by the defeat of national armies and the loss of Arab Palestine, while Israeli official histories seek to reaffirm a sort of Zionist manifest destiny while diminishing responsibility for the negative consequences of the war. This practice has led a recent generation of critical scholars to view the official histories of 1948 as a fabric of myths.

Since the late 1980s, a group of Israeli scholars has led a charge on Israel's foundational myths. The new critical Israeli history was catalyzed by Israel's invasion of Lebanon in 1982, when the Likud government sought to establish historic continuity between their controversial actions in Lebanon and the actions of Israel's founding fathers in Palestine in 1948.

Significantly, in defending the actions of his government, then-Prime Minister Menahem Begin referred to the policies of David Ben-Gurion, Israel's first prime minister, in 1948. Begin claimed that the only difference between them was that Ben-Gurion had resorted to subterfuge, whereas he was carrying out his policy openly. He cited Ben-Gurion's plan to divide Lebanon by setting up a Christian state north of the Litani River, his relentless efforts to prevent the creation of a Palestinian state, and, during the 1948 war, his wholesale destruction of Arab villages and townships within the borders of Israel and the expulsion of their inhabitants from the country – all in the interest of establishing a homogeneous Jewish state.[3]

Begin's remarks inadvertently set in motion a reassessment of Israel's origins. The War of Independence, as the 1948 War is called in Israel, had always transcended controversy. Researchers, motivated in many cases to clear Ben-Gurion's name and discredit Begin, began to look into these charges of wholesale destruction of villages and expulsions. They were aided by a liberal archival policy by which government documents are released to public scrutiny after the passage of thirty years, which made available a vast quantity of documentation on the 1948 War and its aftermath. The Israeli archives proved most revealing.

Simha Flapan set the agenda when he reduced the historiography on the foundation of the state of Israel in 1948 to seven myths: That the Zionists accepted the UN partition resolution and planned for peace; that the Arabs rejected the partition and launched the war; that the Palestinians fled voluntarily intending reconquest; that the Arab states had united to expel the Jews from Palestine; that the Arab invasion made war inevitable; that a defenseless Israel faced destruction by the Arab Goliath; and that Israel subsequently sought peace but no Arab leader responded. Other Israeli scholars developed these themes more extensively. Benny Morris provided the first documentary evidence to demonstrate Israeli responsibility for the flight of the Palestinians from their homes.[4] Avi Shlaim overturned the myth of the Arab Goliath and documented peace overtures to Israel by King ʿAbdullah of Jordan and even the Syrian leader Husni al-Zaʿim.[5] Ilan Pappé demonstrated that Britain, far from seeking to prevent the creation of a Jewish state as argued by Zionist historiography, sought instead to prevent the establishment of a Palestinian state.[6] The sociological consequences of the state's myth-making have in turn been scrutinized by Zeev Sternhell.[7] These works have provoked enormous controversy within Israel and their authors have become a self-conscious group referred to as the "new historians" or "critical sociologists."[8]

A critical tradition has always existed in the Arab histories of 1948, though the criticism in any given country was more often directed against the actions of *other* Arab states. Arab intellectuals have, since the immediate aftermath of the war they dubbed "the catastrophe" (*al-Nakba*), sought to explain their defeat in the shortcomings of Arab society generally. Constantine Zurayq, Sati' al-Husri, Musa al-'Alami and George Hanna were among the most influential of these intellectuals, and their works gained wide circulation in the Arab world. "Yet these books," Walid al-Khalidi argues, "were not able to eradicate and bury forever our myths of what took place in the 1948 War, in spite of their wide circulation." While Khalidi characterizes both the Israeli and the Arab historiography of the 1948 War in similar terms, his summary of the Arab myths is worth citing at length.

The most prominent of the Arab myths of the 1948 War, most of which continue to be circulated down to the present day, portray the Zionist forces as mere terrorist gangs which had been surrounded in all directions by the Arab armies in the first phase of the war (15 May–11 June). The Egyptian vanguard had reached the southern suburbs of Tel Aviv, the Iraqi advanced forces had come very close to the Mediterranean coast to the west of Qalqiliya and Tulkarm, and the Jordanian Arab Legion had reached the eastern suburbs of Tel Aviv. All that was needed was a few more days to deal the enemy the mortal blow which would decide the matter once and for all, when international pressure escalated into threats and menaces and imposed the first truce on the Arabs. Thus the Zionist entity snatched victory from the jaws of inevitable defeat.[9]

Israeli scholars have turned their interests to Arab historiography, perhaps in consequence of their own historical self-examination. Emmanuel Sivan, in his analysis of Arab political myths, considered such recurrent themes as the Crusades as a symbol of an on-going battle between Muslim Arabs and their enemies in the holy land of Palestine, and the symbolic significance of Jerusalem, as two examples of particular relevance to Arab thought in the aftermath of the Palestine War.[10] Avraham Sela, who has studied the Arab historiography of 1948 most extensively, has drawn parallels between Arab and Israeli narratives. Like the earlier Israeli histories of 1948, he argues, "Arab historiography of the 1948 war consists predominantly of non-scholarly literature based more upon collective memory than critical historiography." Unable to reach military parity with Israel or to fulfill its Arab nationalist agenda of liberating Palestine, Sela argues, "the history of the 1948 war is an essential part of the 'unfinished business' of Arab nationalism."[11]

Arab states and Arab nationalism

One explanation for the persistence of national myths in the Arab histories of 1948 lies in the distinction between a narrower nation-state nationalism and a broader supra-national Arab nationalism. The colonial experience of the interwar years had put paid to the greater Arab kingdom envisaged by the Hashemite Sharif Husayn ibn ʿAli and his sons in the first world war. The division of the Fertile Crescent into discrete states under British and French Mandates meant that nationalist struggles went on within the boundaries of the new Arab states rather than at the pan-Arab level. History was thus employed to instill patriotism in Egyptians, Iraqis, Jordanians, Lebanese, and Syrians, though not to the exclusion of their collective identity as Arabs. By the time these states were gaining their independence in the aftermath of the second world war, political elites had emerged with interests to protect within the boundaries drawn by the colonial authorities. Furthermore, there was no popular champion of pan-Arab nationalism. Amir ʿAbdullah's calls for a Greater Syrian union carried little ideological appeal at the grass roots level and were seen instead as a bid for Transjordan's territorial expansion. Pan-Arabism figured only symbolically in the official rhetoric of Egypt, Syria, Lebanon, or Iraq.[12] Nor did the Arab League, founded in March 1945, serve to transcend individual national interests.

It should come as no surprise that the Arab states fought the Palestine War in strictly national terms, guided by domestic agendas and national interests. While all Arab leaders spoke of the necessity of protecting Arab Palestine from partition, King Faruq put Egyptian interests first, King ʿAbdullah the interests of Transjordan, President Quwwatli the interests of Syria, as did the other leaders the interests of their countries. Fearful for internal stability within their countries, several Arab leaders committed only a fraction of their armed forces to the "common struggle" against Israel. It was not that Arab chiefs-of-staff failed to coordinate their battle plans; rather they refused outright to place their own troops under another state's command. Far from raising the banner of the Arab nation, the Arab armies nearly came to blows over the size and placement of their respective national flags when troops from different states were billeted in the same town. No one country was willing to risk its forces to come to the rescue of a "fraternal" Arab state under Israeli attack. And when they had had enough, each Arab state negotiated its own armistice with Israel with no concern for inter-Arab coordination.

By the time the first accounts of the Palestine War were being penned in the 1950s, Arab nationalism had become the dominant nationalist discourse in the Arab world. The defeat in Palestine and the toppling of the *ancien régime*s responsible for "the catastrophe" had galvanized public opinion behind the pan-Arab agenda. Arab Nationalism now had a popular champion of remarkable charisma. Egyptian president Gamal ʿAbd al-Nasir enjoyed grass-roots support not just in his own country but across the Arab lands. The Arab nationalists execrated the narrow self-interest of the Arab leaders of 1948, and turned angrily against their successors in Jordan, Syria, Lebanon, and Iraq. However, the Arab nationalists proved no more effective in achieving the liberation of Palestine or the defeat of Israel than had their predecessors. This led to two tendencies in the history writing on 1948: the defensive Arab states adopted "an apologetic mode, geared towards enhancing political legitimacy" while the Arab Nationalists wrote in "a mode of self-examination that sought to elicit historical lessons and motivate radical social, political, or ideological change in preparation for the 'next round' against Israel."[13] Neither placed much importance on the historical accuracy of their accounts.

A victor's privilege

While there is certainly scope for new Arab histories of the Palestine War, Arab intellectuals lack the material for the task. Unlike in Israel, there is no thirty-year rule which governs the declassification of government archives. Archival material on the Palestine War is still not available in Egypt, Jordan, Iraq, Syria or Lebanon, and there is no immediate prospect for its declassification. This has forced writers to return to available sources with at most a new interpretation reflecting changes in political realities over the fifty years which separate us from the events of the Palestine War. Palestinian historian Walid Khalidi has written a series of works marking the half century since the UN Partition Resolution and the 1948 War on the basis of the documentation he personally has gathered over the years, without a footnote or reference embellishing his texts.[14] Egyptian journalist Muhammad Hasanayn Haykal was driven back to his own war diaries for his reassessment of the Palestine War.[15] Even where archival materials exist, such as the papers of the Hashemite Court in Jordan, access has been strictly limited to historians of demonstrated loyalty to edit and publish documents which reinforce the Jordanian government's official line on the Palestine War.[16] Arab scholars would find no support for critical revisions of their national historiography. Indeed, many Arab countries limit free expression in ways which are prohibitive to critical scholarship.

And so a decade after the publication of the first major Israeli revisionist histories of the Palestine War there is still no analogous literature by scholars from the Arab side.

The link between a national historical narrative and the political legitimacy of the state makes any challenge to official truths controversial. The arguments put forward by the new Israeli historians have provoked tremendous debate in Israel, spilling out of academic forums into the press and public consciousness. The fact that the challenge has come from Israeli academics, who have found their most controversial material in Israeli archives, has made the findings of the new Israeli historians all the more disturbing to domestic opinion in Israel.

Yet the freedom of this debate is a measure of the security of Israeli political institutions. It takes a great deal of political stability for the right of free expression to be preserved over state-sanctioned truths. Perhaps because Israel emerged victorious in 1948 and in subsequent Arab–Israeli conflicts, new historians can challenge the consensus of public memory captured by the traditional historians without jeopardizing public belief in the legitimacy of the civil and military institutions of the state of Israel. The old aphorism, that history is written by the victors, doesn't quite apply. Given that the defeated Arab states have written their own histories of the Palestine War, perhaps it is more accurate to say that the *critical revision* of a nation's history is a victor's privilege.

By the fiftieth anniversary of the Palestine War, Egypt had been at peace with Israel for twenty years and Jordan for four years. The Palestinians and the Israelis had exchanged recognition and established a framework for peace which permitted the Palestine Liberation Organization's chairman, Yasir 'Arafat, to return to a narrow autonomy in parts of the Gaza Strip and the West Bank. With the end of hostilities, a new level of interaction between Arabs and Israelis undermined the aims which informed the earlier historical traditions of the Arab–Israeli conflict. With no prospect of the liberation of Palestine or another round of war with Israel, the ideological underpinnings of the old history are irrelevant. The old fabric of myths is now almost subversive of the direction taken by the former confrontation states. To say that the Arabs need to embark on a critical examination of their history is not a simplistic call to imitate the historical debates which have taken place in Israel since 1988. Rather, it is an acknowledgment that a history which is no longer credible serves neither to legitimate the state nor to inspire or inform its citizenry. The contributors to this book propose as a first step the rewriting of the Palestine War.

Rewriting the Palestine War

This book re-examines the role of all participants in the Palestine War on the basis of archival sources where they exist, and on new materials which have entered the public domain such as memoirs and other published primary sources. The collection brings together leading Israeli new historians with prominent Arab and Western scholars of the Middle East, to revisit 1948 from the perspective of each of the countries involved in the war. In many cases, authors address issues raised by the Israeli new historians on the conduct of war and diplomacy between Israel and the Arab states. However, the essays on the Arab states have drawn deliberately on local sources to re-examine the history from an Arab perspective. In many cases, the paucity of new materials limits the scope of revision. The authors present their work in the hope that official documents will be made available in Arab archives to permit a more thorough revision of the Arab–Israeli conflict.

This collection contains essays on all of the Arab states that took part in the Palestine War bar one: Lebanon. Despite the editors' best efforts it proved impossible to find a contributor to examine Lebanon's role in the war. Lebanese–Israeli relations remain an extremely sensitive topic in the last active front of the Arab–Israeli conflict, exacerbated by a history of Maronite cooperation with Zionism, the Israeli occupation of a large strip of South Lebanon, and Syria's influence over Lebanese foreign policy. Two studies have been published on the Zionist–Maronite "special relationship" on the basis of Israeli sources. Laura Eisenberg has examined the diplomacy which led to a still-born Zionist–Maronite treaty in 1946,[17] and Kirsten Schulze has looked at the persistence of Israeli attempts to intervene in internal Lebanese affairs.[18] Both works have been translated into Arabic and published in Beirut, though ominously Schulze's book was seized upon by Lebanese censors and its author accused by the state's security forces for "instigating sectarian strife."[19] Neither work has much to say about Lebanon's military role in the 1948 War, which was minimal. Lebanon committed only a token contingent of under 1,000 troops who crossed into the northern Galilee only to be repulsed by Israeli forces who in turn occupied a strip of South Lebanon until the two sides signed an armistice agreement on 23 March 1949. However, Lebanon played an important political role in the lead-up to the war. The Lebanese prime minister, Riyad al-Sulh, was strident in his rhetoric for a comprehensive victory in Palestine. Indeed, Sulh was criticized by other leaders for taking the hardest line in Arab League meetings while his country made the smallest commitment to the battlefield. The conservatism of President Bishara al-Khuri, the stridency of his prime minister, the nature of Maronite–Zionist relations and the Lebanese experiences in battle and under brief Israeli occupation provide the material for a fascinating *Lebanese* history of 1948 which seemingly must await a more auspicious political climate.

Most of the essays in the book address a national history – Palestine, Israel, Egypt, Jordan, Iraq, and Syria. Two exceptions are Benny Morris' re-examination of the birth of the Palestinian refugee problem, and Laila Parsons' study of the Druze in the Palestine War. Morris' original study provoked tremendous controversy, both from those Israelis who believed he was discrediting his country and from Palestinians who argued that the archival material Morris uncovered was more damning of Israeli actions than Morris' conclusions that "the Palestinian refugee problem was born of war, not by design."[20] In the years since the publication of *The Birth*, a considerable body of new Israeli documents has been declassified, particularly the archives of the Israeli Defense Forces and the Defense Ministry. In his reassessment of the Palestinian exodus of 1948, Morris addresses one of the most controversial points raised by his earlier critics: Zionist thinking on "transfer," or the expulsion of Palestinians from lands to be included in the projected Jewish state. Morris documents a shift in Zionist thinking on the subject from "haphazard" to a "virtual consensus in support of the notion from 1937 on" which "contributed to what happened in 1948." The second part of his essay examines the expulsion of Palestinians from the northern Galilee in Operation Hiram (28–31 October 1948), with clear evidence of atrocities committed by Israeli forces against the Palestinian villagers. However, Morris continues to refuse to link "transfer thinking" to a *policy* of expulsion, denying that "any overall expulsory policy decision was taken by the Yishuv's executive bodies . . . in the course of the 1948 War."

Laila Parsons disputes this conclusion on the basis of Israeli actions toward the Druze, also focusing on Operation Hiram. Parsons documents a special relationship between the Yishuv and the Druze in the Mandate period which developed into a "secret wartime alliance" by 1948. The numerous examples of Druze–Israeli cooperation in the course of the war, and the fact that no Druze were expelled from their towns or villages, she argues, undermines Morris' claims of the randomness of the expulsion of Palestinians. Indeed, even in one village where the Palestinian Druze broke their pre-battle agreement and fought against the IDF, the Druze villagers were not expelled following the battle. If the Druze were allowed to remain by design, Parsons argues, this implied "at least a partially coherent policy to expel

Muslims." Clearly the wealth of documentation in the Israeli archives still leaves scope for differences of interpretation between scholars.

In a concluding essay, Edward Said examines the consequences of the 1948 War fifty years on. The imbalance between Isreali military and institutional strength and Palestinian efforts at state formation within Gaza and parts of the West Bank puts in question the viability of the two-state solution envisaged by the United Nations Partition Resolution in 1947. The best solution for the Palestinians, Said argues, might well be a bi-national state. With few champions for this vision on either the Israeli or Palestinian sides, Said's idea comes well before its time. Indeed, it might gain ground when, in half a century's time, a new generation of scholars chooses to revisit the Palestine War at its centenary.

Notes

1 Simha Flapan, *The Birth of Israel: Myths and Realities* (New York, 1987); Avraham Sela, "Arab Historiography of the 1948 War: The Quest for Legitimacy," in Laurence J. Silberstein, ed., *New Perspectives on Israeli History: The Early Years of the State* (New York, 1991), pp. 124–54.
2 E.J. Hobsbawm analyzes the analogous fostering of patriotism in Europe in his *Nations and Nationalism since 1780: Programme, Myth, Reality* (Cambridge, 1990), pp. 85–91. For the different uses of history to achieve civic loyalty in the French Third Republic and the German Second Empire see Hobsbawm's "Mass-Producing Traditions: Europe, 1870–1914," in Eric Hobsbawm and Terence Ranger, eds., *The Invention of Tradition* (Cambridge, 1984), pp. 272–274.
3 Flapan, *Birth of Israel*, p. 5.
4 *The Birth of the Palestinian Refugee Problem, 1947–1949* (Cambridge, 1988).
5 *Collusion across the Jordan: King Abdullah, the Zionist Movement, and the Partition of Palestine* (Oxford, 1988).
6 *Britain and the Arab–Israeli Conflict, 1948–51* (London, 1988).
7 *The Founding Myths of Israel: Nationalism, Socialism, and the Making of the Jewish State* (Princeton NY, 1998).
8 Benny Morris, "The New Historiography: Israel and its Past," in Morris, *1948 and After: Israel and the Palestinians* (Oxford, 1994), pp. 1–48; Avi Shlaim, "The Debate About 1948," *International Journal of Middle East Studies* 27 (1995) 287–304.
9 Walid al-Khalidi, *Khamsun 'aman 'ala harb 1948, ula al-hurub al-sihyuniyya al-'arabiyya* [Fifty Years since the 1948 War, the First of the Arab–Zionist wars] (Beirut, 1998), pp. 13–14.
10 *Mythes Politiques Arabes* (Paris, 1995).
11 Sela, "Arab Historiography," pp. 125, 146.
12 Sylvia G. Haim, ed., *Arab Nationalism: An Anthology* (Berkeley CA, 1962); Michael Doran, *Pan-Arabism before Nasser: Egyptian Power Politics and the Palestine Question* (New York, 1999).

13 Sela, "Arab Historiography," p. 125.

14 *Al-Sihyuniyya fi mi'at 'am, 1897–1997* [A Century of Zionism] (Beirut, 1998); *Khamsun 'aman 'ala taqsim filastin, 1947–1997* [Fifty Years Since the Partition of Palestine] (Beirut, 1998); *Dayr Yasin* (Beirut, 1998); *Khamsun 'aman 'ala harb 1948* [Fifty Years Since the 1948 War] (Beirut, 1998).

15 *Al-'Urush wa'l-juyush: kadhalik infajara al-sira'a fi filastin*, vol. 1 [Thrones and Armies: Thus Erupted the Struggle in Palestine] (Cairo, 1998).

16 Muhammad Adnan al-Bakhit, Hind Abu al-Sha'ir and Nawfan Raja al-Suwariyya, eds., *Al-Watha'iq al-Hashimiyya: awraq 'Abdullah bin al-Husayn* [The Hashemite Documents: The Papers of 'Abdullah bin al-Husayn], vol. 5, Palestine 1948 (Amman, 1995).

17 *My Enemy's Enemy: Lebanon in the Early Zionist Imagination, 1900–1948* (Detroit MI, 1994).

18 *Israel's Covert Diplomacy in Lebanon* (London, 1998).

19 As reported in the English-language Lebanese newspaper, *The Daily Star*, 27 February 1999.

20 Morris, *The Birth*, p. 286. Among Israeli critics, Ben-Gurion biographer Shabtai Teveth published a series of articles in the Israeli daily *Ha'aretz* (7, 14, 21 April and 19 May 1989) and "Charging Israel with Original Sin," *Commentary* (September, 1989); among those who argue Morris did not go far enough, see Norman Finkelstein, "Myths, Old and New," and Nur Masalha, "A Critique of Benny Morris," *Journal of Palestine Studies* 21/1 (1991) 66–97.

1   The Palestinians and 1948: the underlying causes of failure

Rashid Khalidi

Between early spring and late fall of 1948, Arab Palestine was radically transformed. At the beginning of that year, Arabs constituted over two-thirds of the population of the country, and were a majority in fifteen of the country's sixteen sub-districts.[1] Beyond this, Arabs owned nearly 90 percent of Palestine's privately owned land.[2] In a few months of heavy fighting in the early spring of 1948, the military forces of a well-organized Jewish population of just over 600,000 people routed those of an Arab majority more than twice its size. In the months that followed, they decisively defeated several Arab armies, which had entered the country on 15 May 1948. Over this turbulent period, more than half of the nearly 1.4 million Palestinian Arabs were driven from or fled their homes. Those Palestinians who did not flee the conquered areas were reduced to a small minority within the new state of Israel (which now controlled about 77 percent of the territory of Mandatory Palestine). At the end of the fighting, Jordan took over the areas of Palestine controlled by its army west of the Jordan River, while the Egyptian army administered the strip it retained around Gaza, adjacent to its borders. In the wake of this catastrophe – *al-Nakba*, as it was inscribed in Palestinian memory[3] – the Palestinians found themselves living under a variety of alien regimes, were dispossessed of the vast bulk of their property, and had lost control over most aspects of their lives.

How and why did this momentous transformation happen? Most conventional accounts of the 1948 War tend to focus on events after 15 May 1948, the date when the state of Israel was founded, and the Arab armies intervened unsuccessfully in Palestine in the wake of the stunning collapse of the Palestinians. In fact, however, the decisive blows to the cohesion of Palestinian society were struck even before 15 May, during the early spring of 1948. Furthermore, it is the central argument of this chapter that the underlying causes of this collapse, and of the larger Palestinian political failure, lay even further in the past, and were related to the constraints on and the structural weaknesses of the Palestinian political institutions, factionalism among the notable stratum which dominated Palestinian society and politics, and grave shortcomings in leadership.[4]

The specific shocks which led Palestinian society to disintegrate in the weeks before 15 May came as the climax of an escalating series of bombings, ambushes, skirmishes, and pitched battles sparked by the passage of United Nations General Assembly resolution 181 on 29 November 1947, which called for the partition of Palestine into an Arab and a Jewish state. During the first few months of this savage civil war, there were successes and subsequent reverses for both sides in heavy fighting in many parts of the country. However, from the beginning of March until mid-May of 1948, the striking superiority of the armed forces of the Zionist movement, and the concomitant weaknesses of their Arab foes began to tell, and they won a series of conclusive victories over the Palestinians. These victories led to the fall of numerous Arab cities and towns, including several of the largest and most important ones, and of hundreds of Palestinian villages, and the capture of a number of strategic roads, junctions, and positions. The main consequence of these crushing defeats in the spring of 1948 was the expulsion of the first wave of Arabs from Palestine.[5] This first exodus, before 15 May 1948, involved perhaps half the eventual total of 750,000 or so Palestinians who became refugees as a result of the fighting of 1948–49.[6]

The fifteenth of May 1948 thus marked not only the birth of the state of Israel, but also the definitive defeat of the Palestinians by their Zionist foes, after decades of struggle between the two sides over control of the country. It also serves to mark the approximate mid-point in the expulsion and flight of roughly half of Palestine's Arab population. This crushing defeat ended any lingering hope that the Arab state called for by the United Nations partition plan would ever see the light of day. Instead the putative Arab state was strangled at birth. It was the victim of the superior military capabilities of the nascent state of Israel, the hostility or indifference of all the great powers and most of the Arab states, the collusion of a number of Arab leaders with Britain and Israel against the Palestinians,[7] and the successive failures of the Palestinians themselves. Important though all these factors were in the defeat of the Palestinians, it is the last one that will be the topic of much of the analysis that follows.

The scope of this defeat must be borne in mind if we are to understand its causes. By the time the fighting ended with the armistices of 1949, more than half the Palestinian people had been uprooted. Those Palestinians who lived in urban areas, who amounted to over 400,000 people at this time or some 30 percent of the total Arab population of the country, were among the first to be dispossessed.[8] Even before the state of Israel had been proclaimed on 15 May 1948, most of the Arab inhabitants of Jaffa and Haifa had been dispersed, and the bulk of their property had been seized.[9] The same thing happened then or very soon afterwards to the Arab residents of the cities and towns of Lydda, Ramla, Acre, Safad, Tiberias, Baysan, and Bir Sabiʿ.[10] Together with Haifa and Jaffa, these centers included about half of the Palestinian urban population of the country, to which must be added the 30,000 Arabs who lived in the western part of Jerusalem and were driven from their homes at the same time. These new refugees from the urban areas of the country generally tended to be those Palestinians with the highest levels of literacy, skills, wealth, and education.

An even worse fate befell the majority of Palestinians who lived in the countryside, where the decades-old struggle for control of land and strategic locations was being decided massively in favor of the Zionists. More than 400 of the over 500 Arab villages in Palestine had been taken over by the Israeli victors by the time the fighting ended with the 1949 armistices between Israel and the Arab states. The inhabitants of these villages were driven out or fled in terror, their land was confiscated, and they were forbidden to return.[11] These were sweeping changes: in the 77 percent of the land area of Palestine which came under Israeli domination, the end result of this process was the creation of a sizable Jewish majority, and the shift of over 18 million of the country's 26 million dunams from Arab to Jewish control.[12] They were long-lasting changes as well: more than half a century later, the basic demographic and property contours created by this seismic event are still extant.

Many explanations have been offered for this debacle, in which Palestinian society crumbled with a rapidity that astonished even its Zionist opponents. The standard semi-official Israeli interpretation of these events – which has decisively shaped the way they have been understood in the West to this day – ascribed responsibility entirely to the Arabs. The core of this explanation was that the Palestinians left because Arab leaders, bent on the destruction of Israel, told them to flee.[13] Over the past decade or so, a number of scholars, most of them Israeli, using Israeli and British archives, have decisively refuted this interpretation in its entirety.[14] In the process they have fundamentally undermined a number of key myths long propagated by Israel.[15]

The Israeli "new historians" have utilized newly discovered evidence from the Zionist and Israeli state archives, and other documents, to confirm in particular these earlier refutations of what turned out to have been entirely baseless claims that Arab leaders told the Palestinians to flee. Much else of importance has been established or clarified by this newly published revisionist history. Nevertheless, given the Israeli and Western sources from which their data were mainly drawn, and their primary focus on Israel, the analyses of the new historians have related primarily to the actions of Israel and the great powers, and only secondarily to those of the Arab states and the Palestinians. In explaining the actions of the Palestinians, these accounts have generally added little, stressing the superior power of the Zionists, the weakness of Arab social and political cohesion, and the flight of the Arab upper and middle classes before the fighting reached its height.[16]

Most Arab histories of what happened in 1948 have tended to stress that the Palestinians were overwhelmed by massively superior force.[17] The focus in these accounts is on the strength of the Zionist forces, the complicity with the Zionists of the withdrawing British, and the invaluable support for them of the United States and the Soviet Union. Other Arab authors stress the alleged collusion between Israel and Transjordan, which fielded by far the most powerful Arab army in Palestine, as well as the relative military weakness of the Arab states and the debilitating internecine divisions among them. Yet others underscore the employment by the Zionist forces of terrorist attacks on civilians, notably at Dayr Yasin,[18] and their intense bombardment of heavily populated urban areas, especially in the major cities of Jaffa, Haifa, and Jerusalem.[19]

There can be no question that the Palestinians, although they outnumbered the Jewish population of Palestine, were facing superior forces on a number of levels. This imbalance in favor of the Yishuv (the Jewish community in Palestine) was naturally not reflected in the traditional Israeli version of the history of the conflict. This version described the Yishuv as outnumbered, beleaguered, and desperate in its conflict with the Palestinians.[20] However, this interpretation cannot be sustained by an objective examination either of the facts or of the results of the conflict. One of the most recent Israeli historians of the Palestine War has recognized the imbalance in favor of the Zionists at this time. This account, which is generally unsympathetic to the Palestinians, describes the lack of trained, regular Palestinian forces, the absence of a centralized command structure or a reliable source of weapons, and other elements of Palestinian military weakness, by contrast with the relatively formidable capabilities of the Zionist forces.[21]

Nevertheless, superior though the Zionist forces were in numerous respects, the Palestinians had several apparent advantages. These included their massive predominance in numbers and the presence of hundreds of Arab villages all over the country, notably along many of its most strategic roads. The Palestinian Arabs also had a cadre of veteran guerrilla fighters and a few competent military leaders who had survived the ferocious British repression of the 1936–39 revolt, and a number of specialists just as willing and able to use terror tactics as any among the Zionists. Finally, they expected that they would receive a degree of support from the surrounding Arab world. If some Jews in Palestine perceived themselves as facing an uphill fight against the Arabs, this was certainly understandable in view of these factors.

Yet when Zionist military capabilities were put to the test against the Palestinians with all their apparent advantages in the decisive battles of the spring of 1948, at the end of the day the Palestinians were not simply beaten, but were routed. Why did this happen? In particular, why were the Palestinians unable to bring such assets as they possessed to bear on the battlefield at the moment of decision? Why were they defeated in virtually all of the important military engagements from late March until the end of the Mandate on 15 May 1948? And why did their defeats in the field lead to the virtual collapse of so much of their society, and the flight of hundreds of thousands of their people?

As we have already noted, in Arab historiography the incapacities and errors of the Palestinians themselves have tended to get relatively little attention – although a few Palestinian historians have tried to examine some of the internal reasons for the Palestinians' failures.[22] Instead, the tendency in this historiography has been to focus on causes external to Palestinian society for an explanation of the disasters which befell it in 1948. But explanations that focus on external factors miss a crucial dimension, that of why the Palestinians were so weak, what they might have done better – even given their numerous enemies and the un-favorable balance of power – and why their defeat was so total. Some Arab historians have avoided such issues partly because they were sensitive ones, directing attention to internal Palestinian divisions that still have a painful echo. This also may have happened because such avenues of analysis were seen as serving the Israeli objective of drawing attention away from Israel's responsibility for the events of 1948, notably its expulsion of the Palestinian refugees. In extreme forms, this tendency produces a narrative of the debacle of 1948 that denies the Palestinians agency in what happened, or indeed any responsibility for their own fate.

Before going further, it is important to stress that for all their flaws, the versions of history produced by this traditional Arab historiography are fundamentally different from the Israeli myths of origin that are currently being deconstructed by the Israeli "new historians." This is true notably because it is not a myth that a determined enemy bent on taking control of their homeland subjected the Palestinians to overwhelming force. It is not a myth, moreover, that as a result of this process the Palestinian people were victims, regardless of what they might have done differently in this situation of formidable difficulty, and of the sins of omission or commission of their leaders. In this, as in so much else in this conflict, there can be no facile equivalence between the two sides, however much some may long for the appearance of Palestinian "new historians" to shatter the "myths" on the Arab side.

Any serious attempt to explain the underlying reasons for the defeat of the Palestinians in 1948, even if it focuses on the less-studied internal causes for this defeat, must do at least two things. First, it must examine events well before that date, since to lay bare the roots of what happened in Palestine in 1948, it is necessary to analyze trends during the preceding decades of the British mandate, if not before that. Second, it must go beyond conventional assertions regarding the debilitating political and military effects of the deep divisions within Palestinian society, and among the elite, and attempt an analysis of these divisions which is not reductionist. Because of the profound impact of the Palestinian revolt of 1936–39 in these and other spheres, it is particularly important to examine this uprising, and the long-lasting effects its failure had on Palestinian society and politics. Finally, such an attempt must explain the striking lack of organization, cohesion, and unanimity in the Palestinian polity before 1948, particularly in view of the contrast with other Arab national movements and with the situation of the Yishuv in the same period. This chapter will make a beginning in some of these directions, although its limited scope naturally precludes a full-scale analysis of all these questions.

The Mandate and the failure of Palestinian institution formation

Palestinian society before 1948 was unquestionably riven by internal divisions, and certainly lacked cohesion in a number of respects. However, in analyzing these internal divisions it is important to avoid the approach which, by comparing Palestinian society exclusively to the Yishuv, concludes with a circular analysis which relates Palestinian political failures to the social backwardness of Palestinian society relative to Jewish society in Palestine. It is more fruitful to compare Palestinian society to other Arab societies, with which it was quite similar, rather than with the Yishuv, with which it was utterly dissimilar in virtually every significant respect.[23] This makes it possible to isolate some of the causes for the political failures of the Palestinian national movement, essentially by comparing the task it faced to those faced by other Arab national movements at the same time.

On the political level, it is necessary to take into account the fact that the emerging Palestinian Arab polity was denied any of the attributes of "stateness," and any access to the levers of state power. In this respect, the Palestinians were completely unlike the Yishuv under the leadership of the Zionist movement, unlike the peoples of Egypt, Iraq, Syria, Lebanon, and Jordan, and unlike the peoples in most other colonial and semi-colonial domains in the Middle East and North Africa in the inter-war years. Specifically, they had no international sanction for their national identity, no accepted and agreed upon context within which their putative nationhood and independence could express themselves, and no means of claiming the political or constitutional position which their majority status should "naturally" have brought them.

The contrast with the situation of most of the other Arab countries at the same time is highly illustrative. By 1946, the Yemen, Saudi Arabia, Egypt, Iraq, Syria, Lebanon, and Transjordan were already inde-pendent states (at least in nominal terms). While Morocco, Tunisia, and most of the Gulf sheikhdoms were European protectorates of different types, they too were at least nominally under the control of their own indigenous governments. Only Algeria (and Libya until the defeat of the Italians during World War II), was a pure colony under direct European rule, where the natives had virtually no rights and little or no control over their own affairs. Algeria and Libya, like Palestine, were the only Arab countries to be the targets of settler colonialism, which reserved most political and other rights to the incoming European settler population, rather than to the indigenous Arab majority. Although Britain and France retained military bases and a measure of control even in nominally independent states in the inter-war period, all of the Arab countries besides Palestine (again with the exception of Libya and Algeria) had recognized indigenous state structures. In every one of them, moreover, it was accepted that sovereignty would ultimately reside with the national majority, in accordance with the Wilsonian principles embodied in the Covenant of the League of Nations. This was true even if in virtually every Arab country before World War II, some of the specific powers and attributes of sovereignty were being temporarily withheld by the colonial powers, and even if there was an ongoing struggle for the transfer of these powers and attributes. Thus the positions of the colonial powers in most Arab countries in this period (whether they were mandates or not) were predicated on the assumption that there existed in each case a people in being or in emergence, with the eventual right to independence and statehood.

The Zionists were in a position analogous to that of these Arab peoples, which was explicitly recognized in the terms of the Mandate for Palestine. The Mandate reprised the wording of the Balfour Declaration in speaking of a "Jewish people" with a right to a "national home," and recognized the Zionist movement, under the name of the Jewish Agency, as a "public body for the purpose of advising and cooperating with the Administration" in order to establish this home.[24] In stark contrast, the Palestinians were both explicitly and by omission denied the same national recognition and institutional framework. The Mandate for Palestine as promulgated by the League of Nations on 24 July 1922 mentioned the "civil and religious rights of the existing non-Jewish communities in Palestine." The wording of this document is significant, for it does not mention the existence of the Palestinians as a people – they are described only as "non-Jewish communities" – nor their political or national rights. In fact, the Palestinian Arabs as such, who constituted over 90 percent of the population of the country when the British occupied in 1917, are not mentioned by name either in the Balfour Declaration or in the terms of the Mandate. This was certainly not a coincidental omission, as was shown by the way that the Mandate was implemented in the years that followed.

The governmental system set up by the British to execute the terms of the Mandate reflected the basic ideas of that document. The Palestinian Arabs were not given access to any significant positions of authority in the British mandatory government. This was in distinction to the other Class A Mandates, governed under their British and French high commissioners by an *amir* and prime minister in Transjordan, a king and prime minister in Iraq, and presidents and prime ministers in Syria and Lebanon. Even when some of those in these positions were no more than puppets or figureheads, they had nominal authority, and sometimes much more. In Palestine the British high commissioner was the highest, indeed the sole, source of authority in the land. There was no parliament or any other elected representative body, and no cabinet, nor were there any responsible Arab officials. Neither were the Palestinians given the right to create their own powerful, autonomous para-state structure, with recognized international reach, as the Zionists were with the Jewish Agency, which the terms of the Mandate specifically enjoined the British to establish and assist. A 1923 British proposal for an Arab Agency to be appointed by the high commissioner (rather than elected as in the Jewish case) was "a pale reflection of the Jewish agency," without sanction in the Mandate, and without international standing.[25]

The significance of the quasi-official status accorded to the Jewish Agency by Britain and the League of Nations through the Mandate cannot be overemphasized. It gave the Zionist movement an international legitimacy and guaranteed access in London and Geneva which were invaluable, besides providing the framework within which the Israeli para-state could be constructed without hindrance, and indeed with ample British support.[26] It is hardly an exaggeration to state that the generous support of the greatest imperial power of the age was an invaluable asset for the Zionist movement in overcoming its Palestinian opponents.

Before 1939 there were a few British attempts to redress this structural imbalance of the Mandate regime which favored the Zionists, such as different proposals for a legislative assembly or for an Arab agency. Whether the Palestinians might have obtained tactical advantage by accepting some of these proposals, and turning the resulting institutions to their advantage, or whether their ability to do so would have suffered from the persistent divisions that plagued their elite, is impossible to say. In any case, these proposals were fatally compromised in Arab eyes by the requirement that they accept the terms of the Mandate, which enshrined the inferior status of the Arab majority by comparison with that of the Jews, and denied them the rights which should flow from majority status. In other words, the Palestinian Arabs were not accorded the right of national self-determination and an internationally accepted status as were the Jews of Palestine and as were the peoples of the other Mandates in Syria, Lebanon, Iraq, and Transjordan. Instead, these British proposals (when not withdrawn or nullified by the British themselves) would have allowed the Palestinians to share with the Jews in some of the functions of government. Unlike the Jews, however, they were to do so not by right, as enshrined in the documents defining the Mandate, but on sufferance, as it were.

These are significant factors in assessing the failures of the Palestinians. They meant that they did not have any access to the uncontested and recognized "neutral" forum or entity that a state or a para-state provides. For the Yishuv and for the other Arab countries under the mandate system, such a forum proved invaluable for the polity to coalesce around or compete for, or as a focus for its action, even if complete control over it was denied by the colonial power. As Issa Khalaf wrote: "More fundamentally than self-governing institutions, the lack of effective power over the state meant that the Palestinian Arab notability which headed the national movement would be unable to use the resources of the state to centralize power in its hands and thereby develop into a cohesive stratum."[27]

Palestinian politics were thus condemned to an even higher level of frustration than politics in the other Arab countries. In the other mandates, there was a constant struggle with the mandatory power over the powers to be accorded to the national government, but there was no question about the existence or potential sovereignty of this government. In Egypt, the British and their Egyptian allies managed to keep the hugely popular Wafd party out of power for more than half of the thirty years from independence in 1922 until 1952, but vital elements of state power were nevertheless in some sense in Egyptian hands. The European powers maintained military forces in the Arab countries against the will of their populations, but the struggle against them was directed from within the state, or could be when control of the state could be won. This struggle for full independence via liberation from foreign military occupation was successful in most Arab countries within a decade of 1945. The Palestinians never had any such advantages. And they proved unable to create their own autonomous forum from which to challenge the colonial authority and its Zionist protégés, for reasons to be examined below.

The failure of the politics of notables

In analyzing the Palestinians' lack of political cohesion, especially in the crucial decade of the 1930s and afterwards, the lack of access to the mechanisms of state and the absence of any other recognized central national forum does not explain everything. As we have seen, however, it is important for understanding the differences between the situation of the Palestinian polity and that of both the Yishuv and the national movements in other Arab states. There were also other important internal factors specific to Palestine, which help to explain why the Palestinians failed so completely on the political and military levels in the years leading up to 1948.

Deprived of access to control of the state and lacking a para-state forum, the Palestinians held a series of congresses which elected an Arab Executive, headed by Musa Kazim Pasha al-Husayni, which was unrecognized and often ignored by the British, and was largely ineffectual until its demise in 1934. The reasons for this are many. They include the divisions among the Palestinian elite, and their near-unanimous belief that they could persuade the British to change their policy of support for

Zionism. This illusion, born of this elite's immersion during the Ottoman period in what Albert Hourani called "the politics of the notables,"[28] whereby they saw themselves as natural intermediaries between local society and the dominant external authority, died hard. As late as 1939, many Palestinian notables apparently seemed to believe that a simple exposition of the justice of the Palestinian case would bring the British to "see reason," abandon Zionism, and grant the Palestinians independence, under their leadership of course.

In this near vacuum, Palestinian Arab politics were increasingly dominated by religious leaderships that had been authorized, encouraged, and subsidized by the British. Indeed the religious-political institutions controlled by these leaders were very much in the nature of an "invented tradition," in the words of Hobsbawm and Ranger.[29] After their occupation of the country, the British created the entirely new post of "grand mufti of Palestine" (*al-mufti al-akbar*), who was also designated the "Mufti of Jerusalem and the Palestine region" (*mufti al-Quds wal-diyar al-filistiniyya*). There previously had been a *mufti* (scholar of recognized authority to deliver interpretations of Islamic law) of Jerusalem, which had always been an important post in the past, but one both limited both in terms of geographical scope and authority to the city of Jerusalem. In the Ottoman and every other Islamic system, the post of *mufti* was always clearly subordinate in power and prestige to that of the *qadi* (or judge).[30] The *qadi* was appointed by the Ottoman state from the ranks of the official Ottoman religious establishment, and almost never came from a local family. The *mufti*, as well as the *qadi*'s deputy, the *na'ib*, who was also chief secretary of the *shari'a* court, were by contrast always local officials.[31] This existing system was completely restructured by the British, who effectively placed the *mufti* above all other religious officials in Palestine.

Similarly, in keeping with their vision of a Palestine composed of three religious communities (only one of which, the Jews, had national rights and status) the British created the Supreme Muslim Shari'a Council in 1921. This was an entirely new body – another invented tradition – which was entrusted with the revenues of the public *awqaf* (Islamic endowments) in Palestine which had formerly been controlled by the Ottoman state, together with a number of other duties.[32] As such it was meant to relieve non-Muslim Great Britain of having to take on directly some of the religious functions that the defunct Ottoman Empire had performed before 1918. In addition to giving the Council control over the considerable public *awqaf* revenues and the patronage which went with them, Britain gave it power to nominate and appoint *qadis*, members of the *Shari'a* Court of Appeal, and local *mufti*s. It could also hire and fire all *awqaf* and *Shari'a* court officials employed with *awqaf* funds.[33]

Into both of these newly created positions of unprecedented power of *mufti* and president of the Supreme Muslim Council, the British placed one man, Hajj Amin al-Husayni.[34] His appointment as *mufti* in 1921 has been a source of fierce controversy ever since. Hajj Amin al-Husayni, whose brother, and three generations of his family before him, had held the post of Hanafi *mufti* of Jerusalem, was appointed by the British high commissioner, Sir Herbert Samuel, ahead of other apparently more qualified, and older, candidates. This was a gamble that this young radical, only recently pardoned for his nationalist activities, would serve British interests by maintaining calm in return for his elevation to the post. Despite constant Zionist complaints about him, it could be argued that the gamble paid off for the British until the mid-1930s, when the *mufti* could no longer contain popular passions. Among all the other leaders of national movements in Arab countries during this period (and among Palestinian leaders), the *mufti* was alone in being a leading religious figure, whose base of power was a "traditional" religious institution, albeit a newly invented one.

Because of the considerable assets which Britain had put in his hands, and his consummate political skill, within a decade Husayni had become the dominant Palestinian political leader, and as such a lightning rod for the dissatisfaction of the Zionists. There is an element of amnesiac historiography in the vilification of the *mufti*, influenced by his subsequent career after 1936. In fact, Husayni served the British exceedingly well for the decade and a half after his appointment, at least until 1936 when he felt obliged to align himself with a growing popular rebellion against his former British masters. One indication of how valuable the British perceived the *mufti* to be is the willingness of the notoriously tight-fisted Mandatory administration to subsidize him. When the revenues of the public *awqaf* properties declined after the Great Depression of 1929, and with it the revenues of the Supreme Muslim Council, the latter were supplemented by direct British subventions starting in 1931, which were naturally kept secret.[35]

Eventually there emerged competing factional, union, and political rivals to the range of institutions that the *mufti* dominated (these institutions included a political party, *al-Hizb al-'Arabi al-Filastini* [the Palestine Arab Party], headed by his cousin, Jamal al-Husayni), but this in the end only increased the factionalism of Palestinian society and politics. Although the Palestinians were able to present a united front to their foes for many years after World War I, the internal divisions among the elite eventually surfaced, ably exploited by the British, with their vast experience of dividing colonized societies in order to rule them more effectively. They were exploited as well by the Zionists, whose intelligence services presumably engaged in undercover activities among the Arabs in these years that have yet to be fully elucidated.[36] Irrespective of what the British and Zionists may have been doing in this regard, the Palestinian notables, deprived of any access to real power and frustrated at every turn by their stronger foes, were hopelessly split. By the 1930s, the Palestinian leadership was polarized between a dominant faction led by the British-appointed mufti, and another even more closely aligned with the British and led by the former mayor of Jerusalem, Raghib al-Nashashibi, which feuded bitterly with one another.[37]

To these and other divisions among the elite must be added another one: that between most of the elite and a growing current of discontent among younger Palestinians, intellectuals, and much of the middle classes. Discontent was also rife among the landless former peasants who were flocking to the cities, especially Haifa and Jaffa, and among many in the countryside, saddled with debt to urban merchants and moneylenders.[38] Some of them were driven off their lands by Zionist land purchases and the resultant evictions, others by the imposition of a policy of "Hebrew labor" (*avoda ivrit*) by the Yishuv, and others by Arab landlords turning land over to more profitable (and less labor-intensive) citrus cultivation. This malaise was gravely accentuated by economic distress in the early 1930s as the worldwide depression hit Palestine, which had become increasingly integrated into the world economy in the preceding decades.

The situation was further aggravated by the impact of rapidly mounting Jewish immigration, as the rise of the Nazis drove thousands of Jews escaping from Europe to seek refuge in Palestine, at a time when most countries coldly shut their doors to them.[39] From 1933 to 1936, the proportion of Jews in the total population of Palestine, which had shrunk or remained stagnant from 1926 to 1932, grew from 18 percent to nearly 30 percent. In the year 1935 alone, at the height of this flood of refugees from Hitler's persecution, almost 62,000 Jewish immigrants arrived in Palestine, a number greater than the entire Jewish population of the country as recently as 1919. Whereas at the beginning of the 1930s, the Zionist project might have appeared to some to be a failure because it seemed that the Jews would never overtake the Arabs in population, a few years later, demographic parity and ultimately Zionist control over the country suddenly seemed to be within the realm of possibility.

The failure of the Arab revolt

The Palestinians naturally had a different view of what the Zionists perceived as a major shift in their favor. In the late 1920s and the early 1930s several sectors of Palestinian society had already grown dissatisfied with the internecine divisions among the notable elite, and the manifest ineffectiveness of its leadership of the national movement. This dissatisfaction had led to various forms of more radical, grass-roots activism. These included support for a policy of boycotting the British, greater anti-British and anti-Zionist activity among youth groups like the Young Men's Muslim Association and various scouting organizations, and the growth in influence of the radical nationalist Independence Party [Hizb al-Istiqlal]. The latter called for a rigorous Indian Congress Party-style boycott of the British, a line which naturally failed to appeal to many of those among the notable class who were on the payroll of the Mandatory Administration, including the *mufti*.[40] Following the out-maneuvering and containment of most of their initiatives by the traditional elite, notably the *mufti* and his cousin Jamal al-Husayni, by the mid-1930s, these discontented elements eventually reacted more forcefully to what they saw as the mounting peril of the growing size and strength of the Yishuv.

In the context of these mounting tensions, a Haifa preacher, Shaykh 'Izz al-Din al-Qassam, a leading figure in several of these radical movements, was killed in a clash with British police near Jenin in November 1935.[41] His partisans and some later biographers describe him as having been engaged in sparking an armed revolt in the north of Palestine. This was the first attempt at an organized, armed revolt against the British since the beginning of the Mandate, in contrast to more spontaneous outbreaks of violence in 1920, 1921, 1929, and 1933. Although British security forces immediately stamped out the attempt, the Syrian-born Qassam had clearly touched a deep chord in the popular imagination. It soon became evident that he was much more closely in tune with important elements of popular Palestinian sentiment than was most of the elite leadership.[42] His death in battle was portrayed as a glorious "martyrdom," and huge crowds followed Qassam to his grave near Haifa, in a demonstration that surprised many observers at the time.[43] It was followed within a few months by the spontaneous outbreak of a nation-wide general strike in April 1936, which lasted until October of the same year, claimed by its partisans as the longest general strike in history.

In the wake of the strike, and the subsequent recommendations of a British Royal Commission for partition of the country into a small Jewish state, and an Arab state to be attached to Jordan, an armed uprising spread through the country beginning in the spring of 1937. The final results of this revolt, and of the general strike that preceded it, are crucial to understanding what happened to the Palestinians in the subsequent decade. Over the next 18 months, the British lost control of large areas of the country, including the older parts of the cities of Jerusalem, Nablus, and Hebron, before a massive campaign of repression by tens of thousands of troops and squadrons of aircraft in 1938–39 was able to restore "order."

The Arab revolt of 1936–39 proved to be a massive failure for the Palestinians, in spite of quite remarkable heroism in the face of daunting odds, and great suffering by much of the Arab population. It obtained no lasting concessions from the British, who in a 1939 White Paper promised that Palestine – by implication a Palestine with an Arab majority – would obtain independence within ten years, a promise which they were ultimately unable to keep. The British promised as well limits on Jewish immigration, a promise that was irrelevant in view of the outbreak of the Second World War, and that proved impossible to implement thereafter following revelation of the Nazi genocide against the Jews, and resultant American pressure. Finally, the White Paper would have placed restrictions on land sales to Jews, but in the event land purchase continued virtually unabated.[44]

Although the Yishuv suffered in various ways during the years of the revolt, on balance it benefited considerably. Arab strikes and boycotts served as justification for completing the implementation of the principle of Hebrew labor which excluded Arab workers from an exclusively Jewish "national" economy, which was substantially fortified as a result. The Arab strike served to provide the pretext that the Zionist leadership needed to demand that the Mandatory authorities permit the construction of a modern port at Tel Aviv. This meant the eventual demise of Jaffa as a port, and with growing control of the Yishuv over the Haifa port, meant that it now dominated even more of the country's basic infrastructure. The Zionist movement benefited as well from the significant assistance in armaments and military organization that Britain provided in order to fight the common Arab enemy: by the end of the 1930s, 6,000 armed Jewish auxiliary police were helping the British to suppress the last embers of the revolt. By 1939, the Yishuv had achieved the demographic weight, control of strategic areas of land,

and much of the weaponry and military organization that would be needed as a springboard for taking over the country within less than a decade.

For the Palestinians, however, the worst effects of the failure of the revolt were on their own society. These effects were manifold and were felt on several different levels. Purely in terms of Arab casualties of approximately 5,000 killed and 10,000 wounded, and those detained, who totaled 5,679 in 1939,[45] the suffering was considerable in an Arab population of about a million: over 10 percent of the adult male population was killed, wounded, imprisoned, or exiled.[46] A high proportion of the Arab casualties included experienced military cadres and enterprising fighters. The British also confiscated large quantities of arms and ammunition during the revolt, and continued to do so during later years.[47] These heavy military losses were to affect the Palestinians profoundly a few years later when Britain handed the Palestine question over to the United Nations, and it became clear that an open battle for control of the country between Arabs and Jews would take place.

As severe as Palestinian military losses were those in the realm of the economy, and the damage done to the country's social fabric and political coherence by years of strikes, boycotts, and British reprisals. The strike of 1936, and the armed uprising which followed it, not only helped the Zionists to reinforce the separate Jewish economy they had already built up in Palestine: by 1936 the sector of the economy of Palestine controlled by Jews was already bigger than that of the Arabs.[48] The events of the years 1936–39 further increased the gap between the two sides in favor of the Yishuv, via a series of self-inflicted wounds on the Arab economy. Arab businesses, especially citrus export, quarrying, transportation, and industry, were severely affected by the revolt, as were the Arab port workers of Jaffa. The rebellion in addition had two other negative economic effects, one of which was the levies imposed on the better-off citizens by the rebels to help them finance their activities. These were often extracted in an arbitrary and haphazard fashion, in keeping with the highly decentralized nature of the revolt, and those raising the money were not always dedicated revolutionaries. The other negative effect was the considerable worsening of the economic situation of many landowners, who in consequence were sometimes forced to sell land, which ended up in Jewish hands, thereby undermining one of the main Palestinian national objectives.

Beyond all of these grim results of the revolt, perhaps its most harmful effects were on the social and political levels. In this time of crisis for the Palestinians, their lack of stateness, the absence of a national focus for their political activity, or of strong, independent political parties or

youth groups, combined with the political hegemony of religious institutions dominated by the *mufti*, proved utterly disastrous. By the end of
the revolt, the traditional Palestinian leadership, which had been obliged
by grass roots pressure to overcome its differences and form a joint
national leadership (the Arab Higher Committee) at the outset of the
general strike in 1936, was shattered. It became even more bitterly
divided by differences over tactics, which were ably exploited by the
British. The British exiled many individual leaders in 1937, and others
fled, some never to return to the country, notably Hajj Amin al-Husayni
himself. The British took over the Supreme Muslim Council, appointing
British officials to supervise it, and depriving the *mufti* of its revenues. In
this situation, leadership fell to the exiled mufti, the leader who in spite
of his distance from the scene of events still had the greatest resources at
his disposal and the most charisma, and who had gradually undermined
or eclipsed or outlived all of his competitors, from his older relative and
rival, Musa Kazim Pasha al-Husayni, to Raghib Bey al-Nashashibi and
Shaykh 'Izz al-Din al-Qassam.

   The revolt thereafter fell victim both to failures at the top – especially
in the *mufti*'s style of leadership, his jealousy of potential rivals, and his
identification of the national cause with himself – and to profound
weaknesses at the base. For reasons related to his own tactical interests,
the *mufti* prevented the rest of the Palestinian leadership from taking
actions it was inclined towards, such as accepting the 1939 White Paper,
which might not have provided strategic victories, but which could have
been to the advantage of the Palestinians. In the case of the White
Paper, it is clear that most of the rest of the Palestinian leadership,
divided though it was, favored acceptance, possibly with conditions.
The *mufti*, surrounded by a few younger and more militant advisors, and
afraid of losing his domination over the national movement, refused,
and carried the day.[49] In exile farther and farther away from Palestine,
and unaware of the devastating impact on the Palestinians of British
repression or of the growth in Zionist strength, the *mufti* was increasingly
out of touch with events on the ground, and his policies became more
and more unrealistic in the years which followed.

   The divided and decentralized nature of the revolt, which at an early
stage helped it to harass the British and throw them off balance
militarily, proved to be a liability in the end. So did the divisions in
Palestinian society between urban factions, rural clans, and individual
leaders, from commanders of rural armed bands to urban notables.[50]
The *mufti*'s tactic of treating those who disagreed with him as traitors,
which at the height of the revolt often meant a death sentence, caused
great suffering and further divided an already fragmented Palestinian

society.[51] This was ultimately a recipe for crushing defeat, given that the Palestinians would need to have been highly united to stand up to the power of a growing Zionist movement, and a British Empire which had not withdrawn from a colonial possession in generations.

Roots of "the Catastrophe"

The net result of the events of the late 1930s was that when the Palestinians faced their most fateful challenge in 1947–49, they were still suffering from the British repression of 1936–39, and were in effect without a unified leadership. Indeed, it might be argued, they were virtually without any leadership at all. The *mufti* was in exile in Beirut after his return from Germany, following a wartime sojourn there which had fatally tainted him in the eyes of many in the West.[52] He remained jealous of any challenge to his dominance of the national movement, although he was even less capable of leading it effectively from a distance than he had been when he was in Palestine. Other leaders, like Jamal al-Husayni, Dr. Husayn Fakhri al-Khalidi, Musa al-ʿAlami, and Raghib Bey Nashashibi could neither take the lead on their own, nor cooperate effectively with one another. The Palestinians still had no functioning national-level institutions, no central para-state mechanisms, no serious financial apparatus, and no centralized military force. The reconstituted Arab Higher Committee, which had in any case been little more than a shell in the late 1930s, was an even less substantial body than before. The lack of representative institutions, which had been one of the worst features of Palestinian politics in the first two decades of the Mandate, now weakened the stature and credibility of the Palestinian leadership, and reduced further its feeble capability to mobilize the populace in the face of the growing strength of the Yishuv.

This essay has argued that the crippling nature of the defeat the Palestinians sustained in 1936–39 was among the main reasons for their failure to overcome the challenges of 1947–48 on the diplomatic, political, or military levels.[53] Although some of the damage of the revolt had been made up by then, notably on the economic plane, the Palestinians were still suffering greatly from its negative after-effects on their national leadership, social cohesion, and military capabilities. They suffered too from having failed utterly in the preceding decades to establish a neutral national forum or representative national institutions that could be the axis around which to organize their struggle against the British and the Zionists. In consequence, the great sacrifices of the 1936–39 revolt, which seems to have been supported by much of Palestinian society at the outset, and which in different circumstances, and with better leadership, might have led to gains, were not only wasted, but in fact gravely weakened the Palestinians for their subsequent ordeal.

Thus the Palestinian catastrophe of 1947–49 was predicated on a series of previous failures. The Palestinians entered the fighting which followed the passage of the UN Partition resolution with a deeply divided leadership, exceedingly limited finances, no centrally organized military forces or centralized administrative organs, and no reliable allies. They faced a Jewish society in Palestine which, although small relative to theirs, was politically unified, had centralized para-state institutions, and was exceedingly well led and extremely highly motivated. The full horrors of the Holocaust had just been revealed, if any further spur to determined action to consummate the objectives of Zionism were needed. The Zionists had already achieved territorial contiguity via land holdings and settlements in the shape of an "N", running north up the coastal strip from Tel Aviv to Haifa, south-east down the Marj Ibn ʿAmir (the Jezreel Valley), and north again up the finger of eastern Galilee.[54] This was the strategic core of the new state, and the springboard for its expansion.

The outcome of the Palestinian–Israeli conflict of 1947–48 was thus a foregone conclusion. The Palestinians had superior numbers, but as we have seen, the Yishuv had more important advantages: a larger and far more diversified economy,[55] better finances,[56] greater firepower, superior organization, and considerable support from the United States and the Soviet Union. All of these factors enabled the nascent Israeli state to triumph over the poorly led, poorly armed, and mainly rural, mainly illiterate Palestinian population of 1.4 million. As I have pointed out elsewhere, the Palestinians have incorporated this and other failures into their national narrative as a case of heroic perseverance against impossible odds.[57] This draws on a Palestinian perception that they have always faced a constellation of enemies so formidable as to be nearly insuperable. Indeed, it is unimaginable that the British Empire would have abandoned Palestine under Arab pressure on the eve of the Second World War, or that the world would have supported the Palestinians against the nascent Israeli state in the wake of the Holocaust.

Nevertheless, a version of history that starts with the insuperable nature of their foes conveniently absolves the Palestinians for any responsibility for their own fate, since, if their enemies were so numerous and powerful, it is little surprise that they were defeated, and no further analysis is required. However, factors such as the poor political calculations, and the disorganization, confusion, and leaderless chaos on the Palestinian side, all of which contributed measurably to the debacle, need to be factored into the Palestinian historical narrative. So too does the fact that the Palestinians, still suffering acutely from the after-effects of the defeat of the 1936–39 revolt, and deprived of a central para-state mechanism, a unified leadership, and representative institutions, in consequence never had a chance of retaining control of their country once they were engaged in an all-out military confrontation with the organized forces of the Yishuv.

Attention to all these considerations has been missing in Palestinian nationalist accounts from the 1960s through the 1970s (with little having changed in much of the historiography since then). Ironically, it might be argued that the "national" element was weak in a national movement led by Hajj Amin al-Husayni, a Muslim cleric in a society with a large Christian minority, who came from a notable family with multiple rivals, and who helped stifle the growth of national political parties like the Istiqlal, and independent grass-roots scouting, union, and religious organizations. In 1936–39 and 1947–48 there appeared to be none of the planning on a national level which the Yishuv engaged in nearly from the beginning of the Zionist movement in the late 1890s, and which was evidenced by the Egyptian and Syrian national revolts of 1919 and 1925–26. For all his dominance of Palestinian politics for nearly two decades, Hajj Amin al-Husayni did not approach the stature of a Saʿd Zaghlul or even a Shukri al-Quwwatli, perhaps most notably because no nationalist political party remotely resembling the Wafd Party, or even the Syrian National Bloc (Kutla Wataniyya), existed in Palestine.

This chapter has paid little attention to the actual course of the fighting in 1947–48. However, in looking at the limited accounts available regarding the Palestinian side of this conflict, one is struck by the extent to which the fighting was a local affair, whereas for the Zionists it was centralized and national. By comparison with 1936–39, indeed, the Palestinians in 1947–49 seem to have been even less organized and even less centralized, and to have had even less of a national focus. Given the analysis in the above pages, we can understand why this may have been the case, and thus some of the basic reasons the Palestinians failed. Perhaps if the Palestinians had managed to hold off their revolt for a decade, or perhaps if they had confronted the British more resolutely or radically earlier on, they might have met with a different outcome. But the might-have-beens of history are ultimately futile. Given the course of Palestinian history until 1948, the underlying causes of what happened in Palestine in that year should be perfectly comprehensible, and the final outcome should not have been unexpected, shocked and surprised though many Palestinians clearly were by it.

Notes

1 The most reliable and careful study of population in Palestine is by Justin McCarthy, *The Population of Palestine: Population Statistics of the Late Ottoman Period and the Mandate* (New York, 1990). He indicates that the Arab population of Palestine was 1,339,773 in 1946, and the Jewish population 602,586 (p. 37). Both had grown larger by 1948. Figures for population by sub-district are from the United Nations report cited in Walid Khalidi, ed., *From Haven to Conquest: Readings in Zionism and the Palestine Problem until 1948* (Beirut, 1971), p. 678, map, p. 671.

2 Khalidi, *From Haven to Conquest*, p. 680, map, p. 673. UN figures, based on British Mandate statistics, show that in 1946 Jews owned 10.6 percent of the privately owned land in Palestine, and Arabs, collectively or privately, owned almost all of the rest. The Arab Office in London, also citing official British figures, calculated that Jews owned no more than 23 percent of arable land in Palestine; cf. *The Future of Palestine* (Geneva, 1947).

3 This is the title of the seminal work by Qustantin Zurayq, *Ma'nat al-nakba* [The Meaning of the Catastrophe] (Beirut, 1948), published as *The Meaning of the Disaster* by R. Bayley Winder (Beirut, 1956).

4 See Issa Khalaf, *Politics in Palestine: Arab Factionalism and Social Disintegration, 1939–1948* (Albany NY, 1991).

5 See Benny Morris, *The Birth of the Palestinian Refugee Problem, 1947–1949* (Cambridge, 1987); and Morris, *1948 and After: Israel and the Palestinians*, rev. ed. (Oxford, 1994). Among the first to publish the results of their research in the Israeli archives regarding the flight of the Palestinian refugees were Tom Segev, *1949: The First Israelis* (New York, 1986), and Simha Flapan, *The Birth of Israel: Myths and Realities* (New York, 1987).

6 The exact number of refugees is hard to ascertain, and has long been highly disputed, in large part for political reasons. Morris, *The Birth*, p. 1, writes of "some 600,000–760,000" refugees. The former figure is very low, while the latter seems more likely to be correct, and is quite close to UN estimates at the time.

7 Avi Shlaim, *Collusion across the Jordan* (Oxford, 1988) is the best source on this aspect of the 1948 war. See also Mary Wilson, *King Abdullah, Britain and the Making of Jordan* (Cambridge, 1987).

8 McCarthy, citing the last British estimates for the country's urban population in 1944, puts the Arab total at 408,000. *Population*, p. 163.

9 On Jaffa, see Mustafa Murad Dabbagh, *Biladuna filastin* [Palestine, Our Country], vol. IV, part 2, *Fil diyar al-yafiyya* [The Jaffa Region] (Beirut, 1972). On Haifa see Mahmoud Yazbak, *Haifa in the Late Ottoman Period, 1864–1914: A Muslim Town in Transition* (Leiden, 1998), and May Seikaly, *Haifa: Transformation of an Arab Society, 1918–1939* (London, 1995).

10 About 199,000 Arabs lived in these cities and towns in 1944, the vast

majority of whom were forced to flee their homes in 1948. McCarthy, *Population*, p. 163.

11 See Walid Khalidi, ed., *All That Remains: The Palestinian Villages Occupied and Depopulated by Israel in 1948* (Washington DC, 1992), which enumerates 418 such villages.

12 Of the 26 million dunams of land in Palestine, about 1.5 million were Jewish owned in 1948. When the fighting ended, they controlled over 20 million. See Hind Amin al-Budayri, *Ard filastin: bayna maza'im al-sihyuniyya wa haqa'iq al-tarikh* [The Land of Palestine: Between the Claims of Zionism and the Facts of History] (Cairo, 1998), Table 23, p. 274.

13 It was Israeli Prime Minister Ben-Gurion himself who thereafter gave canonical form to these allegations in a 1961 speech, as is pointed out by Ilan Pappé in *The Making of the Arab–Israeli Conflict, 1947–1951* (London, 1994), pp. 88–89.

14 Benny Morris, *The Birth*, Tom Segev, *1949*, Simha Flapan, *The Birth Of Israel*, and Avi Shlaim, *Collusion*, all contributed significantly to this process, as did Ilan Pappé, in *The Making*, and others, including Michael Palumbo, *The Palestinian Catastrophe* (London, 1987).

15 In some cases these more recent authors reprised and amplified the analysis of earlier writers such as Walid Khalidi and Erskine Childers in their responses decades ago to the received Israeli version of what happened in 1948. These first refutations of the Israeli version of events include: Walid Khalidi, "Plan *Dalet*: The Zionist Master Plan for the Conquest of Palestine," *Middle East Forum* 37 (November 1961) 22–28; "The Fall of Haifa," *Middle East Forum* 35 (December 1959) 22–32; "Why Did the Palestinians Leave?" *Middle East Forum* 34 (July 1959) 21–24, 35; Erskine Childers, "The Other Exodus," *The Spectator*, no. 6933 (12 May 1961) 672–75, and "The Wordless Wish: From Citizens to Refugees," in Ibrahim Abu Lughod, ed., *The Transformation of Palestine* (Evanston IL, 1971), pp. 165–202. Khalidi's seminal "Plan *Dalet*" article, together with the 1961 correspondence about it and Childers' work, and a number of appendices, were reproduced in *The Journal of Palestine Studies* 18 (Autumn 1988) 4–70.

16 See, for example, Morris, *The Birth*, pp. 128–31.

17 Among the more popular and influential accounts of these events are A.W. Kayyali, *Palestine: A Modern History* (London, 1978), which was published in Arabic in numerous editions, and Naji 'Allush, *al-Muqawama al-'arabiyya fi filastin* [The Arab Resistance in Palestine] (Beirut, 1968). See also Ghassan Kanafani, *Thawrat 1936–39 fi filastin: khalfiyyat wa tafasil wa tahlil* [The Revolt of 1936–39 in Palestine: Background, Details and Analysis] (Beirut, 1974).

18 Walid Khalidi has published a definitive account of the Dayr Yasin massacre: *Dayr Yasin: al-Jum'a, 9/4/1948* [Dayr Yasin: Friday, 9/4/1948] (Beirut, 1998). Khalidi bases his description on the testimony of dozens of survivors, as well as on contemporary and more recently published accounts of these events.

19 See, for example, Khalidi, *From Haven to Conquest*, pp. 1–62.

20 See, for example, Chaim Weizmann, *Trial and Error: The Autobiography of Chaim Weizmann* (London, 1949), pp. 573–89.

21 Haim Levenberg, *The Military Preparations of the Arab Community of Palestine, 1945–1948* (London, 1993).
22 These include Issa Khalaf, *Politics in Palestine*; Philip Mattar, *The Mufti of Jerusalem: Al-Hajj Amin al-Husayni and the Palestinian National Movement* (New York, 1988); and Rashid Khalidi, *Palestinian Identity: The Construction of Modern National Consciousness* (New York, 1997).
23 For an approach which compares Palestinian society during the Mandate to other Middle Eastern societies at comparable stages of development, see R. Khalidi, 'Arab Society in Mandatory Palestine: The Half-Full Glass?" paper presented to conference on "New Approaches to the Study of Ottoman and Arab Societies, 18th-mid-20th Centuries," Boğaziçi University, Istanbul, May 1999.
24 The text of the Mandate can be found in J.C. Hurewitz, ed., *The Middle East and North Africa in World Politics: A Documentary Record*, vol. II (New Haven CT, 1979), pp. 305–9.
25 Ann Mosely Lesch, *Arab Politics in Palestine, 1917–1939: The Frustration of a Nationalist Movement* (Ithaca NY, 1979), pp. 186–87.
26 The degree of this support in the economic sphere alone during the first decade of the Mandate can be gauged from Barbara Smith, *The Roots of Separation in Palestine: British Economic Policy, 1920–1929* (Syracuse NY, 1995).
27 Khalaf, *Politics in Palestine*, p. 236.
28 Albert Hourani, "Ottoman Reform and the Politics of Notables," in W. Polk and R. Chambers, eds., *Beginnings of Modernization in the Middle East: The Nineteenth Century* (Chicago IL, 1968), pp. 41–68.
29 Eric Hobsbawm and Terence Ranger, eds., *The Invention of Tradition* (Cambridge, 1983).
30 This point is made for Haifa by Yazbak, *Haifa in the Late Ottoman Period*.
31 For details of how this system worked in Jerusalem during the late Ottoman period, see R. Khalidi, *Palestinian Identity*, pp. 65–69.
32 Public *awqaf* revenues are dedicated to charitable and other public service purposes; see Yitzhak Reiter, *Islamic Endowments in Jerusalem under British Mandate* (London, 1996).
33 Great Britain. *Parliamentary Command Papers*, Cmd. 5479. "Palestine Royal Commission Report" (the "Peel report") (London, 1937), paras. 80–82.
34 The best treatment of the *mufti* is in Mattar, *Mufti of Jerusalem*.
35 For more details on these secret British subsidies, cf. Weldon Matthews, "The Arab Istiqlal Party in Palestine, 1927–1934" (Ph.D. dissertation, University of Chicago, 1998). For more on the increase in British subsidies to the Supreme Muslim Council in the early 1930s, see Reiter, *Islamic Endowments*, pp. 30–33.
36 Zachary Lockman's *Comrades and Enemies: Arab and Jewish Workers in Palestine, 1906–1948* (Berkeley CA, 1996) has illuminating material on Reuven Shiloah, the founder of the Mossad, who in addition to organizing spy networks in the Arab countries in the 1930s was also a labor organizer among Palestinian Arabs.
37 A biography of Raghib al-Nashashibi, by the journalist Nasser Eddin Nashashibi, *Jerusalem's Other Voice: Ragheb Nashashibi and Moderation in*

Palestinian Politics, 1920–1948 (Exeter, 1990), must be used with care, but includes much primary material.

38 The rural operations of some of these merchants and money-lenders in the late nineteenth century are outlined in Bishara Doumani, *Rediscovering Palestine: The Merchants and Peasants of Jabal Nablus, 1700–1900* (Berkeley CA, 1995).

39 While Palestine took in 232,524 Jewish immigrants between 1932 and 1943, the United States, with its the wide-open spaces, was only willing to accept 170,883 during the same period: W. Khalidi, *From Haven to Conquest*, Appendix VI, Table C, p. 855.

40 For details, see Matthews, "The Arab Istiqlal Party."

41 The best short study of Qassam is S. Abdullah Schleifer, "The Life and Thought of 'Izz-id-Din al-Qassam," *The Islamic Quarterly* 22 (1979) 61–81. See also his "'Izz al-Din al-Qassam: Preacher and *Mujahid*," in E. Burke III, ed., *Struggle and Survival in the Modern Middle East* (Berkeley CA, 1993), pp. 164–78. There is a huge literature on Qassam in Arabic, which attests to the importance that he came to have after his death to a broad range of political and intellectual trends, most recently the Islamists.

42 While many Palestinians revered him, then and later, and his memory was used for their purposes by many others, Qassam's memory was reviled by his contemporary opponents, in a manner which has left a strong trace in official British- and Zionist-influenced historiography. Thus John Marlowe's *Rebellion in Palestine* (London, 1946), which reflects a pro-Zionist British view, describes his actions (p. 145) as "the exploits of a brigand." Marcel Roubicek writes in a similar vein in *Echo of the Bugle: Extinct Military and Constabulary Forces in Palestine and Transjordan, 1915–1967* (Jerusalem, 1974), p. 53.

43 See the diaries of the young nationalist Akram Zu'aytir for a contemporary reaction to the funeral: *Al-Haraka al-wataniyya al-filistiniyya 1935–1939: yawmiyyat Akram Zu'aytir* [The Palestinian National Movement 1935–1939: The diaries of Akram Zu'aytir] (Beirut, 1980), pp. 27 ff. The Arabic press of the months which followed is replete with echoes of Qassam's death.

44 Between 1939 and 1946, Jewish land purchases amounted to about 145,000 dunams, nearly 10 percent of the total amount of land purchased in Palestine by the Zionist movement before 1948: W. Khalidi, *From Haven to Conquest*, Appendix I, pp. 842–43.

45 *Ibid.*, Appendix IV, pp. 846–49.

46 This calculation is based on the figures in W. Khalidi, *From Haven to Conquest*, Table A4–5, p. 104, which indicates that less than 40 percent of the male Muslim population (and a slightly larger proportion of the male Christian population) was between the ages of 20 and 60 in 1940.

47 This is clear from the figures in W. Khalidi, *From Haven to Conquest*, Appendix III, p. 845, which indicate that the British confiscated over 13,200 firearms from Arabs from 1936 until 1945. During the same period, confiscations from Jews totaled 521 weapons.

48 Robert Nathan, Oscar Gass, and Daniel Creamer, *Palestine: Problem and Promise, An Economic Study* (Washington DC, 1946), Table 1, p. 148. On the Jewish economy in Palestine cf. Smith, *Roots of Separation*.

49 Khalaf, *Politics in Palestine*, pp. 74–77.

50 Khalaf, *Politics in Palestine*, provides the most accurate perspective on how these intra-elite conflicts continued in the years after the crushing of the revolt.

51 In his unpublished autobiography, the newspaper publisher 'Isa al-'Isa details the results of his conflict with the *mufti*, which led to the burning of his house and his flight to Beirut in 1937. See 'Isa al-'Isa, "*Min dhikrayat al-madi*" [Memories of the past] (unpublished manuscript). See also Noha Tadros, "*Min dhikrayat al-Madi*, Souvenirs: autobiographie et representation de soi. 'Issa al 'Issa (journaliste palestinien 1878–1950)" (Ph.D. dissertation, Institut National des Langues et Civilisations Orientales, Paris, 1999). A similar story about his father, Shaykh Muhi al-Din 'Abd al-Shafi, who was a member of the Supreme Muslim Shari'a Council, was related by Dr. Haydar Abd al-Shafi in an interview: Gaza, 9 August 1999.

52 The *mufti*'s wartime connections with the Nazis were grist for the propaganda mills of the Zionist movement, which laid the basis for a long-lasting portrayal of Palestinian nationalism as intrinsically anti-Semitic. See e.g., Joseph Schectman, *The Mufti and the Fuhrer: The Rise and Fall of Haj Amin el-Husseini* (New York, 1965).

53 See Levenberg, *Military Preparations*, for a generally accurate but somewhat confused account of the background to the Palestinian defeats of 1947–48.

54 See Khalidi, *Palestinian Identity*, for more details of how these areas were acquired.

55 Nathan, Gass and Creamer, in *Palestine: Problem and Promise*, table, p. 148, show that the Jewish share of national income in 1936 was already larger than that of the Arabs (£P18m vs.£P16m). The disparity was even greater by 1948.

56 The economy of the Yishuv was not simply larger and more dynamic: it could command far greater financial resources than could that of the Palestinian Arabs. According to Zeev Sternhell, during the 1920s "the annual inflow of Jewish capital was on average 41.5 percent larger than the Jewish net domestic product (NDP) . . . its ratio to NDP did not fall below 33 percent in any of the pre-World War II years and was kept at about 15 percent in all but one year since 1941." *The Founding Myths of Israel: Nationalism, Socialism, and the Making of the Jewish State* (Princeton NJ, 1998), p. 217.

57 The word which perhaps best sums up this sense in which failure has been surmounted and survived, which in itself is a sort of victory, is *sumud*, commonly translated as "steadfastness," but encompassing all the meanings just suggested. The word was ubiquitous in Palestinian narratives both of the various stages of the fighting in Lebanon from the late 1960s until 1982, and of resistance to the occupation in the West Bank and Gaza Strip from 1967 until the *intifada* began in 1987. For more details, see R. Khalidi, *Palestinian Identity*, pp. 177–209.

2 Revisiting the Palestinian exodus of 1948

Benny Morris

Over the years, the history of the Arab–Zionist conflict has undergone interpretative innovation. The massive declassification of archival documentation in the West and in Israel made possible the historiographic breakthrough of the late 1980s that is now commonly called the "new historiography." And it is the further declassificatory initiative in Israel today that compels a fresh look at much of what was published in the late 1980s and early 1990s. I am speaking specifically of the opening of certain private and institutional papers, of the protocols of Israel's Cabinet meetings between 1948 and 1953, with additional years now in the works, and, most significantly, of the massive declassification of the documentation stored in the Haganah Archive in Tel Aviv and the Israel Defense Forces and Defense Ministry Archive (IDFA) in Givatayim. A certain amount of material is still being held back, but on average more than 95 percent of each file is being made available. The archive's small staff cannot meet the academic community's needs and, so far, less than 10 percent of the 140,000 files covering the years 1947–56 have been opened. But as most of the now declassified files relate to the 1948 War and, more specifically, to its operational side, it can be said that a great proportion of the important material on 1948 in the IDFA is now available.

Looking through these new materials, both military and civilian, has compelled a fresh look at the creation of the Palestinian refugee problem. When writing *The Birth of the Palestinian Refugee Problem 1947–1949* in the mid-1980s, I had no access to the materials in the IDFA or Haganah Archive and precious little to first-hand military materials deposited elsewhere. None the less, the new materials I have seen over the past few years tend to confirm and reinforce the major lines of description and analysis, and the conclusions, in *The Birth* and in a subsequent volume, *1948 and After*, published in 1990.

These main conclusions were that the refugeedom of the 700,000 Palestinians was essentially a product of the war, of the shelling, shooting, and bombing, and of the fears that these generated. But the flight of the Palestinians was also due to their incompetent, self-serving, and venal leadership, a leadership that failed to prepare properly for war, then plunged headlong into it, and, finally fled at the first whiff of grapeshot, leaving behind leaderless, bewildered, and defeated communities, which then also took flight. Concomitantly, the months of fighting caused the collapse of Palestinian urban society, creating joblessness, increased food prices, and poverty. The gradual exodus, which began with the upper and middle classes, was pushed along by the Haganah, the Irgun Zvai Leumi (IZL or simply "Irgun," lit. National Military Organization), the Lohamei Herut Yisrael (LHI or simply "Stern Gang," lit. Freedom Fighters of Israel), and IDF expulsions at specific sites; by orders in certain areas and towns by local Arab officials and Arab troops to groups of Palestinians – such as women and children – or to specific communities to leave their homes and clear the battlefield; and to Israeli atrocities which unnerved and panicked neighboring communities. The Arab states also contributed to the Palestinians' refugeedom by failing at certain crucial junctures to give the Palestinians clear signals about whether or not to leave and, subsequently, by invading Palestine and then rejecting a succession of proposed compromises and by failing to absorb the refugees in their own countries.

Above all, let me reiterate, the refugee problem was caused by attacks by Jewish forces on Arab villages and towns and by the inhabitants' fear of such attacks, compounded by expulsions, atrocities, and rumors of atrocities – and by the crucial Israeli Cabinet decision in June 1948 to bar a refugee return.[1]

The declassification of the new material none the less necessitates a widening and deepening of description and analysis regarding various aspects of the exodus. I have already begun to probe and write anew about certain episodes and processes and will continue to do this – ultimately producing a revised edition of *The Birth* which will be more accurate, comprehensive, and deeper than the original.

For good or ill, the newly opened material generally tends to reinforce the version of events of those who would stress the Yishuv's and Israel's part in the propulsion of the Palestinian Arabs out of the areas that became the State of Israel rather than that of those who would reduce Israeli responsibility for what happened. Let me quickly add, first that this upshot seems to me natural in that it was precisely those materials that cast Israel in a bad light that Israel's official and semi-official archival repositories took care not to reveal. And, second, I suspect that if and when the Arab states open their archives for 1948 to researchers, the material there may serve to "adjust" the balance and increase our awareness of the direct and indirect responsibility of these states for the tragedy that engulfed Palestine and the Palestinians (i.e., Arab responsibility for unleashing the two stages of the 1948 War, irresponsibility with regard to the emergent refugee problem, orders to specific Arab communities to leave, and so on).

I would like to focus on two subjects to illustrate the importance of the new material: first, transfer thinking among the Zionist leaders in the decade leading up to 1948, and second, the expulsions and atrocities in the central upper Galilee during and immediately after Operation Hiram in October–November 1948. Some of the material relating to the first subject may have been open to researchers in the early and mid-1980s, when *The Birth* was being written, but I was not then aware of its existence.

Transfer thinking, 1937–1947

Among the first criticisms of *The Birth* by Palestinian and pro-Palestinian scholars (such as Nur Masalha and Norman Finkelstein) was that it ignored or underplayed the role of pre-1948 proposals and thinking about transfer among the Zionist leadership in what actually happened in 1948. More recently, Zionist and pro-Zionist critics (such as Shabtai Teveth and Efraim Karsh) have either flatly denied that the Zionist leaders ever seriously entertained the idea of transfer or, at the least, charged that *The Birth* exaggerated the quantity and quality of such transfer thinking and asserted that there was no connection between the occasional whimsical toying with the idea and what transpired in 1948. The controversy here is really about the nature of Zionism and about the degree of Zionist premeditation in what occurred in 1948.

The question goes to the heart of Zionism and to the root of the Zionist–Arab conflict. From the start, the Zionists wished to make the area of Palestine a Jewish state. Unfortunately, the country contained a native Arab population of 500,000 at the start of the Zionist influx around 1882 and of 1.3 million in 1947. How was a round peg to fit into a square hole? How was a Jewish minority – of some 60,000–80,000 in 1914 and 650,000 in 1947 – to gain control of a country populated by an antagonistic Arab majority? Several solutions offered themselves.

The first and most important was through *Aliya* or further Jewish immigration. Gradually the minority would demographically overwhelm the native majority, despite the Arabs' higher birth rates; once the Jews were in a majority, a Jewish state would naturally ensue. Unfortunately, the Ottoman Turks and subsequently, from a certain point on, their British imperial successors, restricted immigration. At the same time, through most of the period, relatively few Diaspora Jews actually wished to immigrate to Palestine. Most, if moving, preferred North America,

Western Europe, and the Commonwealth states. A Jewish majority in Palestine would not come to pass through immigration.

A second solution lay the way of South Africa: the establishment of an apartheid state, with a settler minority lording it over a large, exploited native majority. But this was anathema to the majority of Zionists, who arrived from Europe with liberal or social-democratic views and aimed to establish an egalitarian or at least democratic polity. Apartheid was out of the question.

A third solution lay the way of partition. By the 1930s many of the Zionist leaders understood that the pace of Jewish immigration was insufficient to lead within the foreseeable future to a Jewish majority – and concluded that, at least temporarily, the Jews would have to forgo sovereignty over the whole land of Israel and make do with only a part of the country. A Jewish majority in the whole of Palestine appeared unattainable. But perhaps the country could be divided in such a way as to create a majority in the part allocated for Jewish sovereignty? The problem with partition, however, was that any way one divided the country – unless one declared the minute area of Tel Aviv and its immediate environs a Jewish state – the state that emerged would necessarily contain an Arab majority or at least a very large Arab minority subversive of and hostile to the Jewish polity to which it had been consigned. Indeed, the Jewish state faced such a problem in the UN Partition Plan of November 1947: it would have had 55 percent Jews and 40–45 percent Arabs. Any way one cut it, partition would be extremely problematic, to say the least. How, for instance, the new state would have dealt with its enormous Arab minority in 1948, had there been no war and no refugee problem, is a good question.

The last and, let me say obvious and most logical, solution to the Zionists' demographic problem lay the way of transfer: you could create a homogeneous Jewish state or at least a state with an overwhelming Jewish majority by moving or transferring all or most of the Arabs out of its prospective territory. And this, in fact, is what happened in 1948.

In *The Birth* I devoted several pages to indicating that transfer was, indeed, something Zionist leaders like David Ben-Gurion had thought about in the decade before the first Arab–Israeli war and I implied that this in some way was preparatory to what actually transpired during the fighting. During the 1990s, I looked afresh at the matter, partly in response to Nur Masalha's book, *Expulsion of the Palestinians*.[2]

My conclusion was and remains that thinking about the transfer of all or part of Palestine's Arabs out of the prospective Jewish state was pervasive among Zionist leadership circles long before 1937, when Lord Peel recommended transfer alongside partition as the only possible solution to the conflict, and continued to exercise the Zionist imagination during the following decade. But how exactly this thinking affected Zionist policy and actions in the course of the 1948 War remains more complicated than some Arab researchers have suggested.

As Masalha has shown, many if not most of Zionism's mainstream leaders expressed at least passing support for the idea of transfer during the movement's first decades. True, as the subject was sensitive, they did not often or usually state this in public. Such utterances would certainly have annoyed Arabs and Turks, and perhaps others. But traces, and more than traces, of support for transfer are well documented. Herzl never referred to the idea in his main published works, *Der Judenstaat* [The Jews' State] and *Altneuland* [Old-New Land]. But in his diary he jotted down, on 12 June 1895, the following passage:

We must expropriate gently . . . We shall try to spirit the penniless population across the border by procuring employment for it in the transit countries, while denying it any employment in our country . . . Both the process of expropriation and the removal of the poor must be carried out discreetly and circumspectly.[3]

Given that the vast majority of Palestine's Arabs at the turn of the century were "poor," Herzl can only have meant some form of massive transfer. But he realized that discretion and circumspection must accompany any such enterprise.

This discretion and circumspection was to characterize Zionist references to the idea of transfer during the following decades. But the July 1937 publication of the Peel Commission report – and its endorsement in principle by the British government – seemed to open the floodgates to a more open, if not quite public, discussion of the idea. Peel's recommendation to transfer at least some 225,000 Arabs out of the lowlands of the proposed Jewish state propelled some of the Zionist leaders into transports of enthusiasm. Immediately with its publication, David Ben-Gurion, the Yishuv's leader, jotted down in his diary:

In my comment on the report immediately after the first reading (from 10.7.37) I ignored a central point whose importance outweighs all the other positive [points] and counterbalances all the report's deficiencies and drawbacks, and if it does not remain a dead letter, it could give us something that we never had before, even when we were independent, including during the First Commonwealth and also during the Second Commonwealth: The compulsory transfer of the Arabs from the valleys proposed for the Jewish state.

I ignored this fundamental point out of a prejudice that this [i.e., transfer] is not possible, and that it is not practicable. But the more I look at the commission's conclusions and the more the gigantic importance of this proposal becomes clear – [the more] I reach the conclusion that the first obstacle to implementing this proposal is – our own failure to come to grips with it and our being prisoners to prejudices and intellectual habits that flourished in our midst in other circumstances.

With the evacuation of the Arab community from the valleys we achieve, for the first time in our history, a real Jewish state – an agricultural body of one or more million people, continuous, heavily populated, at one with its land which is completely its own. We achieve the possibility of a giant national settlement, on a large area that is *all in the hands of the state* . . . As with a magic wand, all the difficulties and defects that preoccupied us until now in our settlement enterprise [will vanish] – the question of Hebrew labor, defense, an organized economy, rational and pre-determined exploitation of the land and water. We are given an opportunity that we never dreamed of and could not dare dream of in our most daring imaginings. This is more than a state, more than [self-] government, [more than] sovereignty – this is a national consolidation in a homeland free of handcuffs and external restraints creating power and solidity and rootedness that are more important than any mere political control . . . A continuous block of two and a half million dunams . . . the possibility of the new settlement of fifty or one hundred thousand families . . . when we have a Jewish state in the country and [outside] a Jewish people 16 million strong . . . nothing will be beyond the capabilities of this combination of forces, possibilities, needs and realities.

And we must first of all cast off the weakness of thought and will and prejudice – that [says that] this transfer is impracticable.

As before, I am aware of the terrible difficulty posed by a foreign force uprooting some 100,000 [*sic*] Arabs from the villages they lived in for hundreds of years – will Britain dare carry this out?

Certainly it will not do it – if we do not want it, and if we do not push it to do it with our force and with the force of our faith. Even if a maximum amount of pressure is applied – it is possible she may still be deterred . . . It is certainly possible – and [nothing] greater than this has been done for our cause in our time [than Peel proposing transfer].

And we did not propose this – the Royal Commission . . . did . . . and we must grab hold of this conclusion [i.e., recommendation] as we grabbed hold of the Balfour Declaration, even more than that – as we grabbed hold of Zionism itself we must cleave to this conclusion, with all our strength and will and faith – because of all the Commission's conclusions, this is the one that alone offers some recompense for the tearing away of other parts of the country [i.e., the commission's apportioning of most of the Land of Israel for Arab sovereignty], and [the proposal] *also has great political logic from the Arab perspective,* as Transjordan needs settlement and an increase of population and development and money, and the English government – the richest of governments – is required by her Royal Commission to provide the funds needed for this, and in the implementation of this transfer is a great blessing for the Arab state – and for us it is a question of life, existence, protection of culture, [Jewish population] increase, freedom and independence . . . What is inconceivable in normal times is possible in revolutionary times; and if at this time the opportunity is missed and what is possible only in such great hours is not carried out – a whole world is lost . . . Any doubt on our part about the necessity of this transfer, any doubt we cast about the possibility of its implementation, any hesitancy on our part about its justice may lose [us] an historic opportunity that may not recur. The transfer clause in my eyes is more important than all our demands for additional land. This is the largest and most important and most vital additional "area" ... We must distinguish between the importance and urgency of our different demands. We must recognize the most important wisdom of any historical work: The wisdom of what comes first and what later.

There are a number of things that [we] struggle for now [but] which we cannot achieve now. For example the Negev. [On the other hand,] the evacuation [of the Arabs from] the [Jezreel] Valley we shall [i.e., must] achieve now – and, if not, perhaps we will never achieve it. If we do not succeed in removing the Arabs from our midst, when a royal commission proposes this to England, and transferring them to the Arab area – it will not be achieveable easily (or perhaps at all) after the [Jewish] state is established, and the rights of the minorities [in it] will [necessarily] be assured, and the whole world that is antagonistic towards us will carefully scrutinize our behavior towards our minorities. This thing must be done now – and the first step – perhaps the *crucial* [step] – *is conditioning ourselves for its implementation.*[4]

These were the words set down by Zionism's leader in his diary. But the following month Ben-Gurion presented the gist of his thinking on the matter in a more public forum, the Twentieth Zionist Congress convened in Zurich specifically to consider the Peel proposals. And there Ben-Gurion once again posited transfer in no uncertain terms: "We do not want to expropriate," he said.

[But] transfer of population has already taken place in the [Jezreel] Valley, in the Sharon [Plain] and in other places. You are aware of the work of the Jewish National Fund in this respect. [The reference is to the sporadic uprooting of Arab tenant-farmer communities from lands purchased by the JNF.] Now a transfer of wholly different dimensions will have to be carried out. In various parts of the country new Jewish settlement will not be possible unless there is a transfer of the Arab fellahin ... It is important that this plan came from the Commission and not from us ... The transfer of population is what makes possible a comprehensive settlement program. Fortunately for us, the Arab people have enormous desolate areas. The growing Jewish power in the country will increase our possibilities to carry out a large transfer. You must remember that this method [i.e., possibility] also contains an important humane and Zionist idea. To transfer parts of a people [i.e., the Arabs] to their own country and to settle empty lands [i.e., Transjordan and Iraq] ...[5]

Despite the fact that the notion of transfer had been proposed by a royal commission and that Ben-Gurion had seen fit to speak of it in the plenum of the Zionist Congress, the subject was still very sensitive. Indeed, a gauge of its continuing sensitivity is to be found in the fact that the Jewish press reports about the Congress' proceedings generally failed to mention that Ben-Gurion, or anyone else, had come out strongly in favor of transfer or indeed had even raised the subject. And when the Zionist Organization published the texts of the addresses the following year, reference to transfer was almost completely excised from every speech. Needless to say, the passage quoted above from Ben-Gurion's speech was completely deleted from this laundered version of the proceedings.[6]

Subsequently, the matter of transfer repeatedly cropped up at the meetings of the Jewish Agency Executive (JAE), the "government" of the Yishuv and the leading body of the Zionist Organization. However, according to the existing protocols, the Executive debated the matter infrequently over the years 1939–47. Usually, the matter was referred to in an isolated sentence or half-sentence, without follow-up. My assumption is that more was said about transfer at these meetings than actually was recorded in the protocol. The issue was highly sensitive – and it was common practice in Zionist bodies to order stenographers to "take a break" and thus to exclude from the record discussion on such matters. But, perhaps, the record does not lie and transfer was simply not discussed often or comprehensively, perhaps because all or most of the JAE members simply felt that there was no need for such debate. At the time, the idea was deemed impractical and, in any case, all or almost all members were in agreement on the matter. The subject was highly sensitive; the less said about it the better as leaks could be highly embarrassing.

None the less, according to Jewish Agency records, in June 1938 transfer was broadly discussed in successive meetings of the JAE. On 7 June, Ben-Gurion proposed that the Zionist movement's future "lines of action" included discussing with the neighboring Arab states "the matter of voluntarily transferring Arab tenant-farmers, laborers and fellahin from the Jewish state to the neighboring states."[7] And on 12 June the matter was roundly discussed. Werner David Senator, a Hebrew University executive, said that the Yishuv must aim for "maximal transfer." Menahem Ussishkin, head of the JNF, said that there was nothing immoral about transferring 60,000 Arab families: "It is the most moral [thing to do]." Berl Katznelson, one of the dominant Mapai Party's leaders, said: "A large transfer must be agreed." And Ben-Gurion said: "I support compulsory transfer. I don't see in it anything immoral."[8]

The consensus or near-consensus in support of transfer – voluntary if possible, compulsory if necessary – was clear. Nor, as some critics have contended, did interest in and support for transfer end or wane when the British government in effect dropped the idea with the publication, in October 1938, of the Woodhead Commission report. The commission had ostensibly been set up the previous January to look into ways of implementing the Peel partition recommendation; but, in effect, its mandate was to bury the Peel proposals and the idea of partition. On 12 December 1938, months after the British government had retreated from partition and transfer, Ben-Gurion jotted down in his diary: "We shall propose to Iraq 10 million Palestine pounds for the transfer of one hundred thousand Arab families from Palestine to Iraq."[9]

Nor did the onset of World War II do much to dampen Ben-Gurion's enthusiasm for transfer. Rather the opposite. Nazi persecution of the Jews only heightened his appreciation of the urgent need for more empty land in Palestine on which to settle Jewish immigrants. Moreover, the spectacle of Nazi exploitation of German minorities in central and Eastern Europe to subvert opposing regimes acted as a spur to Zionist thinking about how the prospective Jewish state must rid itself, *ab initio*, of its prospective subversive Arab minority; and the war itself provided precedents and models of actual ethnic transfers that served to rationalize the demographic and geopolitical situation in various nation states. As Ben-Gurion saw things, more such transfers were on the cards in the post-war European settlement. The fact that Her Majesty's government in 1938 had shied away from the idea of transfer was no reason to abandon hope.

In October 1941, Ben-Gurion expatiated at length about the need for and practicalities of transfer in a memorandum outlining future Zionist policy. He believed that parts of Palestine's Arab population – "the Druse, several of the Beduin tribes in the Jordan Valley and the South, the Circassians, and perhaps also the Matawalis [Shi'ites of northern Galilee]" would "not mind being transferred, under favourable conditions, to some neighbouring country." Moreover, "it would . . . be probably not too difficult" to transfer tenant-farmers and landless laborers out of the country. But a complete transfer of the bulk of the Arab population could only be carried out by force, by "ruthless compulsion," in Ben-Gurion's phrase. However, recent European history, Ben-Gurion pointed out, had demonstrated that a massive, compulsory transfer of populations was possible – and the ongoing world war had made the idea of transfer even more popular as the surest and most practical way to solve the difficult and dangerous problem of national minorities. The post-war settlement in Europe, he envisioned, would include massive population transfers. But the Zionists must take care not to preach openly or advocate compulsory transfer, as this would be impolitic and would antagonize many in the West. At the same time, Ben-Gurion reasoned, the Zionist movement should do nothing to hamper those in the West who were busy advocating transfer as a necessary element in a solution to the Palestine problem.[10]

Ben-Gurion was not the only Zionist leader who kept anxiously, not to say obsessively, mulling over the possibilities of transfer. Chaim Weizmann, president of the Zionist Organization and the movement's liberal elder statesman, repeatedly pressed the idea on various interlocutors. The following is a description – possibly penned by Lewis Namier, one of Weizmann's aides – of Weizmann's talk with Soviet ambassador to London Ivan Maisky in January 1941. The talk focused on the post-war settlement in Palestine:

Dr. Weizmann said he had had . . . a very interesting talk with M. Maisky . . . Mr. Maisky said there would have to be an exchange of populations. Dr. Weizmann said that if half a million Arabs could be transferred, two million Jews could be put in their place. That, of course, would be a first instalment; what might happen afterwards was a matter for history. Mr. Maisky's comment was that they in Russia had also had to deal with exchanges of population. Dr. Weizmann said that the distance they had to deal with in Palestine would be smaller; they would be transferring the Arabs only into Iraq or Transjordan. Mr. Maisky asked whether some difficulties might not arise in transferring a hill-country population to the plains, and Dr. Weizmann replied that a beginning might be made with the Arabs from the Jordan Valley; but anyhow conditions in Transjordan were not so very different from the Palestine hill-country . . . Dr. Weizmann explained that they were unable to deal with [the Arabs] as, for instance, the Russian authorities would deal with a backward element in their population in the USSR. Nor would they desire to do so.[11]

The possibility of solving the problem of Palestine had in effect been shelved by Britain, the Zionist movement, and the Arabs during the Second World War; the world had more pressing problems. So, for the duration of the global conflict, talk of the practicalities of transfer was pointless. None the less, the matter came up from time to time in internal Zionist deliberations. For example, on 7 May 1944 the JAE discussed the British Labour Party Executive's resolution supporting transfer as part of a solution to the Palestine conundrum. Moshe Shertok (Sharett), the director of the Jewish Agency's political department, soon to be the state of Israel's first foreign minister and second prime minister, began: "The transfer can be the archstone, the final stage in the political development, but on no account the starting point. By doing this [i.e., by talking prematurely about transfer] we are mobilizing enormous forces against the idea and subverting [its implementation] in advance . . ." And he continued: "What will happen once the Jewish state is established – it is very possible that the result will be transfer of Arabs."

Ben-Gurion followed Shertok:

When I heard these things [i.e., about the Labour Party Executive's resolution] . . . I had some difficult thoughts . . . [But] I reached the conclusion that it is best that this remain [i.e., that the resolution remain as part of Labour's official platform] . . . Were we asked what should be our program, I would find it inconceiveable to tell them transfer . . . because talk on the subject might cause harm in two ways: (a) It could cause [us] harm in public opinion in the world, because it might give the impression that there is no room [for more Jews] in Palestine without ejecting the Arabs . . . (b) [such declarations in support of transfer] would force the Arabs onto . . . their hind legs [i.e., would shock and stir them up].

None the less, declared Ben-Gurion: "Transfer of Arabs is easier than any other type of transfer. There are Arab states in the area . . . and it is clear that if the Arabs [of Palestine] are sent [to the Arabs countries] this will better their situation and not the contrary . . ."[12] The rest of the JAE members followed suit. Yitzhak Gruenbaum, who would be Israel's first interior minister in 1948, declared:

To my mind there is an Arab consideration in favour of transfer. That is, in the increase of population of Iraq by [additional] Arabs. It is the function of the Jews occasionally to make the Gentiles [goyim] aware of things they did not until then perceive . . . If for example it is possible to create artificially in Iraq conditions that will magnetize the Arabs of Palestine to emigrate to Iraq, I do not see in it any iniquity or crime . . .[13]

Eliahu Dobkin, a Mapai stalwart and director of the Jewish Agency's immigration department, said: "There will be in the country a large [Arab] minority and it must be ejected. There is no room for our internal inhibitions [in this matter]. . ." Eliezer Kaplan, the number-three man in Mapai who would become Israel's first finance minister, said: "Regarding the matter of transfer I have only one request: Let us not start arguing among ourselves . . . This will cause us the most damage externally." Dov Joseph, the Agency's legal adviser (and soon to be Israel's justice minister), chimed in: "I agree with Mr. Kaplan." Werner David Senator said: "I do not regard the question of transfer as a moral or immoral problem . . . It is not a matter I would refuse to consider . . ."[14]

Ben-Gurion returned to the transfer theme the following month, when he proposed bringing 1 million Jewish immigrants to Palestine's shores "immediately." The religious Mizrahi Party's Moshe Hayim Shapira said that the matter would force the Yishuv to consider transferring Arabs. Ben-Gurion replied:

I am opposed that any proposal for transfer should come from our side. I do not reject transfer on moral grounds and I do not reject it on political grounds. If there is a chance for it [I support it]; with regard to the Druse it is possible. It is possible to move all the Druse voluntarily to Jabal Druse [in Syria]. The other [Arabs] – I don't know. But it must not be a Jewish proposal. . .[15]

What is the importance of these expressions of support for transfer in the decade before 1948? How do they connect to what actually happened during the first Arab–Israeli war? Some researchers – such as Masalha – will have us believe that there was a direct, causal, one-to-one link between the earlier thinking and the subsequent actions. My feeling is that the connection is more subtle and indirect.

The haphazard thinking about transfer before 1937 and the virtual consensus in support of the notion from 1937 on contributed to what happened in 1948 in the sense that they conditioned the Zionist leadership, and below it, the officials and officers who managed the new state's civilian and military agencies, for the transfer that took place. To one degree or another, these men all arrived at 1948, in no small measure owing to the continuous anti-Zionist Arab violence which played out against the growing persecution of Diaspora Jewry in central and eastern Europe, with a mindset which was open to the idea and implementation of transfer and expulsion. And the transfer that occurred – which encountered almost no serious opposition from any part of the Yishuv – transpired smoothly in large measure because of this pre-conditioning, though also because all or almost all came to understand, after the Arabs of Palestine had initiated the war and after the Arab states invaded Palestine, that transfer was what the Jewish state's survival and future well-being demanded.

One last point on this subject. Much more work needs to be done on the Yishuv's attitude to transfer. So far, only the surface of the available documentation has been scratched. The diaries and letters of various Zionist leaders and officials and the files of various Zionist bodies between 1881 and 1937 need to be thoroughly combed. So must the protocols of various political bodies – the Mapai Centre, the political committees of other parties – and the diaries and correspondence of the leaders and officials for the period 1937–47. Of particular interest might be the papers from 1937–47 of the majors and colonels and generals of 1948 who actually carried out the transfer, such as Yigal Allon and Yitzhak Sadeh and Moshe Carmel.

Expulsion and atrocity in Operation Hiram, 1948

Nothing that I have seen in Israeli archives during the past decade indicates the existence before 1948 of a Zionist master plan to expel the Arabs of Palestine. Nor, in looking at the materials from 1948, is there anything to show that such a plan existed and was systematically unleashed and implemented in the course of the war, or that any overall expulsory policy decision was taken by the Yishuv's executive bodies – the Jewish Agency Executive, the Defence Committee, the People's Administration, or the Provisional Government of Israel – in the course

of the 1948 War (apart from the June–July 1948 Cabinet decision to bar
a refugee return).

None the less, expulsion was in the air in the war of 1948. From April
on, Palestinian Arabs were the target of a series of concrete expulsions
from individual villages, clusters of villages, and towns. The readiness
among the Israeli commanders and officials to expel fluctuated in
relation to the local conditions and to the national military situation
(certainly there was greater willingness to expel after the Arab states
invaded Palestine on 15 May, putting the Yishuv's very existence
temporarily in question), the character and outlook of the Israeli
commanders, and the nature of the Arab villagers and townspeople
involved (traditional anti-Zionists or "friendly" Arabs, Muslims,
Christians, Druse, etc.), topographical conditions, and so on.

Clearly, the readiness to resort to compulsory transfer grew in the
Yishuv's bureaucracies and among its military units in the course of the
first months of fighting, and as the fighting became more desperate,
bloody and widespread, with Ben-Gurion himself setting the tone and
indicating direction, usually resorting to a nod and a wink if not actually
issuing explicit orders. Given his deep awareness of historical processes
and the mechanics and importance of historiography, Ben-Gurion was
very careful, in speech and writing, not to leave too clear a spoor in his
wake.

Ben-Gurion apart, the documentation that has come to light or been
declassified during the past ten years offers a great deal of additional
information about the expulsions of 1948. The departure of Arab
communities from some sites, departures that were described in *The
Birth* as due to fear or IDF military attack or were simply unexplained,
now appear to have been tinged if not characterized by Haganah or IDF
expulsion orders and actions (for example, Ein Hod near Haifa and
Isdud, today's Ashdod, near Ashkelon). This means that the proportion
of the 700,000 Arabs who took to the roads as a result of expulsions
rather than as a result of straightforward military attack or fear of attack,
etc. is greater than indicated in *The Birth*. Similarly, the new documentation has revealed atrocities that I had not been aware of while writing
The Birth (for example, at al-Husayniyya, north of the Sea of Galilee, in
March, and at Burayr, north of Beersheba, in May). These atrocities are
important in understanding the precipitation of various phases of the
Arab exodus.

Let me add that with respect to both expulsions and atrocities, we can
expect additional revelations as the years pass and as more Israeli
records become available. As things stand, the IDFA has a standing
policy guideline not to open material explicitly describing expulsions

and atrocities. Thus, much IDF material on these subjects remains closed. But IDFA officials, like all officials, occasionally overlook a document with an explicit description or, more frequently, relent when it comes to implicit or indirect descriptions. Thus, the archive may declassify a document carrying an order to expel but keep sealed the following document in which the local commander details how he carried out the order. Similarly, the IDFA will generally declassify a document which uses euphemisms such as to "move" (*le'haziz*) or "evacuate" (*le'fanot*) a community while keeping closed a document employing the more explicit term to "expel" (*le'garesh*).

Occasionally, the new documentation compels a revision of *The Birth* with respect not to a specific site but to a whole campaign and a large area. A case in point is "Operation Hiram" (28–31 October) and its immediate aftermath, when the IDF overran the central upper Galilee held by the Arab Liberation Army and a battalion of regular Syrian Army troops. In *The Birth* I wrote that

neither before, during nor immediately after Operation . . . Hiram did the Cabinet . . . decide or instruct the IDF to drive out the Arab population from the areas it was about to conquer or had conquered. Nor, as far as the evidence shows, did the heads of the defence establishment issue any general orders to the advancing brigades to expel or otherwise harm the civilian population in their path. Nor, as far as can be ascertained, did any general orders issue from the headquarters of the . . . operation or from the headquarters of the . . . brigades involved to their battalions and companies to this purpose.[16]

In the book I described a chaotic situation in which the IDF units involved were not directed by a central guideline or a consistent policy, and each acted differently – here leaving an Arab community in place, there expelling one, in certain villages committing atrocities, occasionally accompanied by an expulsion, in other places acting benignly. I reached this conclusion on the basis of the demographic situation after Operation Hiram, in which a large number of communities, both Christian and Muslim, remained *in situ*, and on two documents: a letter of 12 November from Ya'akov Shimoni, acting director of the Israel Foreign Ministry's Middle East Affairs Department, to Eliahu (Elias) Sasson, the departmental director who was then in Paris; and a letter, six days later, from Shimoni to the ministry director general, Walter Eytan.

Shimoni, a former intelligence executive and a man well-versed in Middle Eastern affairs, wrote Sasson:

Too many hands have stirred the [Hiram] broth . . . So it was that the attitude towards the Arab inhabitants of the Galilee and towards the Arab refugees [temporarily] living in the Galilee villages or near them was haphazard and different from place to place according to the initiative of this or that commander or government official. Here people were expelled and there people were left in place, here the surrender of villages was accepted (and with it a sort of commitment to allow the inhabitants to remain and to protect them) and there [officers] refused to accept surrender, here Christians benefited from positive discrimination, and there [the army] dealt with Christians and Muslims the same way and without distinction. So it was, too, that refugees who had fled in the panic-filled first moments of the conquest were allowed to return to their places. Our advice [to the army] and our view [i.e., the view of the Middle East Affairs Department of the Foreign Ministry], which were not acted upon, are certainly clear to you: We asked that [the army] make an effort during the conquest that no Arab inhabitants remain in the Galilee and certainly that no refugeees from other places remain there . . .[17]

To Eytan, Shimoni wrote:

After [i.e., during] two trips around the [newly conquered areas of the] Galilee by Ezra Danin [special adviser on Arab Affairs at the Foreign Ministry], Zvi Meckler (of the Political [i.e., intelligence] Department [of the Ministry]), Shmuel Ya'ari (of the Syrian and Lebanese section in my department) and myself . . . we heard from all the commanders with whom we had contact that during the operations in the Galilee and in Lebanon[18] they had *no clear orders, no clear line* [italics in the original] concerning behavior towards the Arabs in the conquered areas – expulsion of the inhabitants or leaving them in place; harsh or soft behavior; discrimination in favor of Christians or not; special treatment of Maronites; special treatment of Matawalis [i.e., Shi'ites], etc., etc. . . . As for those acts of cruelty perpetrated [by the IDF] – certainly some of them were carried out for reasons not connected to these considerations; but I have no doubt that some of them would not have happened had the conquering army had a clear . . . policy regarding behavior [toward civilian populations].[19]

The demographic situation in the wake of the operation on the face of it reinforced these descriptions. Many villagers, both Christian and Muslim, stayed put and were left in place – and they and their descendants today constitute the core of Israel's current almost 1 million strong Arab minority.

In an interview I conducted in 1985 with General Moshe Carmel, OC Northern Front (Command) during Hiram, he explained that he had never adopted a policy of expulsion *vis-à-vis* Arab communities he had conquered in the battles of 1948, though he admitted that in a number of localities he had authorized expulsions for military reasons. But Carmel had not told me the truth and Shimoni had been somewhat misinformed – so it emerges from newly released documents in the IDFA. There was a central directive by Northern Front to clear the conquered pocket of its Arab inhabitants, though Carmel had shied clear of using the explicit word "to expel" (*le'garesh*). It is possible that the "advice" proffered by the Foreign Ministry (as mentioned by

Shimoni) to the army command influenced the issuance of this directive.

On the morning of 31 October 1948, Carmel radioed all his brigade and district commanders: "Do all in your power to clear quickly and immediately from the areas conquered all hostile elements in accordance with the orders issued. The inhabitants should be assisted to leave the conquered areas."[20] On 10 November, Carmel added the following, somewhat "softer," order: "(B) [The troops] should continue to assist the inhabitants wishing to leave the areas conquered by us. This is urgent and must be carried out swiftly. (C) A strip five kilometers deep behind the border between us and Lebanon must be empty of [Arab] inhabitants."[21]

There can be no doubt that, in the circumstances, the brigade and district OCs understood Carmel's first order, of 31 October (and perhaps also his follow-up of 10 November), as a general directive to expel. Clearly this is how Major Yitzhak Moda'i (who in the 1980s rose to national prominence as a Likud politician and served as Israel's finance minister) understood the order. In his classified, comprehensive analysis of Operation Hiram based mainly on IDF archival material, written for IDF History Branch in the late 1950s, Moda'i devoted a great deal of space to the question of why most of the Arab population in the conquered pocket remained *in situ*, when most of the inhabitants fled or were driven out of areas previously overrun by the IDF. Moda'i wrote:

One could have believed that the Arab population in the Galilee simply wasn't forced – as were the inhabitants of other parts of the country – to flee for their lives by the intimidator [i.e., Israel]. But from testimony by commanders and men and from official reports . . . it is clear that our forces in the Galilee did not act with restraint and that their treatment of the inhabitants could in no way be construed as a factor [motivating them] to stay in their villages.

Although [Northern] Front's and the Brigade HQ's operational orders for Operation Hiram make no mention of the local population [and its prospective treatment],[22] all were aware of General Staff\Operations stand on this score.

Moda'i refers his readers to the order by Yigael Yadin, IDF OC Operations, from 18 August 1948, stating "that we are not interested in Arab inhabitants [in Israel] and their return [to Israeli territory] must be prevented at all costs." Moda'i then quotes Carmel's order of 31 October ("the inhabitants should be assisted to leave the areas conquered"), and concludes: "It appears, therefore, that the Arab population in the Galilee by and large stayed put in its villages, despite the fact that our forces tried to throw it out, often using means which were illegal and not gentle." Moda'i suggests a number of explanations for the fact that the bulk of the population stayed put:

(A) The [Arab] Liberation Army's opposition to [civilian] flight on the eve of the operation. [The central-upper Galilee pocket conquered by the IDF in Hiram had been held by the ALA, supported by a regular Syrian Army battalion.]

(B) The mountainous terrain of the Galilee areas [i.e., certain villages failed to hear about the IDF campaign until after it had been accomplished and the topography made flight, especially with baggage, very difficult] and the nature of the villagers.

(C) The presence of a friendly population which was promised good treatment by us in advance and which was not subjected to ill-treatment in the course of the operation [i.e., Maronites and Druse].

(D) The speed with which our forces took over the Galilee's roads.

(E) A lack of initiative on the part of our forces which enabled a great number of villagers to return to their homes, after they had first evacuated.

Moda'i also speaks explicitly of:

the lack of a clear and predetermined order, instructing [the troops] to get rid of the inhabitants (if that, indeed, was the aim), the Arabs or the Muslims in the Galilee, [and the absence of] a precise definition of the [appropriate] attitude to be employed towards the various religious and ethnic groups, an ignoring, in the planning and the implementation of the operation, of the question [i.e., problem] posed by the [presence of the] Arab inhabitants, and the fact that no forces were prepared in advance to ensure that a "vacuum" would not be created, which would enable the inhabitants to return to their homes – these are the reasons that gave rise to the fact [i.e., continued presence] of the Arab community in the Galilee.[23]

To these explanations one should, in my view, add that by the end of October 1948 the inhabitants of the "pocket" had heard about the trials and tribulations of their fellow countrymen who had gone into exile during the previous months and had become impoverished refugees. They concluded that, on balance, they would probably be better off staying put. Moreover, by Hiram most of the Palestinians probably understood that they and the Arab states had lost the war and that the refugees would not be allowed back to their homes. One must also pay attention to the date of Carmel's order – 31 October. By the morning of that day Operation Hiram had almost been concluded; that is, by the time the battalions and companies had received Carmel's order, they had already overrun most of the pocket's villages and advanced beyond them. To expel the population of a village during or immediately after its conquest was one thing; to go back to a village hours or days after it had been subdued and throw out its inhabitants was something else (though, to be sure, there were expulsions also after the campaign ended). Carmel's order had been issued at 10:00. Presumably additional time would have had to elapse until it reached the battalion and company OCs who would have had to carry it out. Lastly, the order itself was couched in soft terms, seeming to leave the commanders in the field with a measure of discretion. Certainly, no commander was subsequently charged with or tried for not expelling – or, for that matter, for expelling – villagers.

None the less, a question arises about events in some of the Galilee pocket villages during the operation and in the following days and weeks. When Shimoni referred to the IDF's "acts of cruelty" and Moda'i to the troops' "lack of restraint" – they were referring to the series of massacres carried out by Carmel's troops in Majd al-Kurum, al-Bi'na, Dayr al-Assad, Nahf, Safsaf, Jish, Sasa, Saliha, Ilabun, and Hula, mostly after the end of the fighting. Perhaps they also refer to the post-Hiram expulsions in the border zone.

The question arises to what degree were these acts the fruit of local initiatives – by platoon, company, and battalion OCs – and to what extent they were a response to directives from on high.

As regards the expulsions from the strip of territory along the Lebanese border in the week after Operation Hiram – including those from Iqrit and Bir'im – there is no doubt that they stemmed from one central, expulsive directive, and Carmel's second cable of 10 November (above) indicates as much.

But what of the massacres? Our knowledge of the details of these massacres is limited, relying mainly on Arab oral and written testimony and some United Nations and Israeli civilian documentation (see Appendix, p. 57).[24] The IDF documents relating to them – reports from the officers in the field and the testimony given to various inquiry commissions which probed the massacres and their final reports (there were at least two, one by IDF Northern Command itself and the other by Israel's attorney general, Ya'akov Shimshon Shapira) – are still classified and unavailable to researchers. But the general lines of what happened are clear.

I am not arguing here that Carmel gave a general order to carry out massacres and that, as a result, a series of massacres were committed. But two things indicate that at least some officers in the field understood Carmel's orders as an authorization to carry out murderous acts that would intimidate the population into flight: the pattern in the actions and their relative profusion; and the absence of any punishment of the perpetrators. The massacres were carried out by battalions of the three main units that participated in Hiram, namely, the (1st) Golani, the 7th, and the (2nd) Carmeli brigades, as well as by second-line garrison battalions who replaced the assaulting brigades in the conquered villages. To the best of my knowledge, none of the soldiers or officers who carried out these war crimes was ever punished.

It is quite possible that the perpetrators looked to Carmel's order of 31 October as inspiration for their actions. The fact that no one was subsequently punished leaves the impression that their interpretation of that order (or accompanying oral instructions or exegesis by officers lower down the chain of command, such as brigade commanders) was sufficiently widespread and well founded so as to deter anyone from bringing them to book. Put simply, Carmel or officers and civilian leaders above him may have been deterred by the possibility or threat that those charged would point an accusatory finger upwards, up the chain of command, to explain the source of their actions.

In any event, the uniform or at least similar nature of the massacres points to a belief, among the perpetrators, of central direction and authorization (and perhaps even to the existence of some form of central guideline). Almost all the massacres followed a similar course: a unit entered a village, rounded up the menfolk in the village square, selected four or ten or fifty of the army-age males (in some places according to prepared lists of persons suspected of helping Qawuqji's or Grand Mufti Hajj Amin al Husayni's forces), lined them up against a wall, and shot them. Some of the massacres were carried out immediately after the conquest of the village by the assaulting troops, though most occurred in the following days. In some cases (as in Majd al Kurum on 5 or 6 November) the massacre occurred ostensibly as part of the unit's efforts to force the villagers to hand over hidden weapons, though more often it seems to have been connected to a process of intimidation geared to provoking the villagers into flight (as in Ilabun, Jish, etc.).

In *The Birth* I assumed that there had been no central order from "on high" to commit the atrocities.[25] The documentation recently declassified in the IDFA seems to corroborate this. Three and a half weeks after Operation Hiram, Carmel issued an "order of the day" to all the units under his command, stating:

Our brilliant victory . . . in the Galilee was marred as some soldiers allowed themselves a shameful outburst by looting and condemnable crimes against the Arab population after its surrender . . . Ill-treatment of the inhabitants, murder and robbery are not a military activity or acts of courage. They are a disgrace to our army . . . The perpetrators of these crimes during the operation and in its wake are standing trial and will be punished . . . [but] it has come to my attention that even now such displays of unrestrained behavior have not completely ceased. These acts must cease immediately, and with all severity [*sic*]. Anyone caught committing another crime will be tried immediately and will be most severely punished. I ask the commanders and troops in Northern Front to help stamp out this corruption. Whoever covers for the criminal is an accomplice in the crime and he too will not be cleared of responsibility . . .

Honor to the the loyal and liberating Hebrew fighter, respect for the pure, protective and crushing Hebrew arms![26]

As stated, this statement appears to point to Carmel's displeasure over these actions, and he even asserts – to the best of my knowledge, without foundation – that soldiers were being put on trial for these crimes. But the profusion of cases (altogether about a dozen massacres occurred), the lack of punishment, the pattern of the events, and the delay in the issuing of this "order of the day," taken together, perhaps point to a more ambiguous conclusion.

I have brought these examples of Zionist thinking about transfer in the decade before 1948 and of Operation Hiram, to demonstrate the importance of the documentation currently being declassified, especially in the IDFA, for a fuller understanding of what transpired in 1948. The newly available documentation, which I will deal with and deploy more fully in the planned revised version of *The Birth*, sheds important, fresh light on different segments and aspects of the first Arab–Israeli war. Without doubt, the crystallization of the consensus in support of transfer among the Zionist leaders helped pave the way for the precipitation of the Palestinian exodus of 1948. Similarly, far more of that exodus was triggered by explicit acts and orders of expulsion by Jewish/ Israeli troops than is indicated in *The Birth*. These are certainly two of the major, if still tentative, conclusions that emerge from the newly released documentation. But more years will have to pass before the declassification process is completed. Even then, black, incomprehensible holes will no doubt remain, areas where knowledge and understanding will remain incomplete. But these areas of darkness will be smaller than those that exist today.

Appendix: The Massacre of 14 Beduin Tribesmen in Eastern Galilee, 2 November 1948

Most IDFA documentation regarding the massacres remains classified. But the classifiers have not been consistently efficient. For example, one report now open to researchers (in IDFA 1096\1949\\65), written on 2 November 1948, apparently by the sergeant-major of "C" Company (the signature is indecipherable), 103rd Battalion, explains and (succinctly) describes the massacre of 14 beduin tribesmen in eastern Galilee on 2 November 1948.

This massacre is not to be confused with the one that occurred in nearby Eilabun three days before, in which 12 villagers were slaughtered by Golani Brigade troops (see The Birth, p. 229). But that massacre too, appears to have been triggered by the death of the two missing IDF soldiers. The Golani troops appear to have found their severed heads in one of the village houses.

Subject: Report on A Search Operation in the Area of ʿArab al Mawasi Near Position 213.

Transmitted by Platoon OC Haim Hayun.

On 2.11.48 at 09:00 hours a force comprising two squads accompanied by the battalion armored squad, commanded by Lt. Z. Kleinman and Haim Hayun, set out from the base at Maghar. When they arrived at the site [of ʿArab al-Mawasi, apparently Khirbet al-Waʿra al-Sauda, 8 km east of Eilabun], they assembled the adult males and demanded their arms. Seven rifles were collected. The force [then] divided in two; one part, commanded by Kleinman, stayed to keep guard over the adult males; the second part, commanded by Hayun, went up to Position 213 [apparently a hilltop some 2 km west of Khirbet Waʿra], where the bones were found of two [IDF] soldiers lost in a previous action at this position. Their identities were determined by articles of clothing that were found nearby. [The bodies were] found headless.

The men set fire to the Arabs' houses and returned to base [i.e., Maghar] with 19 Arab adult males. At the base the men [i.e., captives] were sorted out and those who took part in hostile actions against our army were identified, and they were sent under command of Haim [Hayun] to a place that had been determined and there 14 of the adult males were liquidated [*veʿsham huslu*]. The rest are being transferred to a prisoner-of-war camp.

Notes

1 An early version of Part I of this essay appeared in Hebrew in Yehiam Weitz, ed., *Bein Hazon LeRiviziya* [Between Vision and Revision] (Jerusalem, 1997). An early version of Part 2 appeared in the *Journal of Palestine Studies* 28 (Winter 1999). See Morris, *The Birth of the Palestinian Refugee Problem, 1947–1949* (Cambridge, 1988), and Morris, *1948 and After: Israel and the Palestinians* (Oxford, 1990).

2 Nur Masalha, *Expulsion of the Palestinians: The Concept of "Transfer" in Zionist Political Thought, 1882–1948* (Washington DC, 1992). Masalha argued that the Zionist leaders, between the turn of the century and the start of the war of 1948, had consistently and systematically espoused a transfer solution to "the Arab problem" – that is, the problem posed by the existence of an Arab majority in a country, Palestine, that they wished to turn into a "Jewish" state. He further argued that the "de-Arabizing" of the country in the course of 1948 – the Palestinian exodus – was the natural culmination and outcome of this transfer thinking and of specific transfer schemes mooted by the Zionist leaders during the previous decades.

3 Theodor Herzl, *The Complete Diaries of Theodor Herzl*, Raphael Patai, ed. (New York, 1960), vol. I, p. 88, (12 June 1895).

4 David Ben-Gurion Diary, 12 July 1937, the Ben-Gurion Archive, Sede Boker, Israel. Emphasis in the original. See also Ben-Gurion diary entry for 20 July 1937.

5 CZA, S5–1543, text of Ben-Gurion's speech, 7 August 1937. It is worth noting that Ben-Gurion here broached the idea that the Yishuv, rather than the British, would carry out the transfer.

6 See the *Twentieth Zionist Congress and the Fifth Session of the Jewish Agency Council, Zurich, 3–21 August 1937, A Stenographic Report, The Executive of the Zionist Organization and the Jewish Agency* (Jerusalem, 1938); and Morris, "A New Look at Central Zionist Documents" (Heb.) *Alpayim* 12 (1996) 73–103.

7 CZA 28, protocol of meeting of the JAE, 7 June 1938.

8 CZA 28, protocol of the joint meeting of the JAE and the Zionist Actions Committee, 12 June 1938.

9 Ben-Gurion Diary, entry for 12 December 1938, BG Archive.

10 Ben-Gurion, "Outlines of Zionist Policy," 15 October 1941, CZA Z4–14632. I am grateful to Professor Yoav Gelber, of Haifa University, for steering me toward this important document.

11 Weizmann Papers, 2271, "Short Minutes of Meeting Held on Thursday, January 30th, 1941, at 77 Great Russell Street, London, W.C.1," ("Present: Dr. Weizmann, Mrs. Dugdale, Professor Namier, Mr. Locker, Mr. Linton").

12 CZA S100/42b, protocol of JAE meeting, 7 May 1944.

13 *Ibid.*

14 *Ibid.*

15 CZA S100/43b, protocol of JAE meeting, 20 June 1944.

16 Morris, *The Birth*, pp. 218–219.

17 ISA, Foreign Ministry Papers (FM), 2570/11, Shimoni to Sasson, 12 November 1948.

18 In Operation Hiram, the IDF also conquered a string of villages on the Lebanese side of the international frontier. (The villages were evacuated by the IDF during the following months, the last of them returning to Lebanese sovereignty after the signing of the Israel–Lebanon General Armistice Agreement in March 1949.)

19 ISA, FM 186/17, Shimoni to Eytan, 18 November 1948.

20 IDFA 715/49//3, Carmel to brigades, districts, 31 October 1948, 10.00 hours.

21 IDFA 4858/49//495, Front "A" (North) to 2nd and 9th brigades, 10 November 1948, 09.00 hours.

22 See IDFA 854/52//321, "Operational Order Operation Hiram," Front "A" to brigades, districts, etc., 26 October 1948. There is no reference in the order to the requisite behavior toward Arab civilian communities in the areas about to be overrun.

23 IDFA 922/75//189, "Operation Hiram," a report by Major Yitzhak Moda'i, undated but from the late 1950s.

24 See Morris, *The Birth*, ch. 7, and Morris, "New look at Central Zionist Documents," pp. 96–97, 101–03. In *The Birth* I wrongly attributed a report delivered by Moshe Erem at the meeting of the Mapam Political Committee on 11 November 1948 about these atrocities to Yisrael Galili. This was corrected in the article in *Alpayim*.

25 Morris, *The Birth*, p. 230.

26 IDFA 437/49//84, Carmel, "Order of the Day," 25 November 1948. It is worth stressing that Carmel certainly knew of the atrocities on the days they occurred or at most a few days after. Why did he wait two to three weeks to issue this "Order of the Day" condemning them? Perhaps, as he says, it was connected to fresh acts of a similar nature; perhaps he had waited for the various inquiries into the events (by Attorney General Ya'akov Shimshon Shapira, or by Northern Front itself) to be completed. Perhaps his order was issued as a way of persuading officers and men to give evidence to these commissions of inquiry. Or perhaps he had simply tried to refrain from issuing any statement in the matter but in the end was compelled, belatedly, to do so by events, his party (Mapam) or something else. There is no way of knowing with the present evidence available.

3   The Druze and the birth of Israel

Laila Parsons

This chapter addresses two questions related to the alliance between the Palestinian Druze and the Zionists during the 1947–49 Arab–Israeli War.[1] The first question is historical: how does the alliance between Druze and Jews during the Palestine War affect our understanding of the history of that brief but hugely important episode in modern Middle Eastern history? In my answer I shall discuss how the experience of the Druze during the war helps us gain a more subtle understanding of the birth of the Palestinian refugee crisis. The second question is historiographical: what do the descriptions of the alliance by its protagonists tell us about their own view of, and approach to, its history? In my answer I shall discuss how prominent figures from both the Druze and the Jewish sides have interpreted their respective histories in such a way as to make their wartime alliance appear inevitable or pre-determined.

So now to the first question. Partly because of the Palestine War's importance to the development of the modern Middle East, the war has been the subject of much recent controversy, specifically between those now labeled "traditionalists" and "new historians." The new historians have sought to dismantle what they regard as the litany of myths surrounding the birth of Israel. One of the most important pieces of new history about the Palestine War has been Benny Morris' book *The Birth of the Palestinian Refugee Problem, 1947–1949*. In this painstakingly researched work Morris succeeded in dismantling many of the traditionalists' myths surrounding the wartime exodus of four-fifths of the Palestinian population from what became the state of Israel. One myth he laid to rest was the notion that the Palestinians were told to leave by the leaders of the neighboring Arab states, and that they were not in any way forced from their homes by the Israeli army. Through his examination of recently declassified military records Morris revealed that military coercion indeed occurred and led to the deliberate expulsion of some Palestinians.

Crucially, however, Morris asserts in his book that this planned coercion lay behind only a small minority of the expulsions. The majority of expulsions were instead the result of what Morris calls the "randomness" of war. In other words, most Palestinians were forced to leave as a result of local military factors rather than of grand political objectives, as a result of tactics rather than of strategy. Morris famously sums up his thesis with the conclusion that the "Palestinian refugee problem was born of war, not by design."[2]

Since it was published, Morris' book has drawn criticism from scholars on both sides of the traditionalist–new history debate. The traditionalists have accused him of distorting the evidence to serve what they see as a hidden, left-wing political agenda. The more pro-Arab members of the new history camp, on the other hand, have accused Morris of not having gone far enough. Specifically, Morris' hypothesis that the refugee crisis arose not on purpose but by accident, as it were, has been described by Norman Finkelstein and Nur Masalha as merely a new myth substituted for the old.[3]

Finkelstein's critique of Morris centers on the premise that Morris' book is internally inconsistent. Finkelstein claims that the moderate conclusion that Morris draws is contradicted by the very evidence cited to support that conclusion. He lists Morris' purported inconsistencies without, however, offering any new evidence of his own. Masalha takes a different tack. Based on his own work on the centrality of the idea of "transfer" to pre-state Zionist political ideology, Masalha challenges Morris' claim that there was no all-encompassing policy to expel Palestinians. Masalha has garnered evidence which shows that many Zionists, both before and during the Palestine War, supported the idea of transferring the Palestinian population as a way to pre-empt the impending problem of governing a large Arab population in a Jewish state. Given this evidence, Masalha argues, why should it be so difficult to infer that what happened to the Palestinians in 1947–49 was not the direct result of the earlier Zionist advocacy of transfer?[4] On the whole, Morris convincingly refutes Finkelstein and Masalha. He picks apart Finkelstein's list of purported inconsistencies point by point. He also claims that Masalha's conclusions are based on the fallacy of *post hoc ergo propter hoc*:

The fact that in the late 1930s Ben Gurion and the majority of Zionist leaders favoured a "transfer" solution to the problem of the prospective Arab minority in the prospective Jewish state, and that during 1947–49 Ben Gurion and most of the Yishuv's leaders wished to see as few Arabs remaining as possible, does not mean that the Yishuv adopted and implemented a policy of expulsion. One can argue that most Arabs, including, probably, most Egyptians, would like to see Israel disappear; but is that the same thing as saying that it is Egyptian (or Jordanian, or Lebanese) policy to destroy Israel?[5]

My own research on the experience of the Palestinian Druze during the Palestine War shows that one part of the story Morris tells in *The Birth* is wrong. To put it less strongly, my research shows that Morris has skirted an issue that undermines the central thesis of his book that the exodus of Palestinian refugees was by accident and not on purpose. What is specifically at issue is whether or not in 1947–49 the Israeli army treated each of the various Palestinian religious communities differently from the others. If a Muslim Palestinian was expelled because he was a Muslim, while a Christian or Druze was allowed to stay because they were Christian or Druze, then this selectivity, this act of choice, would indicate that at least a degree of intentionality or design had infected the process of expulsion. Here is what Morris says in *The Birth*:

No clear guidelines were issued to the commanders of the advancing IDF columns about how to treat each religious or ethnic group they encountered. What emerged roughly conformed to a pattern as if such "instinctive" guidelines had been followed by both the IDF and the different conquered communities . . . The demographic outcome generally corresponded to the circumstances of the military advance. Roughly, villages which had put up a fight or a stiff fight against IDF units were depopulated: their inhabitants, fearing retribution for their martial ardour, or declining to live under Jewish rule, fled, or in some cases, were expelled. The facts of resistance or peaceful surrender, moreover, roughly corresponded to the religious-ethnic character of the villages. In general, wholly or largely Muslim villages tended to put up a fight. Christian villagers tended to surrender without a fight or without assisting Qawuqji's units. In mixed villages where the IDF encountered resistance the Christians by and large stayed put while the Muslims fled or were forced to leave. Druze and Circassian villagers nowhere resisted IDF advance.[6]

On the surface Morris' hypothesis is plausible. It seems reasonable enough to attribute the disproportionately high number of Muslim to Christian refugees to a corresponding resistance and passivity during battle. After all, war is a chaotic business and military decisions made in the heat of battle, or in the immediate aftermath of a battle when emotions are still running high, might not reflect a calm, rational, coordinated policy, but instead derive from the personality and individual experience of a particular commanding officer.

When it comes to the Druze, however, Morris' "randomness" hypothesis hits troubled waters. As a result of my own research in the Israeli archives I can claim with confidence that a consistently pro-Druze bias existed in Israeli policy, and that this bias in policy was sufficiently articulated to commanders on the ground that they felt constrained to implement it. I have narrated the development of the Druze–Jewish alliance elsewhere: from Druze neutrality during the

1936–39 Arab Revolt, to the Zionists' unrealized plan of the late 1930s to transfer the entire Palestinian Druze population to Jebel Druze in Syria, to the defection to the IDF in the early summer of 1948 of soldiers from the Arab Liberation Army's (mainly Syrian) Druze Battalion.[7] For now, I shall merely make two general points about the alliance, and then focus on two events that most vividly illustrate the degree of collusion between Druze and Zionists.

The general points are, first of all, that Israeli attempts to cultivate the friendship of the Palestinian Druze community both before the war, that is, during the British Mandate period, as well as during the war itself, were part of a nascent Israeli policy of cultivating links with different minority groups throughout the Middle East. In fact, one of the keenest exponents of this policy – loosely based on the principle of "my enemy's enemy is my friend" – was Ben-Gurion himself. This policy also guided Israel's relations with the Maronite Christians of Lebanon, for example. In the 1930s one Jewish Agency official described this policy as "a way to establish spots of light and inspiration in the dark Arab sea all around us."[8]

The second general point is that the Israelis' particular interest in the Palestinian Druze arose primarily because the Palestinian Druze were seen as a conduit to their far more numerous and powerful co-religionists in Syria. Arabists in the Jewish Agency and subsequently in Israel's Foreign Affairs ministry, as well as various secret agents, recruited individual Palestinian Druze to pass messages along to the Druze leaders in Syria.

As for the two events that most vividly illustrate the degree of collusion between Druze and Zionists, the first is really more of a process than an event: the gradual formation of a predominantly Druze "Unit of the Minorities" in the IDF. The origins of this unit lay in the early summer of 1948, when elements of the Arab Liberation Army's Druze battalion defected to the IDF. These Druze defectors, mainly from Syria, as well as some Palestinian Druze, mainly from the villages of Daliyat al-Karmil and Isfiya on Mount Carmel, constituted the bulk of the Unit of the Minorities. Far smaller numbers of Beduin and Circassians filled the remaining ranks. The unit was attached to the Oded Brigade of the IDF and saw action in Operation Hiram in October 1948. The establishment of the Unit of the Minorities was a radical step for the Israelis, and one with at least as many political as military ramifications. Militarily a unit of this size could not make a decisive difference to the Israeli war effort. In political terms, however, the incorporation into the IDF of an Arabic-speaking unit, many of whose members had been fighting on the enemy side only a few months before, was a propaganda coup. The political advantages of such a recruitment, particularly in terms of solidifying the Druze–Jewish alliance, were significant. Certainly for those Druze recruited into the unit it was an irrevocable act.[9]

The second event that illustrates the degree of collusion between Druze and Zionists involved Druze civilians rather than Druze soldiers, and occurred in the middle of the war, during Operation Dekel, a campaign whose objective was the capture of the large Palestinian town of Nazareth. During Operation Dekel, which saw significant Israeli gains, the IDF successfully occupied the mixed Muslim-Druze-Christian town of Shafaʿamr. Documents from the Israeli Archives, as well as memoirs by participants, show that the Israeli brigade that took the town in the summer of 1948 held secret meetings with its Druze leaders before the battle. During those meetings the Druze agreed to fake a defense of their quarter of the town so that the IDF could sweep through the town much more quickly than the Muslim and Christian defenders were expecting. In the words of the commander of the IDF Brigade:

Everything went according to plan. While the Muslim quarter was being shelled the assault force approached the walls. They and the Druze "Defenders" fired harmlessly over each other's heads. The attackers quickly passed through Druze lines entering the village and capturing the Muslim quarter from the rear. Within a short time the whole town was in our hands.[10]

The faked battle of Shafaʿamr and the consequent capture of Nazareth gave momentum to the Druze–Jewish alliance, demonstrating such success that its potential benefits came to be discussed not only by IDF officers on the ground, but also by officials in the Israeli Foreign Ministry. Those Foreign Ministry officials who, during the Mandate and early war periods, had been skeptical about pursuing friendly relations with the Druze, were now shown concrete military advantages. In a memo, Yaʿcov Shimʿoni, deputy director of the Middle East Affairs Department in the Foreign Ministry, reported to Reuven Shiloah in the Political Department: "We had no military surprises in the Galilee thanks to a network of information gathering and to the conquest of Shafaʿamr which came as a result of good relations [with the Druze] and the organisation of the operation from within."[11]

Those on the Israeli side who were suspicious of Druze motivations could no longer ignore the potential usefulness of Druze support. This is revealed in an exchange of letters between Itzhak Avira, a *kibbutznik* who had worked for Hagana Intelligence, and Ezra Danin, at the time advisor on Arab affairs to the Foreign Ministry. The two men were friends. Avira had visited Shafaʿamr in the days following its conquest and was disturbed by the IDF's preferential treatment toward the Druze:

I made a brief visit to Shafaʿamr. There I saw the faces of Druze who are not only walking freely in the town but also seem to rejoice in the Muslim calamity, Muslims who have been deported and whose property has been dispersed. Ezra, do not suspect that I am at all angry about our army's occupations and the way it is conducting its operations. I just see a danger in assuming that a Druze or a Christian is "kosher" and a Muslim is "non-kosher".

Danin replied that:

Concerning the attitude of the Druze and their treachery they are not different from the Muslims and they are perhaps even worse. What determines their position is their choice or lack of it. The Muslims have backing whereas these Druze are weak; we can use their lack of choice while we are fighting alone in this war.[12]

There are many other examples of cooperation between the Israeli military and the Druze but the above should suffice to illustrate the degree of the collusion. With regard to Benny Morris' randomness hypothesis, the point is that the existence of this special relationship between Druze and Jews makes it difficult to believe that the fact that no Druze were expelled from their towns or villages can be put down to chance.

Let me turn to a few examples that indicate how exactly Morris' randomness hypothesis is undermined by the experience of the Druze. In the northern mixed Christian–Druze village of al-Rama, the Israeli forces occupying the village expelled the Christians but allowed the Druze to stay. One villager later recounted:

The people of al-Rama were ordered to assemble in the centre of the village. A Jewish soldier stood on the top of the rise and addressed us. He ordered the Druze present among us to go back to their homes, suggesting they report to him in case any of their possessions were missing. Then he ordered the rest of us to leave to Lebanon threatening death to those taking any of their belongings with them.[13]

Strangely, Morris himself cites the example of al-Rama as evidence *for* his randomness theory, because, as he points out, the Christians were expelled *despite* the fact that they had not resisted the occupation. Morris does not seem interested in the implications of the fact that the Druze were allowed to stay.[14] To my mind, the opposite fates of the Druze and Christian villagers is clear evidence of design, not of randomness. However, the example that poses the most serious problem for Morris' randomness hypothesis is the battle for the Druze village of Yanuh and its aftermath, in the closing days of the war. Morris does not mention this battle in his book.

The battle for Yanuh occurred during Operation Hiram, the last big Israeli campaign in the north, whose aim was to clear out the last pockets of Arab resistance still active in the Galilee. During Operation Hiram the Druze villagers of Yanuh resisted IDF occupation, in spite of the fact that village representatives had made a secret agreement before the battle not to resist – similar, in fact, to the pre-battle pact made at Shafaʿamr. Now, the archival reports on the battle disagree as to why exactly the agreement fell apart. Whichever explanation is true, however, Israeli sources are unanimous in portraying IDF losses at Yanuh as resulting from the treachery of the Druze villagers.

This perception of Yanuh's treachery came to color the relationship between the villagers of Yanuh and the Israeli authorities in the months following the battle. During that period of transition from war to peace, the Palestinian Druze as a whole were brought more and more under the official umbrella of the state. Yanuh was different. In January 1949, after the fighting in the north had died out, the question of opening a school in Yanuh arose in Israel's newly established Ministry of the Minorities. Yehuda Blum, then minister for education, gave a clear indication of Israeli policy towards Yanuh when he stated in a letter to a Minorities Affairs Ministry official: "As is well known the village of Yanuh has betrayed us. To the best of my knowledge the military authority is not "taking care of" [his inverted commas] this village. If the policy of the government towards this village changes I would like to know so I can take care of the question of the children's education."[15] The striking thing about Yanuh is that in spite of the Israelis' clearly articulated sense of betrayal, the villagers there were not expelled following the battle.

This poses a problem for Morris' randomness hypothesis. On the one hand, there were certain cases, such as those of al-Rama and another village called ʿIlabun, where Christians who had not resisted IDF attack were expelled anyway. On the other hand, the Druze villagers of Yanuh, who had resisted, were not expelled. Nor, for that matter, were Druze from any other village expelled. Given these two very different experiences, it requires a leap of faith to maintain, as Morris does, that considerations of religion or ethnicity played no role in determining which Palestinians got expelled and which were allowed to remain. At the very least, this apparent paradox – some villagers who do not resist are expelled, while other villagers who do resist are allowed to remain – shifts the burden of proof to those, such as Morris, who would deny that an explicit and official pro-Druze policy existed, at least on the part of the IDF commanders on the ground.

Morris cites what he refers to as the "Druze" village of ʿAmqa in support of his randomness thesis. ʿAmqa was attacked and its inhabitants expelled during the war, and Morris describes it as "the only Druse [sic] village in the Western Galilee so shelled and evacuated."[16] If ʿAmqa had indeed been a Druze village at the time, it would provide clear evidence in support of Morris' randomness hypothesis. But ʿAmqa was not a Druze village. ʿAmqa had been Druze during the period of Ottoman rule over Palestine but was resettled by Muslims before 1890 when contemporaneous sources confirm it as being a Muslim village. In 1948 ʿAmqa had not been inhabited by Druze for over fifty years. Morris cites two sources for his assertions about ʿAmqa, Nafez Nazzal's *The Palestinian Exodus from the Galilee, 1948* and Tzadok Eshel's *Hativat Carmeli beMilhemet haKomemiut* [*The Carmeli Brigade in the War of Independence*]. Although both sources mention ʿAmqa neither identifies it as a Druze village. So with a slip of the pen – understandable given the huge number of sources regarding individual villages that Morris had to collate – Morris offers an example of Druze expulsion which did not in fact occur.[17]

So let me reiterate: Benny Morris makes two important errors with regard to the history of the Druze in the Palestine War. The first is his claim that Druze villagers nowhere resisted the IDF. In fact, the Druze villagers of Yanuh resisted the IDF. Morris' second error is his claim that some Druze, the inhabitants of the village of ʿAmqa, were expelled during the war. In fact, the inhabitants of ʿAmqa were Muslims, not Druze. In my opinion, these errors undermine Morris' broader claim that the Israeli army's expulsion of Palestinian villagers during Operation Hiram is best characterized by randomness, not design.

The experience of the Druze is particularly relevant to the debate between Morris and Finkelstein. Finkelstein's main criticism of Morris concerns the question of whether or not one can properly speak of an overarching policy of expulsion during the war. Finkelstein claims that the evidence Morris himself presents is decisive enough to justify concluding that such a policy existed. One of Morris' responses to this criticism is to cite the example of Operation Hiram. If there had been a policy of expulsion, Morris reasons, then Operation Hiram – a well-organized and highly successful military campaign launched at the end of the war when Israel was winning on all fronts – would have been the perfect framework in which to carry out expulsions. Yet the fact is that only one-half of the Palestinian population in Operation Hiram's theater of operations left or were expelled. In other words, Morris argues that if expulsion had indeed been a fully articulated, comprehensive policy, then Operation Hiram, more than any other, was the occasion for it to be implemented.[18]

Morris has convinced me that there was no generally articulated, overarching policy of expulsion in the war, at least in the sense in which Morris understands the term "policy." But if I am right in showing that there was a policy not to expel the Druze during Operation Hiram, then that implies at least a partially coherent policy to expel the Muslims and Christians. If you have a policy not to do something it implies that you also have a position on what you are doing. At the very least it implies that there was some awareness of expulsion as a policy issue. Now the debate between Finkelstein and Masalha on the one hand and Morris on the other hand is in some ways clouded by the fact that not one of them really defines what he means by "policy." This is an important point. For Morris, a policy seems to consist of a set of clear and direct orders drawn up by Ben-Gurion and his senior staff and issued to all the commanding officers in the field. By contrast, Finkelstein and Masalha imply that the mere fact that certain officials in the top echelons of the Israeli establishment were on record as saying that it would not be a bad thing if the Palestinians left, was enough to constitute a policy.

In my opinion, Morris' criteria of what constitutes a policy are too strict and Finkelstein's and Masalha's are too loose. When I use the term "policy" to describe the Israeli attitude towards the Druze I am referring to something that lies between these two extremes, namely, an articulated awareness amongst Israeli commanding officers and military intelligence agents that the Druze were friends and should be treated specially. It seems clear to me that during the course of the war relations between the Jews and the Druze reached a point of critical mass whereby individual instances of Druze support for the Jews and of Jewish support for the Druze were sufficiently numerous that they came to be interpreted as representing the intentions of the two communities as a whole.

This is why the Druze were special. There may have been instances of individual Christian and Muslim collaboration with the Jews, but only Druze–Jewish cooperation gelled into something more than just the sum of its parts. That is to say, the relationship between Druze and Jews got to the stage where it began to produce what American businessmen call "synergy," a new reality that was suddenly in the process of being created. In light of this definition of "policy" I feel confident in asserting that during Operation Hiram a pro-Druze policy existed, even though my evidence, while compelling, remains circumstantial. I have not found the "smoking gun."

To be fair to Morris, it is true that the years since the debate with Finkelstein and Masalha have seen an evolution of his views. In his contribution to this volume Morris articulates his new views on the two issues that were at the center of his debates with Finkelstein and

Masalha. With regard to the issue of how many Palestinians left their homes as a direct result of Hagana and IDF expulsions, versus those who left out of a general sense of fear caused by the war, Morris now asserts that the "proportion of the 700,000 Arabs who took to the roads as a result of the expulsions rather than as a result of straightforward military attack or fear of attack is greater than indicated in *The Birth*."[19] Morris also appears to have tempered his position on transfer. While rejecting Masalha's strong claim of a direct causal link between pre-war Zionist thinking on transfer and the expulsion of Palestinians during the war, Morris now accepts a weaker version of that claim: he says that the "virtual consensus in support of the notion [of transfer] from 1937 on contributed to what happened in 1948 in the sense that they conditioned the Zionist leadership, and, below it, the officials and officers who managed the new state's civilian and military agencies, for the transfer that took place."[20]

What caused Morris to revise his opinions was not the argumentation of Finkelstein and Masalha, however, but rather his discovery of newly declassified IDF documents, in particular a directive issued on 31 October and 10 November, during Operation Hiram, by Moshe Carmel – the operational commander of Israeli forces on the northern front – to clear out the Palestinian inhabitants.[21] In his debate with Finkelstein, let us recall, Morris argued that the fact that so many Palestinians remained during Operation Hiram was itself clear evidence that no policy of expulsion existed. In his revised view, however, that old argument has disappeared. Morris now appeals to Yitzhak Moda'i's formerly classified analysis of Operation Hiram to unravel the puzzle of how so many Palestinians could remain during Operation Hiram despite what he now admits was a clearly articulated policy of expulsion.

With regard to the question of a master plan to expel Palestinians during the war as a whole, however, Morris sticks to the original position articulated in *The Birth*: given the absence in the Israeli archives of any evidence of such a master plan, we must conclude that no such plan existed. But such a preoccupation with the existence or non-existence of an ultimate "smoking gun" document begs the following question: given Morris' significant changes of view over the past ten years on the question of the proportion of Palestinians who were forcibly expelled to those who left of their own accord; given the newly declassified evidence he presents of a clearly articulated policy of expulsion during Operation Hiram; and given the evidence I have just presented of preferential treatment towards the Druze during the war, which buttresses the arguments for design and against randomness in the process of expulsion; is it not possible that the debate has now reached the stage where the protagonists are no longer talking about substance but about labels? I suspect that we may never uncover a master plan of expulsion; probably there never was one. But at what point do lots of little policies add up to a big policy? Perhaps, as the declassification of IDF documents continues, more and more little policies of expulsion will be uncovered, and Morris will eventually conclude that he must entirely abandon his original position that the refugee crisis was "born of war, not by design."

The invention of a common past

Now to a question of historiography rather than history. In this, the second part of my chapter, I shall examine how the alliance between the Druze and the Jews has been portrayed by the protagonists themselves. I should begin by saying that one of the clearest conclusions I drew from my research was that the alliance between Jews and Druze during the 1947–49 War arose primarily because of local military and economic factors that were specific to the Mandate and war periods and local to the Galilee and, to a lesser extent, to Syria. And as I have already mentioned, the alliance with the Druze was, from the perspective of Jewish Agency and Israeli officials, one facet of a broader policy of cultivating links with minority groups throughout the Middle East.

The Druze perspective on the alliance is more complex and difficult to analyze. First of all, it would be too much of a generalization to claim that the Druze as a whole made a coherent and all-encompassing decision to support the Jews. Instead, it would be more precise to say that there existed a number of politically active, pro-Jewish Druze families who established contact with Jewish officials in the early 1930s and during the 1936–39 Arab Revolt, and whose pro-Jewish activities brought economic advantages to the Druze community at large, particularly during the Palestine War when times were bad. During the war, for example, the Druze were allowed by the Israeli military authorities to harvest their crops. Some Druze were also granted special permits to move about freely, to bring in provisions from the cities, and to set up schools, all as a direct result of their pro-Jewish position.

Yet despite these clear but prosaic advantages – social and economic to the Druze, military and political to the Jews – many of the prominent figures involved in both sides of the alliance appear to have interpreted their respective histories in such a way that their war-time alliance could be viewed as inevitable or pre-determined. In other words, they presented the past – including the ancient past – as comprising a series of clear markers leading inexorably toward their mid-twentieth-century alliance.[22] For example, in an article written five years after the end of the war, Itzhak Ben Tzvi, the Jewish Agency Arabist responsible for much of the initial Zionist contact with the Druze during the British Mandate period, stated that:

Druze friendship [i.e., towards the Jews], rooted in ancient tradition and similarity of fate, should be highly valued. It should be cultivated and historical ties strengthened. The case of the Druze provides an example of a small nation fighting staunchly against its malevolent foes and at the same time appreciating its friends and well wishers. Let us not treat this matter as of little account.[23]

Ben Tzvi's point appears to be that Israelis should view the Druze–Jewish alliance during the Palestine War as possessing historical depth and context, as resulting from a pattern of behavior that can be traced back through the centuries. One of the main pieces of evidence Ben Tzvi offers to substantiate his claim is a single paragraph written by the twelfth-century Hispano-Jewish traveler Benjamin of Tudela. In his book, entitled *Sefer Hamassa'ot* [*The Itinerary*], Benjamin describes his journey through Europe and the Middle East between the years 1167 and 1172. During his travels in the Levant, Benjamin came across some Druze living in the Shuf mountains. After describing the Druze as "pagans of a lawless character" who were "steeped in vice" (descriptions which Ben Tzvi happens not to have cited), Benjamin goes on to point out that, despite all this, the Druze in the Shuf did maintain good commercial relations with the Jewish community nearby. According to Benjamin this was because the Druze "like the Jews."[24]

In making so much of Benjamin of Tudela's remark, Ben Tzvi may have been following the lead of Eliahu Epstein, another Jewish Agency Arabist. In an article written in 1939 entitled "The Druse people – Druse community in Palestine – Traditional friendship to the Jews," Epstein wrote: "[The] historical record provides many striking examples of Druse helpfulness and friendliness towards the Jews . . . Benjamin of Tudela wrote in the journal of his journey that 'they love the Jews'."[25] Although Benjamin's observations are an interesting footnote to early Druze history, his comments, of course, reveal no more than that a cordial trading relationship happened to have existed in the twelfth century between the Druze of the Shuf and a few local Jewish artisans. It would be very difficult to prove anything other than a coincidental historical connection between an apparently isolated Druze–Jewish trading relationship and their twentieth-century political and military alliance.

Efforts to create a shared history were not confined to the Jewish side. In November 1948, immediately following the Israeli conquest of the

Galilee in Operation Hiram, the Israeli minister for the minorities, Bechor Shalom Shitrit, visited the Druze villages recently placed under Israeli occupation. In the important village of Julis, from which the spiritual leaders of the Druze in the Galilee have traditionally come, Salman Tarif, a prominent Druze shaykh, delivered a welcoming speech to the visiting Israeli delegation. His speech was summarized by Shitrit in a memo sent to the Israeli Foreign Office:

After welcoming us he [i.e., Salman Tarif] elaborated on the notion of the closeness between the Druze sect and the people of Israel and he especially emphasized that the friendship between the people of the Druze community and the people of Israel is not a new one, but an ancient one; not only are the relations ones of friendship but they are also familial relations, because we are after all in-laws. The familial relationship derives from the marriage of Moses to Tzipora the daughter of Jethro, the priest of the Medianites. According to Druze belief and tradition Nabi Shuʿayb is none other than Jethro. He mentioned the story about the daughter of the priest of Median who drew water in order to give it to the flocks of their father, but the herdsmen drove them off. It was Moses who saved them and gave water to their goats, and it was as a result of this act that the priest of Median was led to give his daughter Tzipora to Moses. He also said that the familial closeness which began in the earliest days of Israeli history has been strengthened in our day through a closeness of blood in the battle by Israel for its country in which the blood of Israel and the blood of the Druze mingled for the liberation of the land.[26]

To claim that the Old Testament's Jethro and the Qurʾan's Shuʿayb were one and the same, thus implying that there is a scriptural, as well as historical, basis for the alliance, is a curious move. The story that the Druze shaykh cites in his speech, that Moses helped Jethro's daughters and was thereupon given Tzipora as a bride, is found only in the Old Testament (Exodus 2:16–21 and 3:1), and not in the Qurʾan. Nor does the Qurʾan, for its part, identify Shuʿayb as Jethro, although some commentators, following al-Tabari (d. 923) and focusing on Sura 7, verse 85, do make the identification of Shuʿayb and Jethro, on the basis of the fact that Shuʿayb is described in the Qurʾan as living amongst the inhabitants of Midian as their brother.[27] In his *Lataʾif al-maʿarif*, al-Thaʿalibi (d. 1037) identifies Tzipora as the daughter of Shuʿayb while praising her for her foresight in picking Moses as a husband. However, in his *Qisas al-anbiyaʾ* [Stories of the Prophets], al-Thaʿlabi (d. 1035) cites various possibilities for Shuʿayb's origins, and Jethro is not one of them.[28]

My intention of course is not to create a textual history of my own but merely to show that the sources are very equivocal about the Druze shaykh's identification of Shuʿayb with Jethro. And of course the main point is surely that since Judaism and Islam share many prophets, any

Jew or Muslim Arab could make the far more compelling claim that as the descendants of Abraham (through, respectively, Isaac and Ishmael), their relation was one of blood rather than of marriage. Indeed, in his famous speech to the Knesset in October 1977, President Anwar Sadat of Egypt stressed the common Abrahamic parentage of the Jews and the Arab Muslims. Just as Salman Tarif had done nearly thirty years previously, Sadat employed a rhetorical device to give historical depth to – and thereby justify – a twentieth-century political and military decision.

We should bear in mind that although in 1948 the Palestinian Druze had managed to end up on the winning side, they faced an uncertain future under their new rulers. Those Palestinians, including the Druze, who remained in possession of their land and houses in the Galilee were anxious not to antagonize the authorities of the new state. Several documents from this period, including personal letters from Druze individuals to the Israeli authorities, attest to the anxiety felt by the Druze that, in spite of their war-time service, they might in the end not prove immune to the wholesale land seizures and clearing of border villages going on around them in the Galilee. In this light the Druze shaykh's speech appears intended to pre-empt such actions by stressing the alliance's "ancient" history.

In contrast to the spotlights that were focused on the snippets of evidence for ancient roots to the modern friendship between Druze and Jews, anti-Jewish material in Druze literature has tended to remain hidden in the shadows. One example of Druze anti-Jewish bias is contained in an epistle ascribed to one of the founders of Druzism, Baha' al-Din, and probably written sometime between 1027 and 1042 while the Druze *da'wa* (that is, the proselytizing campaign) was still active. The epistle is addressed to Christians in an attempt to convert them to Druzism. In the epistle Baha' al-Din chastizes the Christians both for having "followed the example of the rebellious Jews who killed and scared the prophets" and for having "forsaken the laws of the people of reality [the Druze] and of the true religion [Druzism], following the example of the priests and chiefs of the Jews in their dealings with the worshipful and kneeling Christians and in their rise to repel by unbelief and apostasy the word of the Lord after it had appeared."[29] I have not cited this passage in order to imply that there is a kind of anti-Jewishness inherent to Druzism. The passage simply shows that those who have sought to establish the existence of a historical, consistently pro-Jewish Druze attitude, have been selective with the evidence.

Those Jewish Agency and Israeli officials keen to encourage an alliance with the Druze had to contend with the fact that on the surface the Druze *seemed* very much like their Christian and Muslim Arab neighbors. It is in their attempts to grapple with this problem that the theological doctrine of *taqiyya* pops up. The principle of *taqiyya* is generally held to be Shi'ite in origin. In Arabic the word means "prudence," "carefulness," or "wariness," and it came to have the sense of hiding one's true beliefs in a time of crisis or persecution; hence the typical English translation "dissimulation." *Taqiyya* is commonly associated not only with mainstream Twelver Shi'ites but also with Isma'ili Shi'ites and the 'Alawites. Because of their Isma'ili Shi'ite origins the Druze have also been associated with *taqiyya*.[30] Now, a number of those involved in promoting Druze–Jewish relations have seized upon *taqiyya* as a convenient device by means of which Druze cooperation with the Jews can be understood.[31]

This way of using *taqiyya* appears most starkly in a Jewish Agency report on Druze history written in 1939 by Eliahu Epstein. At the time, Epstein was serving as head of the Middle East Section of the Jewish Agency. His report was written as briefing material for a plan hatched in the 1930s to transfer the entire Palestinian Druze population to Jabal Druze in southern Syria. In 1939 Epstein published an abridged version of this official report as the *Palestine and Near East Economic Magazine* article I mentioned earlier. His writings should be seen in the context of the Agency's growing desire to promote friendly relations with the Druze, a desire that was spurred on by the fact that the Palestinian Druze had, by and large, ignored Muslim calls to join in attacks on Jews during the 1936–39 Arab Revolt. Epstein's view of *taqiyya* was as follows:

In particular the Druze are careful not to reveal the secrets of their religion to strangers, and with them as with the Nusayriyya who live in the Alawi region of Syria – the tenet of *taqiyya* is accepted. It obligates the Druze for known reasons to take the guise of a different religion externally – usually the ruling religion in their area – in order to keep the secrets of their religion safe from interference by strangers and also to ensure by this the existence of the Druze at a time of danger from the jealous enemy of another religion. Because of this it can be understood why the Druze have for generations called themselves Muslims . . . it was only a disguise that did not hurt the virtue or the good name of the Druze who changed his religion among his people. The lives of these Marranos were accompanied by great spiritual and material suffering, and there developed among the Druze feelings of extreme jealousy and suppressed hate towards those rulers among their neighbours to whose religion and customs the Druze were forced to adhere – in particular, of course, the Muslims.[32]

In this passage the effect of Epstein's use of *taqiyya* is to pry the Druze away from the larger Muslim culture surrounding them. Given that the Arab nationalist movement during the 1936–39 Revolt was predominantly Muslim, the further implication seems to be that the Druze should not even really be viewed as Arabs. In other words, Epstein's message to his Jewish Agency colleagues (in the report) and the Jewish community at large (in the article) appears to be that while the Druze may seem to be like Muslim Arabs, and while they may seem to be participating in Muslim Arab culture, they are in fact just pretending. They are practising *taqiyya*.

In fact, Epstein goes one step further and compares the Druze to the Marranos, Spanish Jews whom the Inquisition forced to convert to Christianity but who secretly preserved their Jewish faith and practice. Epstein's argument thus comes full circle: the Druze are not only unlike the Muslim Arabs, they are like the Jews, since their experience of persecution (and their subsequent dissimulation) at the hands of a brutish majority is analogous to that of the Jews. In 1939, in the immediate aftermath of the Arab revolt, when Jewish feelings of fear and hostility were particularly strong, Epstein's appeals to a sense of shared history between Druze and Jews were likely to have had a powerful effect. In short, Epstein's report, a seemingly academic discussion of Druze history and theology, tells us more about the political history of the period in which he wrote it than it does about the Druze themselves.

In Epstein's article the bankruptcy of this use of *taqiyya* is plain, for it can be, and has been, used to prove opposites. On the one hand, those whose interests lay in promoting an alliance with the Druze called upon *taqiyya* to show that while the Druze may dress like Arabs, eat like Arabs, and speak like Arabs, they are, in fact, only pretending to be Arabs. On the other hand, those interested in scuppering an alliance with the Druze could equally call upon *taqiyya* to show that while the Druze may seem to be friendly to the Jews now, they are, in fact, only pretending to be friendly.

It is important to note, however, that Epstein's use of *taqiyya* in analyzing the Druze was symptomatic of a broader Orientalist tendency to appeal to theological tenets when explaining political events in the modern era. My suspicion is that Epstein took his lead from the famous Lebanese Orientalist Philip Hitti. In his *Origins of the Druze People and Religion*, published in New York in 1928, Hitti put *taqiyya* to use in very similar ways. For example, when confronted by the mass of evidence that contradicted his notion that the Druze people were of Persian or Kurdish origin, Hitti says:

The prevailing idea among the Druzes themselves today is that they are of Arab stock. This hypothesis conforms to the general local tradition, but is in contradiction to the results obtained in this study. In his Huxley Memorial Lecture, "The Early Inhabitants of Western Asia", Professor Felix von Luschan, the famous anthropologist of the University of Berlin, states that he measured the skulls of fifty-nine adult male Druzes and "not one single man fell, as regards his cephalic index, within the range of the real Arab." Evidently the Druze claim of Arab descent is the result of their application of the principle of dissimulation (*taqiyyah*) to their racial problem, they being a small minority amidst an Arab majority which has always been in the ascendancy. According to this principle, one is not only ethically justified but is under obligation, when the exigencies of the case require, to conceal the reality of his religion, or race, and feign other religious or racial relationships.[33]

According to this view, whatever a Druze does, whether it be in the thirteenth century or in the twentieth, whether he be fighting alongside or against a crusader or a Saracen, an Israeli, or a nationalist Arab, he is always practising *taqiyya*. Johnny Druze cannot help but dissimulate since it is in his nature.

Conclusion

In conclusion, let me recapitulate the two parts of this chapter. The main point of the first part is that an analysis of the experience of the Palestinian Druze in the 1947–49 Arab–Israeli War throws light on the causes of one of the most important events in modern Middle Eastern history: the exodus of Palestinian Arabs from their homes during that war. Specifically, the Druze experience provides evidence that undermines Benny Morris' claim, expressed in *The Birth of the Palestinian Refugee Problem*, that the expulsion of Palestinian Arabs from the Galilee during Operation Hiram is best characterized by randomness rather than design, and reinforces Morris' revised view, expressed in this volume, that the expulsion during Operation Hiram was purposeful.

The main point of the second part of the chapter is that attempts to create a common Druze and Jewish past appear to fall into the category of "invented traditions", and will, therefore, be of interest to scholars concerned with issues relating to nationalism and to the creation of national identities. What I have argued here is that the relationship between Druze and Jews during the Palestine War was rooted in the specific political, economic, and military conditions obtaining in the Galilee during the first half of the twentieth century, and that there was nothing "traditional" about it.

Notes

1 For a full account of this alliance see Laila Parsons, *The Druze between Palestine and Israel, 1947–1949* (London, 2000).
2 Benny Morris, *The Birth of the Palestinian Refugee Problem, 1947–1949* (Cambridge, 1987), p. 286.

3 Norman Finkelstein, "Myths, Old and New," *Journal of Palestine Studies* 21/ 1 (1991) 67.

4 Nur Masalha, "A Critique of Benny Morris," *Journal of Palestine Studies* 21/1 (1991) 90–97.

5 Benny Morris, "Response to Finkelstein and Masalha," *Journal of Palestine Studies* 21/1 (1991) 103.

6 Morris, *The Birth*, p. 225.

7 See Parsons, *The Druze*, or, in condensed form, "The Palestinian Druze in the 1947–49 Arab–Israeli War," *Israel Studies* 2/1 (1997) 72–93.

8 These words were included in a report written by Aharon Haim Cohen, an intelligence officer attached to the Joint Bureau for Arab Affairs, 2 November 1937, S25/6638, CZA.

9 5 August 1948, 195/105, HA. This document is a long intelligence report written by Yehoshua Palmon entitled "Our activities amongst the Druze." It includes some information on the Druze unit. See also Shim'oni to Sasson, 19 August and 16 September 1948, 2570/11, FM:ISA; August 1948, 2289/ 50/3339, IDFA; and 1318/20, MAM:ISA. This last document is an undated list of local Druze recruits and the number of family members they support. See also David Koren, *Kesher Ne'eman* [Steadfast Alliance] (Tel Aviv, 1991), 63, and Yoav Gelber, "Druze and Jews in the War of 1948," *Middle Eastern Studies* 31 (1995) 446–60. For more on the defection of the Syrian officers and troops see Parsons, *The Druze*, pp. 69–74.

10 Ben Dunkelman, *Dual Allegiance: An Autobiography* (New York, 1976), p. 261.

11 Ya'cov Shimoni to Reuven Shiloah, 13 September 1948, 2565/8, FM:ISA.

12 Itzhak Avira to Ezra Danin, 29 July 1948, 2570/11, FM:ISA; Ezra Danin to Itzhak Avira, 16 August 1948, 2570/11, FM:ISA.

13 Eyewitness testimony cited in Nafez Nazzal, *The Palestinian Exodus from the Galilee, 1948* (Beirut, 1978), pp. 32–33.

14 Benny Morris, *The Birth*, p. 227.

15 Yehuda Blum to Y. Burlah, 21 January 1949, 302/78, MAM:ISA. The pre-battle agreement between the villagers of Yanuh and the IDF is described in Army Investigation Division to Yadin (i.e., Yigal Yadin, then chief of operations), 27 September 1948, 2384/50/10, IDFA. For an interesting account of the battle drawn from eyewitness accounts see Raja Sa'id Faraj, *Duruz filastin fi fatrat al-intidab al-britani* [*The Druze of Palestine in the Period of the British Mandate*] (Daliyat al-Karmil, 1991), pp. 98–111.

16 Morris, *The Birth*, p. 199.

17 Both Falah and Firro are unclear about when exactly 'Amqa was resettled. Falah identifies 'Amqa as one of a group of villages resettled in the nineteenth century, and Firro describes it on a map of Druze settlements in Palestine as having been resettled by Muslims before 1890. Salman Falah, "A History of the Druze Settlements in Palestine during the Ottoman Period," in Moshe Maoz (ed.), *Studies on Palestine during the Ottoman Period* (Jerusalem, 1975), pp. 44–45; Kais Firro, *A History of the Druzes* (Leiden, 1992), p. 44. For Morris' sources for 'Amqa see Tzadok Eshel, *Hativat Carmeli beMilhemet haKomemiut* [*The Carmeli Brigade in the War of Independence*] (Tel Aviv, 1973), p. 210; Nazzal, *Palestinian Exodus*, pp. 71–74.

18 Morris, "Response to Finkelstein and Masalha," p. 101.

19 See Morris' chapter in this volume, p. 49.

20 Ibid.

21 See Morris' chapter in this volume and Benny Morris, "Operation Hiram Revisited: A Correction," *Journal of Palestine Studies*, 28/2 (1999) 68–76.

22 Parts of an earlier version of this section of the chapter also appear in Laila Parsons, "The Druze, the Jews and the Creation of a Shared History," in Ron Nettler and Suha Taji-Farouki, eds., *Muslim–Jewish Encounters: Intellectual Traditions and Modern Politics* (London, 1998), pp. 131–48. Some of this section's themes are also treated in an interesting way by Kais Firro, in the introduction to his *The Druzes in the Jewish State* (Leiden, 1999).

23 Itzhak Ben Tzvi, "The Druze community in Israel," *Israel Exploration Journal* 4/2 (1954) 76.

24 Benjamin of Tudela, *Sefer hamassa'ot* [The Itinerary], M. N. Adler (ed.) (London, 1907) "khaf."

25 Eliahu Epstein, "The Druse People – Druse Community in Palestine – Traditional Friendship to the Jews," *Palestine Near East and Economic Magazine* 29 (1939).

26 Bechor Shalom Shitrit, memorandum on "Visits in the North," 30 November 1948, 2565/8, MAM:ISA.

27 Al-Tabari, *Ta'rikh al-rusul wa-al-muluk* [The History of the Prophets and Kings] M. de Goeje, ed. (Leiden, 1879–1901), vol. I, p. 365.

28 Al-Tha'alibi, *Lata'if al-ma'arif* [The Delights of Knowledge], P. de Jong, ed., (Leiden, 1867), p. 52; al-Tha'labi, *Qisas al-anbiya'* [Stories of the Prophets] (Cairo, 1929), pp. 111–12.

29 "Excerpt from Baha' al-Din's epistle entitled Christianity," translated in Philip K. Hitti, *The Origins of the Druze People and Religion, with Extracts from the Sacred Writings* (New York, 1928), p. 69.

30 For an excellent analysis of the role of *taqiyya* in Shi'ism see Etan Kohlberg, "Some Imami-Shi'i views on Taqiyya," *Journal of the American Oriental Society* 95 (1975) 395–402. In the article Kohlberg seems to favor the functional over the normative approach to *taqiyya*: "the different Imami-Shi'i attitudes to *taqiyya* were shaped as much by the political and historical circumstances as by the growth of an increasingly intricate body of Shi'i doctrine'" p. 395.

31 In addition to protagonists such as Epstein, a number of present-day scholars – for example, Haim Blanc and Aharon Layish – have explained Druze behavior as springing from *taqiyya*. Blanc describes *taqiyya vis-à-vis* the Druze as being "an age-old, deeply ingrained custom, almost a cultural trait" and goes on to claim that the "most recent instance of this outward assimilation may be seen in present day Israel." Layish states baldly that Druze political behavior "is guided by *taqiyya*." Haim Blanc, "Druze particularism: modern aspects of an old problem," *Middle Eastern Affairs* 3/11 (1952) 317. Aharon Layish, "Taqiyya among the Druzes," *Asian and African Studies* 19/13 (1985) 275.

32 Eliahu Epstein, report on "The Druze in Eretz Israel," S25/6638, CZA.

33 Hitti, *Origins*, p. 14.

Avi Shlaim

"A nation," said the French philosopher Ernest Renan, "is a group of people united by a mistaken view about the past and a hatred of their neighbors." Throughout the ages, the use of myths about the past has been a potent instrument of forging a nation. The Zionist movement is not unique in propagating a simplified and varnished version of the past in the process of nation-building. But it does provide a strikingly successful example of the use of myths for the dual purpose of promoting internal unity and enlisting international sympathy and support for the state of Israel.

The traditional Zionist version of the Arab–Israeli conflict places the responsibility on the Arab side. Israel is portrayed as the innocent victim of unremitting Arab hostility and Arab aggression. In this respect, traditional Zionist accounts of the emergence of Israel form a natural sequel to the history of the Jewish people, with its emphasis on the weakness, vulnerability, and numerical inferiority of the Jews in relation to their adversaries. The American Jewish historian Salo Baron once referred to this as the lachrymose view of Jewish history. This view tends to present Jewish history as a long series of trials and tribulations culminating in the Holocaust.

The War of Independence constituted a glorious contrast to the centuries of powerlessness, persecution, and humiliation. Yet the traditional Zionist narrative of the events surrounding the birth of the state of Israel was still constructed around the notion of the Jews as the victims. This narrative presents the 1948 war as a simple, bipolar no-holds-barred struggle between a monolithic and malevolent Arab adversary and a tiny peace-loving Jewish community. The biblical image of David and Goliath is frequently evoked in this narrative. Little Israel is portrayed as fighting with its back to the wall against a huge, well-armed and overbearing Arab adversary. Israel's victory in this war is treated as verging on the miraculous, and as resulting from the determination and heroism of the Jewish fighters rather than from disunity and disarray on the Arab side. This heroic version of the War of Independence has proved so enduring and resistant to revision precisely because it corresponds to the collective memory of the generation of 1948. It is also the version of history that Israeli children are taught at school. Consequently, few ideas are as deeply ingrained in the mind of the Israeli public as that summed up by the Hebrew phrase, *me'atim mul rabim*, or "the few against the many."

One of the most persistent myths surrounding the birth of the State of Israel is that in 1948 the newly-born state faced a monolithic and implacably hostile Arab coalition. This coalition was believed to be united behind one central aim: the destruction of the infant Jewish state. As there is no commonly accepted term for the liquidation of a state, Yehoshafat Harkabi, a leading Israeli student of the Arab–Israeli conflict, proposed calling it "politicide" – the murder of the *politeia*, the political entity. The aim of the Arabs, Harkabi asserted, was politicidal. Linked to this aim, according to Harkabi, was a second aim, that of genocide – "to throw the Jews into the sea" as the popular phrase put it.[1] Harkabi's view is just one example of the widely held belief that in 1948 the Yishuv, the pre-state Jewish community in Palestine, faced not just verbal threats but a real danger of annihilation from the regular armies of the neighboring Arab states. The true story of the first Arab–Israeli war, as the "new historians" who emerged on the scene in the late 1980s tried to show, was considerably more complicated.[2]

The argument advanced in this chapter, in a nutshell, is that the Arab coalition facing Israel in 1947–49 was far from monolithic; that within this coalition there was no agreement on war aims; that the inability of the Arabs to coordinate their diplomatic and military moves was partly responsible for their defeat; that throughout the conflict Israel had the military edge over its Arab adversaries; and, finally, and most importantly, that Israel's leaders were aware of the divisions inside the Arab coalition and that they exploited these divisions to the full in waging the war and in extending the borders of their state.

The military balance

As far as the military balance is concerned, it was always assumed that the Arabs enjoyed overwhelming numerical superiority. The war was accordingly depicted as one between the few against the many, as a desperate, tenacious, and heroic struggle for survival against horrifyingly heavy odds. The desperate plight and the heroism of the Jewish fighters are not in question. Nor is the fact that they had inferior military hardware at their disposal, at least until the first truce, when illicit arms supplies from Czechoslovakia decisively tipped the scales in their favor.

But in mid-May 1948 the total number of Arab troops, both regular and irregular, operating in the Palestine theater was under 25,000, whereas the Israel Defense Force (IDF) fielded over 35,000 troops. By mid-July the IDF mobilized 65,000 men under arms, and by December its numbers had reached a peak of 96,441. The Arab states also reinforced their armies, but they could not match this rate of increase. Thus, at each stage of the war, the IDF outnumbered all the Arab forces arrayed against it, and, after the first round of fighting, it outgunned them too. The final outcome of the war was therefore not a miracle but a faithful reflection of the underlying military balance in the Palestine theater. In this war, as in most wars, the stronger side prevailed.[3]

The Arab forces, both regular and irregular, mobilized to do battle against the emergent Jewish state were nowhere as powerful or united as they appeared to be in Arab and Jewish propaganda. In the first phase of the conflict, from the passage of the United Nations partition resolution on 29 November 1947 until the proclamation of statehood on 14 May 1948, the Yishuv had to defend itself against attacks from Palestinian irregulars and volunteers from the Arab world. Following the proclamation of the state of Israel, however, the neighboring Arab states and Iraq committed their regular armies to the battle against the Jewish state. Contact with regular armies undoubtedly came as a shock to the Haganah, the paramilitary organization of the Yishuv which was in the process of being transformed into the IDF. Yet, the Jewish propaganda machine greatly exaggerated the size and quality of the invading forces. A typical account of the war of independence, by a prominent Israeli diplomat, goes as follows: "Five Arab armies and contingents from two more, equipped with modern tanks, artillery, and warplanes . . . invaded Israel from north, east, and south. Total war was forced on the Yishuv under the most difficult conditions."[4]

The five Arab states who joined in the invasion of Palestine were Egypt, Transjordan, Syria, Lebanon, and Iraq; while the two contingents came from Saudi Arabia and Yemen. All these states, however, only sent an expeditionary force to Palestine, keeping the bulk of their army at home. The expeditionary forces were hampered by long lines of communication, the absence of reliable intelligence about their enemy, poor leadership, poor coordination, and very poor planning for the campaign that lay ahead of them. The Palestinian irregulars, known as the Holy War Army, were led by Hasan Salama and 'Abd al-Qadir al-Husayni. The Arab Liberation Army consisted of around 4,000 Arab volunteers for the Holy War in Palestine. They were funded by the Arab League, trained in bases in southern Syria, and led by the Syrian adventurer Fawzi al-Qawuqji. Qawuqji's strong points were politics and public relations rather than military leadership. The Arab politicians who appointed him valued him more as a known enemy and therefore potential counter-weight to the grand mufti, Hajj Amin al-Husayni, than as the most promising military leader to lead the fight against the Jews. The *mufti* certainly saw this appointment as an attempt by his rivals in the League to undermine his influence over the future of Palestine.[5]

The Arab coalition was beset by profound internal political differences. The Arab League, since its foundation in 1945, was the highest forum for the making of pan-Arab policy on Palestine. But the Arab League was divided between a Hashemite bloc consisting of Transjordan and Iraq and an anti-Hashemite bloc led by Egypt and Saudi Arabia. Dynastic rivalries played a major part in shaping Arab approaches to Palestine. King ʿAbdullah of Transjordan was driven by a long-standing ambition to make himself the master of Greater Syria which included, in addition to Transjordan, Syria, Lebanon, and Palestine. King Faruq saw ʿAbdullah's ambition as a direct threat to Egypt's leadership in the Arab world. The rulers of Syria and Lebanon saw in King ʿAbdullah a threat to the independence of their countries and they also suspected him of being in cahoots with the enemy. Each Arab state was moved by its own dynastic or national interests. Arab rulers were as concerned with curbing each other as they were in fighting the common enemy. Under these circumstances it was virtually impossible to reach any real consensus on the means and ends of the Arab intervention in Palestine. Consequently, far from confronting a single enemy with a clear purpose and a clear plan of action, the Yishuv faced a loose coalition consisting of the Arab League, independent Arab states, irregular Palestinian forces, and an assortment of volunteers. The Arab coalition was one of the most divided, disorganized, and ramshackle coalitions in the entire history of warfare.

Separate and conflicting national interests were hidden behind the fig-leaf of securing Palestine for the Palestinians. The Palestine problem was the first major test of the Arab League and the Arab League failed it miserably. The actions of the League were taken ostensibly in support of the Palestinian claim for independence in the whole of Palestine. But the League remained curiously unwilling to allow the Palestinians to assume control over their own destiny. For ʿAbd al-Rahman ʿAzzam, the secretary-general of the Arab League, the *mufti* was "the Menachem Begin of the Arabs." ʿAzzam Pasha told a British journalist (who relayed it to a Jewish official), that the Arab League's policy "was intended to squeeze the *mufti* out."[6]

At Arab League meetings, the *mufti* argued against intervention in

Palestine by the regular Arab armies, but his pleas were ignored.[7] All the *mufti* asked for was financial support and arms and these were promised to him but delivered only in negligible quantities. It is misleading, therefore, to claim that all the resources of the Arab League were placed at the disposal of the Palestinians. On the contrary, the Arab League let the Palestinians down in their hour of greatest need. As Yezid Sayigh, the distinguished historian of the Palestinian armed struggle, put it: "Reluctance to commit major resources to the conflict and mutual distrust provoked constant disputes over diplomacy and strategy, leading to incessant behind-the-scenes manoeuvring, half-hearted and poorly conceived military intervention, and, ultimately, defeat on the battlefield."[8]

The Hashemite connection

The weakest link in the chain of hostile Arab states that surrounded the Yishuv on all sides was Transjordan. Ever since the creation of the Amirate of Transjordan by Britain in 1921, the Jewish Agency strove to cultivate friendly relations with its Hashemite ruler, ʿAbdullah ibn Husayn. The irreconcilable conflict between the Jewish and Arab national movements in Palestine provided the setting for the emergence of the special relations between the Zionists and ʿAbdullah, who became king in 1946 when Transjordan gained formal independence. Failure to reach an understanding with their Palestinian neighbors spurred the Zionist leaders to seek a counterweight to local hostility in better relations with the neighboring Arab countries. Indeed, the attempt to bypass the Palestine Arabs and forge links with the rulers of the Arab states became a central feature of Zionist diplomacy in the 1930s and 1940s.

The friendship between the Hashemite ruler and the Zionist movement was cemented by a common enemy in the shape of the grand mufti, Hajj Amin al-Husayni, the leader of the Palestinian national movement. For the *mufti* had not only put his forces on a collision course with the Jews; he was also ʿAbdullah's principal rival for control over Palestine. Both sides perceived Palestinian nationalism as a threat and therefore had a common interest in suppressing it.[9] From the Zionist point of view, ʿAbdullah was an immensely valuable ally. First and foremost, he was the only Arab ruler who was prepared to accept the partition of Palestine and to live in peace with a Jewish state after the conflict had been settled. Second, his small army, the Arab Legion, was the best trained and most professional of the armies of the Arab states. Third, ʿAbdullah and his aides and agents were a source of information about the other Arab countries involved in the Palestine problem. Last but not least, through ʿAbdullah the Zionists could generate mistrust, foment rivalry, and leak poison to weaken the coalition of their Arab adversaries.

In 1947, as the conflict over Palestine entered the crucial stage, the contacts between the Jewish side and King ʿAbdullah intensified. Golda Meir of the Jewish Agency had a secret meeting with ʿAbdullah in Naharayim on 17 November 1947. At this meeting they reached a preliminary agreement to coordinate their diplomatic and military strategies, to forestall the *mufti*, and to endeavor to prevent the other Arab states from intervening directly in Palestine.[10] Twelve days later, on 29 November, the United Nations pronounced its verdict in favor of dividing the area of the British mandate into two states, one Jewish and one Arab. This made it possible to firm up the tentative understanding reached at Naharayim. In return for ʿAbdullah's promise not to enter the area assigned by the UN to the Jewish state, the Jewish Agency agreed to the annexation by Transjordan of most of the area earmarked for the Arab state. Precise borders were not drawn and Jerusalem was not even discussed as under the UN plan it was to remain a *corpus separatum* under international control. Nor was the agreement ever put down in writing. The Jewish Agency tried to tie ʿAbdullah down to a written agreement but he was evasive. Yet, according to Yaacov Shimoni, a senior official in the Political Department of the Jewish Agency, despite ʿAbdullah's evasions, the understanding with him was:

entirely clear in its general spirit. We would agree to the conquest of the Arab part of Palestine by ʿAbdullah. We would not stand in his way. We would not help him, would not seize it and hand it over to him. He would have to take it by his own means and stratagems but we would not disturb him. He, for his part, would not prevent us from establishing the state of Israel, from dividing the country, taking our share and establishing a state in it. Now his vagueness, his ambiguity, consisted of declining to write anything, to draft anything which would bind him. To this he did not agree. But to the end, until the last minute, he always said again and again: "perhaps you would settle for less than complete independence and statehood, for full autonomy, or a Jewish canton under the roof of the Hashemite crown." He did try to raise this idea every now and again and, of course, always met with a blank wall. We told him we were talking about complete, full, and total independence and are not prepared to discuss anything else. And to this he seemed resigned but without ever saying: "OK, an independent state." He did not say that, he did not commit himself, he was not precise. But such was the spirit of the agreement and it was totally unambiguous.

Incidentally, the agreement included a provision that if ʿAbdullah succeeded in capturing Syria, and realized his dream of Greater Syria – something we did not think he had the power to do – we would not disturb him. We did not believe either in the strength of his faction in Syria. But the agreement included a provision that if he did accomplish it, we would not stand in his way. But regarding the Arab part of Palestine, we did think it was serious and that he had every chance of taking it, all the more so since the Arabs of Palestine, with their official leadership, did not want to establish a state at all. That meant that we were not interfering with anybody. It was they who refused. Had they accepted a state, we might not have entered into the conspiracy. I do not know. But the fact was that they refused, so there was a complete power vacuum here and we agreed that he will go in and take the Arab part, provided he consented to the establishment of our state and to a joint declaration that there will be peaceful relations between us and him after the dust settles. That was the spirit of the agreement. A text did not exist.[11]

Neutralizing the Arab Liberation Army

King 'Abdullah was the Zionists' principal vehicle for fomenting further tension and antagonism within the ranks of the conflict-ridden Arab coalition, but he was not the only one. Fawzi al-Qawuqji, the commander of the Arab Liberation Army, was another weak link in the chain of hostile Arab forces. The first companies of the ALA started infiltrating into Palestine in January 1948 while Qawuqji himself did not arrive until March. Qawuqji's anti-Husayni political orientation provided an opportunity for a dialogue across the battle lines that were rapidly taking shape in Palestine as the British mandate was approaching its inglorious end.

Yehoshua ("Josh") Palmon was one of the Haganah's ablest intelligence officers and a fluent Arabic speaker. From close observation of factional Arab politics, Palmon was aware of the bitter grudge which Qawuqji bore the *mufti*. In 1947 Palmon discovered wartime German documents bearing on this feud and he passed them on to Qawuqji. These documents confirmed Qawuqji's suspicion that it was the *mufti* who had instigated his arrest and incarceration by the German authorities. Qawuqji expressed a desire to meet Palmon but, on being appointed to command the ALA, he dropped the idea. From officers who arrived in Palestine before their chief, however, Palmon learnt that Qawuqji was not hell-bent on fighting the Jews. He apparently realized that such a war would be neither short nor easy and he was said to be open to suggestions for averting it.[12]

David Ben-Gurion, the chairman of the Jewish Agency Executive, approved Palmon's plan for a secret meeting to try and persuade Qawuqji to keep out of the fight between the Haganah and the *mufti*'s forces provided no promises were made to limit their own freedom of action to retaliate against any armed gangs.[13] Palmon went to see Qawuqji at the latter's headquarters in the village of Nur al-Shams on 1 April. After a great deal of beating about the bush, Palmon got down to the real business of the meeting which was to turn inter-Arab rivalries to the advantage of his side. A solution could have been found to the problem of Palestine, he said, had it not been for the *mufti*. Qawuqji launched into a diatribe against the *mufti*'s wicked ambitions, violent methods, and selfish lieutenants. When Palmon mentioned ʿAbd al-Qadir al-Husayni, the *mufti*'s cousin, and Hasan Salama, Qawuqji interjected that they could not count on any help from him and, indeed, he hoped that the Jews would teach them a good lesson. Palmon then suggested that the Haganah and the ALA should refrain from attacking each other and plan instead to negotiate, following the departure of the British. Qawuqji agreed but explained frankly that he needed to score one military victory in order to establish his credentials. Palmon could not promise to hand him a victory on a silver plate. If Jews were attacked, he said, they would fight back. Nevertheless, he went away with a clear impression that Qawuqji would remain neutral in the event of a Jewish attack on the *mufti*'s forces in Palestine.[14]

The extent of Palmon's success in neutralizing the ALA became clear only as events unfolded. On 4 April the Haganah launched Operation Nahshon to open the Tel Aviv–Jerusalem road which had been blocked by the Palestinian irregulars. First, Hasan Salama's headquarters in Ramla was blown up. Although an ALA contingent with heavy guns was present in the neighborhood, it did not go to the rescue. Qawuqji was as good (or as bad) as his word to Palmon. Next was the battle for the Qastal, a strategic point overlooking the road to Jerusalem, which changed hands several times amid fierce fighting. ʿAbd al-Qadir al-Husayni telephoned Qawuqji to ask for an urgent supply of arms and ammunition to beat off the Jewish offensive. Thanks to the Arab League, Qawuqji had large stocks of war material but, according to the Haganah listening post which monitored the call, he replied that he had none.[15] ʿAbd al-Qadir al-Husayni himself was killed in the battle for Qastal on 9 April. He was by far the ablest and most charismatic of the *mufti*'s military commanders and his death marked the collapse of the Husayni forces in Palestine.

The road to war

The tide now turned decisively in favor of the Jewish forces. The mixed towns of Tiberias, Haifa, Safad, and Jaffa fell into Jewish hands in rapid succession and the first waves of Palestinian refugees were set in motion. With the collapse of Palestinian resistance, the Arab governments, and especially that of Transjordan, were subjected to mounting popular pressure to send their armies to Palestine to check the Jewish military offensive. King 'Abdullah was unable to withstand this pressure. The flood of refugees reaching Transjordan pushed the Arab Legion toward greater participation in the affairs of Palestine. The tacit agreement that 'Abdullah had reached with the Jewish Agency enabled him to pose as the protector of the Arabs in Palestine while keeping his army out of the areas that the UN had earmarked for the Jewish state. This balancing act, however, became increasingly difficult to maintain. Suspecting 'Abdullah of collaboration with the Zionists, the anti-Hashemite states in the Arab League began to lean towards intervention with regular armies in Palestine, if only to curb 'Abdullah's territorial ambition and stall his bid for hegemony in the region. On 30 April the Political Committee of the Arab League decided that all the Arab states must prepare their armies for the invasion of Palestine on 15 May, the day after expiry of the British mandate. Under pressure from Transjordan and Iraq, King 'Abdullah was appointed as commander-in-chief of the invading forces.[16]

To the Jewish leaders it looked as if 'Abdullah was about to throw in his lot with the rest of the Arab world. So Golda Meir was sent on 10 May on a secret mission to Amman to warn the king against doing that. 'Abdullah looked depressed and nervous. Meir flatly rejected his offer of autonomy for the Jewish parts under his crown and insisted that they adhere to their original plan for an independent Jewish state and the annexation of the Arab part to Transjordan. 'Abdullah did not deny that this was the agreement but the situation in Palestine had changed radically, he explained, and now he was one of five; he had no choice but to join with the other Arab states in the invasion of Palestine. Meir was adamant: if 'Abdullah was going back on their agreement and if he wanted war, then they would meet after the war and after the Jewish state had been established. The meeting ended on a frosty note but 'Abdullah's parting words to Ezra Danin, who accompanied and translated for Golda Meir, were a plea not to break off contact, come what may. It was nearly midnight when Mrs. Meir and her escort set off on the dangerous journey back home to report the failure of her mission and the inevitability of an invasion.[17]

In Zionist historiography the meeting of 10 May is usually presented as proof of the unreliability of Israel's only friend among the Arabs and as confirmation that Israel stood alone against an all-out offensive by a united Arab world. Golda Meir herself helped to propagate the view that King 'Abdullah broke his word to her; that the meeting ended in total disagreement; and that they parted as enemies.[18] The king's explanation of the constraints that forced him to intervene were seized upon as evidence of treachery and betrayal on his part. In essence, the Zionist charge against 'Abdullah is that when the moment of truth arrived, he revoked his pledge not to attack the Jewish state and threw in his lot with the rest of the Arab world.[19] This charge helped to sustain the legend that grew up around the outbreak of war as a carefully orchestrated all-Arab invasion plan directed at strangling the Jewish state at birth.

The truth about the second 'Abdullah-Golda meeting is rather more nuanced than this self-serving Zionist account would have us believe. A more balanced assessment of 'Abdullah's position was presented by Yaacov Shimoni at the meeting of the Arab Section of the Political Department of the Jewish Agency on 13 May in Jerusalem: "His Majesty has not entirely betrayed the agreement, nor is he entirely loyal to it, but something in the middle."[20] Even Meir's own account of her mission, given to her colleagues on the Provisional State Council shortly after her return from Amman, was nowhere as unsympathetic or unflattering as the account she included much later in her memoirs. From her own contemporary report on her mission, a number of important, but frequently overlooked points, emerge. First, 'Abdullah did not go back on his word: he only stressed that circumstances had changed. Second, 'Abdullah did not say he wanted war: it was Golda Meir who threatened him with dire consequences in the event of war. Third, they did not part as enemies. On the contrary, 'Abdullah seemed anxious to maintain contact with the Jewish side even after the outbreak of hostilities. 'Abdullah needed to send his army across the River Jordan in order to gain control over the Arab part of Palestine contiguous with his kingdom. He did not say anything about attacking the Jewish forces in their own territory. The distinction was a subtle one and Golda Meir was not renowned for her subtlety.

Part of the problem was that 'Abdullah had to pretend to be going along with the other members of the Arab League who had unanimously rejected the UN partition plan and were bitterly opposed to the establishment of a Jewish state. What is more, the military experts of the Arab League had worked out a unified plan for invasion. This plan was all the more dangerous because it was geared to the real capabilities of the regular Arab armies rather than to the wild rhetoric about throwing the Jews into the sea. But the forces actually made available by the Arab states for the campaign in Palestine were well below the level demanded by the Military Committee of the Arab League. Moreover, King 'Abdullah wrecked the invasion plan by making last-minute changes. His objective in ordering his army across the River Jordan was not to prevent the establishment of a Jewish state but to make himself master of the Arab part of Palestine. 'Abdullah never wanted the other Arab armies to intervene in Palestine. Their plan was to prevent partition; his plan was to effect partition. His plan assumed and even required a Jewish presence in Palestine although his preference was for Jewish autonomy under his crown. By concentrating his forces on the West Bank, 'Abdullah intended to eliminate once and for all any possibility of an independent Palestinian state and to present his Arab partners with annexation as a *fait accompli*.

As the troops marched into Palestine, the politicians of the Arab League continued their backstage manoeuvers, labyrinthine intrigues, and sordid attempts to stab each other in the back – all in the name of the highest pan-Arab ideals. Politics did not end when the war started but was inextricably mixed with it from the moment the first shot was fired until the guns finally fell silent and beyond.[21] On 15 May, the day of the invasion, an event took place which presaged much of what was to follow and exposed the lengths to which the Arab politicians were prepared to go in their attempts to outwit their partners. Syrian President Shukri al-Quwwatli sent a message to King 'Abdullah saying it was necessary to halt the advance into Palestine and to provide the Palestinians instead with all possible arms and funds. 'Abdullah suspected that this was a ploy to find out his true intentions. His answer was a flat rejection of this proposal.[22] His army had already been given its marching orders. The die was cast.

If King 'Abdullah's relations with his fellow Arab leaders had sunk to one of their lowest points, his contact with the Jewish Agency had been severed altogether. The momentum generated by popular Arab pressure for the liberation of Palestine was unstoppable. The Jews were in a similarly truculent and uncompromising mood: they had proclaimed their state and they were determined to fight for it, whatever the cost. It was an ultimatum that Mrs. Meir had gone to give King 'Abdullah, not sympathy or help in dealing with his inter-Arab problems. The Hashemite–Zionist accord, which had been thirty years in the making, looked about to unravel amid bitter recriminations. Five Arab armies were on the move, dashing the hope of a peaceful partition of Palestine that lay at the heart of this accord. As the soldiers took charge on both sides, the prospects of salvaging anything from the ruins of the Zionist–Hashemite accord looked at best uncertain.

The invasion

The first round of fighting, from 15 May until 11 June, was a critical period during which the fate of the newly born Jewish state seemed to hang in the balance. During this period the Jewish community suffered heavy casualties, civilian as well as military; it reeled from the shock of contact with regular Arab armies; and it suffered an ordeal which left indelible marks on the national psyche. For the people who lived through this ordeal, the sense of being *me'atim mul rabim*, the few against the many, could not have been more real. During this period, the IDF was locked in a battle on all fronts, against the five invading armies. The IDF had numerical superiority in manpower over all the Arab expeditionary forces put together, but it suffered from a chronic weakness in firepower, a weakness that was not rectified until the arrival of illicit arms shipments from the Eastern bloc during the first truce. The sense of isolation and vulnerability was overwhelming. And it was during this relatively brief but deeply traumatic period that the collective Israeli memory of the 1948 War was formed.[23]

Israel's political and military leaders, however, had a more realistic picture of the intentions and capabilities of their adversaries. David Ben-Gurion, who became prime minister and defense minister after independence, expected 'Abdullah to take over the Arab part of Palestine in accordance with the tacit agreement that Golda Meir had reached with him in November 1947. So he could not have been altogether surprised to learn from Mrs. Meir in May 1948 that 'Abdullah intended to invade Palestine. The real question was whether 'Abdullah's bid to capture Arab Palestine would involve him in an armed clash with the Israeli forces.

Ben-Gurion did not have to wait long for an answer to this question. No sooner had the Arab armies marched into Palestine, when the Arab Legion and the IDF came to blows. Some of the fiercest battles of the entire war were fought between these two armies in and around Jerusalem. Even before the end of the British mandate, an incident took place which cast a long shadow over relations between the Yishuv and Transjordan. An Arab Legion detachment launched an all-out attack, with armored cars and canons, on Gush Etzion, a bloc of four Jewish settlements astride the Jerusalem–Hebron road. After the defenders surrendered, some were massacred by Arab villagers from the Hebron area and the rest were taken captive by the Arab Legion.[24] The Etzion bloc was an enclave in the middle of a purely Arab area which had been assigned to the Arab state by the UN. Nevertheless, this ferocious assault could not be easily reconciled with 'Abdullah's earlier protestations of friendship or professed desire to avert military hostilities.

In Jerusalem the initiative was seized by the Jewish side. As soon as the British evacuated the city, a vigorous offensive was launched to capture the Arab and mixed quarters of the city and form a solid area going all the way to the Old City walls. Glubb Pasha, the British commander of the Arab Legion, adopted a defensive strategy which was intended to avert a head-on collision with the Jewish forces. According to his account, the Arab Legion crossed the Jordan on 15 May to help the Arabs defend the area of Judea and Samaria allocated to them. They were strictly forbidden to enter Jerusalem or to enter any area allotted to the Jewish state in the partition plan. But on 16 May the Jewish forces tried to break into the Old City, prompting urgent calls for help from the Arab defenders. On 17 May, King 'Abdullah ordered Glubb Pasha to send a force to defend the Old City.[25] Fierce fighting ensued. The legionnaires inflicted very heavy damage and civilian casualties by shelling the New City, the Jewish quarters of Jerusalem. On 28 May, the Jewish Quarter inside the Old City finally surrendered to the Arab Legion.

After the Jewish offensive in Jerusalem had been halted, the focal point of the battle moved to Latrun, a hill spur with fortifications, that dominated the main route from Tel Aviv to Jerusalem. Like Gush Etzion, Latrun lay in the area allotted by the UN to the Arab state. But Latrun's strategic importance was such that Ben-Gurion was determined to capture it. Against the advice of his generals, he ordered three frontal attacks on Latrun, on 25 and 30 May and on 9 June. The Arab Legion beat off all these attacks and inflicted very heavy losses on the hastily improvised and ill-equipped Jewish forces.

Any lingering hope that Transjordan would act differently to the rest of the Arab countries went up in smoke as a result of the costly clashes in and around Jerusalem. Yigael Yadin, the IDF chief of operations, roundly rejected the claim that there had ever been any collusion between the Jewish Agency and the ruler of Transjordan, let alone collusion during the 1948 War:

Contrary to the view of many historians, I do not believe that there was an agreement or even an understanding between Ben-Gurion and 'Abdullah. He may have had wishful thoughts . . . but until 15 May 1948, he did not build on it and did not assume that an agreement with 'Abdullah would neutralize the Arab Legion. On the contrary, his estimate was that the clash with the Legion was inevitable. Even if Ben-Gurion had an understanding or hopes, they evaporated the moment 'Abdullah marched on Jerusalem. First there was the assault on Kfar Etzion, then the capture of positions in Latrun in order to dominate the road to Jerusalem, and then there was the entry into Jerusalem. From these moves it was clear that 'Abdullah intended to capture Jerusalem.[26]

Yadin's testimony cannot be dismissed lightly for it reflected the unanimous view of the IDF General Staff that the link with Transjordan had no influence on Israel's military conduct during the War of Independence. As Major-General Moshe Carmel, the commander of the northern front, put it: "All of us felt that *à la guerre come à la guerre* and that we had to act against all the Arab forces that had invaded the country."[27] What may be questioned is the assumption of Israel's military leaders that 'Abdullah intended to capture Jerusalem.

One of the many paradoxes of the 1948 War was that the greatest understanding – that between Israel and Transjordan – was followed upon the outbreak of war by the bloodiest battles. One explanation of this paradox is that within the context of the tacit understanding between the two sides, there was plenty of scope for misunderstandings. Jerusalem was the most likely area for misunderstandings to arise both because of its symbolic and strategic importance, and because the fact that it was to form a separate enclave under an international regime permitted both sides to keep their fears and their hopes to themselves. In the first round of fighting, which ended when the UN-decreed truce took effect on 11 June, Transjordan and Israel looked like the worst of enemies. During the rest of the war, however, they were, in the apt phrase of one Israeli writer, "the best of enemies."[28]

The other Arab armies were not as effective as the Arab Legion in the first round of fighting. There was little coordination between the invading armies and virtually no cooperation. Although there was one headquarters for all the invading armies, headed by an Iraqi general, Nur al-Din Mahmud, it had no effective control over those armies, and the military operations did not follow the agreed plan. Having accomplished the initial thrust into Palestine, each army feared that it would be cut off by the enemy from the rear. Consequently, one after the other, the Arab armies took up defensive positions. The Egyptian army sent two columns from their forward bases in Sinai. One advanced north along the coastal road in the direction of Tel Aviv. Its advance was slowed down by its attempts, mostly abortive, to capture Jewish settlements scattered in the northern Negev. It continued its advance, by-passing these settlements, until it was stopped on 29 May by the Negev Brigade in Ashdod, 20 miles from Tel Aviv. The second column, which included volunteers from the Muslim Brotherhood, proceeded towards Jerusalem through Beersheba, Hebron, and Bethlehem. It was stopped at Kibbutz Ramat Rahel at the southern edge of Jerusalem on 24 May. An Arab Legion unit was stationed nearby but it extended no assistance to the Egyptian fighters. Thus, after only 10 days of fighting, the Egyptian advance was halted.

The Iraqi army, despite considerable logistical difficulties, managed to assemble a sizeable force, with tanks and artillery, for the invasion of Palestine. In the first three days following the end of the mandate, the Iraqi army launched attacks on three Jewish settlements, all of which were repulsed. Having given up the attempt to capture Jewish settlements, the Iraqi army retreated, regrouped, and took up defensive positions in "the triangle" defined by the large Arab cities of Jenin, Nablus, and Tulkarem. When attacked by IDF units, in Jenin for example, it held its ground. It also launched occasional forays into Jewish territory, but none of them lasted more than a few hours. Although its westernmost point was less than 10 miles from the Mediterranean, the Iraqi army made no attempt to push to the sea and cut Israel in two. One reason for the relative passivity of the Iraqi military leaders was the fear of being cut off by the enemy. Another reason was their mistrust of the Arab Legion or, more precisely, of its foreign commander Glubb Pasha. Salih Sa'ib al-Jubury, the Iraqi chief of staff, claimed that it was the failure of the Arab Legion to carry out the mission assigned to it in the overall invasion plan that exposed his own army to attacks from the Israelis and prevented it from achieving its aims. According to al-Jubury, the Legion acted independently throughout, with terrible results for the general Arab war effort.[29]

In the north, the Syrians crossed into Israel just south of the Sea of Galilee and captured Zemah, Sha'ar ha-Golan, and Massadah before being stopped at Degania. They retreated, regrouped, and launched another offensive a week later north of the Sea of Galilee. This time they captured Mishmar Hayardem, establishing a foothold on the Israeli side of the Jordan river, from which the IDF was unable to dislodge them. While the Syrians were fighting in the Jordan Valley, the Lebanese forces broke through the eastern gateway from Lebanon to Israel and captured Malkiya and Kadesh. IDF operations behind the lines and against villages inside Lebanon succeeded in halting the Lebanese offensive. By the end of May the IDF had recaptured Malkiya and Kadesh and forced the Lebanese army on the defensive.

All in all, the combined and simultaneous Arab invasion turned out to be less well-coordinated, less determined, and less effective than Israel's leaders had feared. Success in withstanding the Arab invasion greatly enhanced Israel's self-confidence. Ben-Gurion was particularly anxious to exploit the IDF's initial successes in order to move on to the offensive and go beyond the UN partition lines. On 24 May, only ten days after the declaration of independence, Ben-Gurion asked the General Staff to prepare an offensive directed at crushing Lebanon, Transjordan, and Syria. In his diary he wrote:

The weak link in the Arab coalition is Lebanon. Muslim rule is artificial and easy to undermine. A Christian state should be established whose southern border would be the Litani. We shall sign a treaty with it. By breaking the power of the Legion and bombing Amman, we shall also finish off Transjordan and then Syria will fall. If Egypt still dares to fight – we shall bomb Port Said, Alexandria and Cairo.[30]

These plans were overambitious. By the end of the first week in June a clear stalemate had developed on the central front and a similarly inconclusive situation prevailed on all the other fronts. The UN truce came into force on 11 June. To the Israelis it came, in Moshe Carmel's words, like dew from heaven. Though they had succeeded in halting the Arab invasion, their fighting forces were stretched to the limit and badly needed a respite to rest, reorganize, and train new recruits. On the Israeli side, the four weeks' truce was also used to bring in large shipments of arms from abroad in contravention of the UN embargo – tanks, armored cars, artillery, and aircraft. On the Arab side, the truce was largely wasted. No serious preparations were made by any of the Arab countries to reorganize and re-equip their armies so that they would be better placed in the event of hostilities being resumed. The UN arms embargo applied in theory to all the combatants but in practice it hurt the Arabs and helped Israel because the Western powers observed it whereas the Soviet bloc did not.[31] Consequently, the first truce was a turning-point in the history of the war. It witnessed a decisive shift in the balance of forces in favor of Israel.

The second round of fighting

Inter-Arab rivalries re-emerged with renewed vigor during the truce. As far as King 'Abdullah was concerned, the war was over. He began to lobby in the Arab world for the incorporation of what was left of Arab Palestine into his kingdom. He made no secret of his view that the resumption of the war would be disastrous to the Arabs. His solution, however, was unacceptable to any of the other members of the Arab coalition. Syria and Lebanon saw 'Abdullah as a permanent threat to their independence, while King Faruq saw him as a growing menace to Egypt's hegemony in the Arab world. Count Folke Bernadotte, the UN mediator, omitted all reference to the UN partition plan, and proposed the partition of mandatory Palestine between Israel and Transjordan. 'Abdullah could have hardly asked for more but since the Arab League and Israel rejected Bernadotte's proposals out of hand, he saw no point in going out on a limb by publicly accepting them.

Having failed to promote a settlement of the Palestine problem, Bernadotte proposed the extension of the truce that was due to expire on 9 July. Once again, Transjordan found itself in a minority of one in the Arab League. All the Arab military leaders pointed to the gravity of their supply positions but the politicians voted not to renew the truce.

To deal with the difficulty of resuming hostilities when their arsenals were depleted, the Arab politicians settled on a defensive strategy of holding on to existing positions. 'Abdullah suspected that the decision was taken with the sinister intention of undermining his diplomatic strategy and embroiling his army in a potentially disastrous war with the Israelis. He therefore summoned Count Bernadotte to Amman to express his extreme unease at the prospect of war breaking out afresh and to urge him to use the full power of the UN to bring about a reversal of the Arab League's warlike decision.[32] But the Egyptians pre-empted by attacking on 8 July, thereby ending the truce and committing the Arab side irreversibly to a second round of fighting.

If 'Abdullah was against a second round of fighting, Glubb Pasha was even more reluctant to be drawn in as his army had only four contact days' worth of ammunition and no replenishments in sight. Indeed, in the second round, the Arab Legion only reacted when it was attacked. When hostilities were resumed, the IDF quickly seized the initiative on the central front with Operation Danny. In the first phase the objective was to capture Lydda and Ramla; in the second it was to open a wide corridor to Jerusalem by capturing Latrun and Ramallah. All these towns had been assigned to the Arab state and fell within the perimeter held by the Arab Legion. On 12 July, Israeli forces captured Lydda and Ramla and forced their inhabitants to flee eastwards. In Latrun, on the other hand, the Israeli offensive was repulsed as was the last minute attempt to capture the Old City of Jerusalem.

The ALA, the Egyptian, Iraqi, Syrian, and Lebanese armies all suffered some reverses in the course of the second round of fighting. The IDF offensive in the north culminated in the capture of Nazareth and in freeing the entire Lower Galilee from enemy forces. On the other hand, the attempt to eject the Syrians from the salient at Mishmar Hayarden was not successful and the fighting ended in stalemate. Israel's overall position improved appreciably as a result of the ten days' fighting. Israel seized the initiative and was to retain it until the end of the war.

The second UN truce came into force on 18 July and, unlike the first truce, it was of indefinite duration. As soon as the guns fell silent, Arab politicians resumed the war of words against one another. The line that the Arab Legion was being prevented from using its full strength against the Jews, both through the treachery of the British officers and the withholding of supplies by the British government, was actively propagated by the Syrian and Iraqi officers and by 'Azzam Pasha. The Iraqi army officers operating in Transjordan were particularly hostile to the British who served in the Arab Legion.[33] The suspicion that Glubb was secretly working to impose on the Arabs London's policy of partition accounted for the virtual breakdown of the relations between the two Hashemite armies and for the Iraqi branch jealously guarding its freedom of action.[34]

Lull in the storm

During the lull in the storm ʿAbdullah kept flirting with the idea of bilateral negotiations with Israel to settle the Palestine problem. Though it did not go as planned, the war had served its basic purpose in enabling him to occupy the central areas of Arab Palestine. Not only was there nothing else to be gained from an appeal to arms, but such an appeal could jeopardize both his territorial gains and his army, the mainstay of his regime and his only defense against his Arab opponents. Accordingly, he shifted his attention from the military to the political arena.

The Israelis had their own reason for wanting to resume direct contact with their old friend. Disunity in the Arab camp gave them considerable room for manoeuver. The Arabs had marched into Palestine together but as they sustained military reverses, each country looked increasingly to its own needs. Each country was licking its wounds and was in no position and in no mood to help the others or to subordinate its interests to the common cause. Under these circumstances, anyone looking for cracks in the wall of Arab unity could easily find them. Israel, with the memory of its military victories still fresh in everybody's mind, was well placed to play off the Arabs against one another.[35] This was the background of the renewal of contact with King ʿAbdullah's emissaries in September 1948.

Rumors that ʿAbdullah was once again in contact with the Jewish leaders further damaged his standing in the Arab world. His many critics suggested that he was prepared to compromise the Arab claim to the whole of Palestine as long as he could acquire part of Palestine for himself. "The internecine struggles of the Arabs," reported Glubb, "are more in the minds of the Arab politicians than the struggle against the Jews. ʿAzzam Pasha, the *mufti* and the Syrian government would sooner see the Jews get the whole of Palestine than that King ʿAbdullah should benefit."[36]

To thwart ʿAbdullah's ambition, the other members of the Arab League, led by Egypt, decided in Alexandria on 6 September to approve the establishment of an Arab government for the whole of Palestine with a seat in Gaza. This was too little and too late. The desire to placate public opinion, critical of the Arab governments for failing to protect the

Palestinians, was a major consideration. The decision to form the Government of All-Palestine in Gaza, and the feeble attempt to create armed forces under its control, furnished the members of the Arab League with the means of divesting themselves of direct responsibility for the prosecution of the war and of withdrawing their armies from Palestine with some protection against popular outcry. Whatever the long-term future of the Arab government of Palestine, its immediate purpose, as conceived by its Egyptian sponsors, was to provide a focal point of opposition to 'Abdullah and serve as an instrument for frustrating his ambition to federate the Arab regions with Transjordan.

But the contrast between the pretensions of the All-Palestine Government and its capability quickly reduced it to the level of farce. It claimed jurisdiction over the whole of Palestine, yet it had no administration, no civil service, no money, and no real army of its own. Even in the small enclave around the town of Gaza its writ ran only by the grace of the Egyptian authorities. Taking advantage of the new government's dependence on them for funds and protection, the Egyptian paymasters manipulated it to undermine 'Abdullah's claim to represent the Palestinians in the Arab League and in international forums. Ostensibly the embryo for an independent Palestinian state, the new government, from the moment of its inception, was thus reduced to the unhappy role of a shuttlecock in the ongoing power struggle between Cairo and Amman.[37]

Israel was content to see the rift develop inside the Arab League but prudently refrained from expressing any opinion in public for or against the All-Palestine Government. Before the Provisional State Council, on 23 September 1948, foreign minister Moshe Sharett described what remained of Arab Palestine as a "geographical expression" rather than a political entity. There were two candidates for ruling this part of Palestine: the *mufti* and King 'Abdullah. In principle, said Sharett, Israel had to prefer a separate government in the Arab part to a merger with Transjordan; in practice, they preferred a merger with Transjordan though their public posture was one of neutrality.[38] In practice, Israel also took advantage of the renewed contacts with 'Abdullah in order to thwart the establishment of a Palestinian state and expand the territory of the Jewish state. As Yaacov Shimoni, the deputy head of the Middle East department in the foreign ministry, candidly confessed:

Sharett knew that we had agreed with 'Abdullah that he will take and annex the Arab part of Palestine and Sharett could not support this ludicrous, impotent, and abortive attempt made by the Egyptians against 'Abdullah. This attempt had nothing to do with us. It was a tactical move by 'Abdullah's enemies to interject something against his creeping annexation. At that time there was no annexation. Formal annexation only occurred in April 1950. But he had started taking and preparing for annexation. So they tried, without any success, to build a countervailing force.

The second point is that at that time Sharett and our men knew what the powerful State of Israel has forgotten in recent years. He understood the meaning of diplomacy and knew how to conduct it. Sharett was definitely aware that publicly we were obliged to accept the Palestinian Arab state and could not say that we were opposed to the establishment of such a state. In the first place, we had accepted the UN resolution which included a Palestinian Arab state. Secondly, this was the right, fair, and decent course and we were obliged to agree to it. The fact that below the surface, behind the curtain, by diplomatic efforts, we reached an agreement with 'Abdullah – an agreement which had not been uncovered but was kept secret at that time – was entirely legitimate but we did not have to talk about it. Sharett knew that our official line had to be in favour of a Palestinian state if the Palestinians could create it. We could not create it for them. But if they could create it, certainly, by all means, we would agree. The fact that he made a deal with 'Abdullah on the side to prevent the creation of such a state, that is diplomacy, that is alright. Sharett behaved in accordance with the rules of diplomacy and politics that are accepted throughout the world.[39]

The war against Egypt

The rivalries among the Arab states that gave rise to the so-called Government of All-Palestine complicated Israel's diplomacy but simplified its strategy. David Ben-Gurion, the man in charge of grand strategy, was constantly on the look-out for divisions and fissures in the enemy camp that might be used to extend Israel's territorial gains. Arab disunity provided the strategic luxury of fighting a war on only one front at a time and the front Ben-Gurion chose to renew the war was the southern front. In early October he asked the General Staff to concentrate the bulk of its forces in the south and to prepare a major offensive to expel the Egyptian army from the Negev. In view of the worsening relations between Egypt and 'Abdullah, he thought it unlikely that the Arab Legion would intervene in such a war.[40]

On 15 October, the IDF broke the truce and launched Operation Yoav to expel the Egyptian forces from the Negev. In a week of fighting, the Israelis captured Beersheba and Bayt Jibrin, and surrounded an Egyptian brigade (which included Major Gamal 'Abd al-Nasir) in Faluja. As Ben-Gurion expected, Transjordan remained neutral in the war between Israel and Egypt. The Arab Legion was in a position to intervene to help the Egyptian brigade trapped in the Faluja pocket but it was directed instead to take Bethlehem and Hebron, which had previously been occupied by the Egyptians. 'Abdullah and Glubb were apparently happy to see the Egyptian army defeated and humiliated.

The formation of the Government of All-Palestine revived the *mufti*'s Holy War Army – *Jaysh al-Jihad al-Muqaddas*. This irregular army endangered Transjordan's control in Arab Palestine. The Transjordan government therefore decided to nip in the bud the challenge posed by this army to its authority. On 3 October, the minister of defense laid down that all armed bodies operating in the areas controlled by the Arab Legion were either to be under its orders or disbanded.[41] Glubb carried out this order promptly and ruthlessly. Suspecting that Arab officers would balk at performing such an unpatriotic task, he sent British officers to surround and forcibly disband the Holy War Army. The operation brought the Arabs to the brink of internecine war when they were supposed to be cooperating against the common enemy. But it effectively neutralized the military power of 'Abdullah's Palestinian rivals. Against this background, the Israeli attack on the Egyptian army was not altogether unwelcome. Glubb privately expressed the hope that the Jewish offensive "may finally knock out the Gaza government and give the gyppies [*sic*] a lesson!" In a letter to Colonel Desmond Goldie, the British commander of the First Brigade, Glubb explained that "if the Jews are going to have a private war with the Egyptians and the Gaza government, we do not want to get involved. The gyppies and the Gaza government are almost as hostile to us as the Jews!"[42]

The Israelis followed up their "private war" in the south by launching a major offensive in the north. Israel's enemies were now being picked off one by one. On 29 October, Operation Hiram unfolded, resulting in the capture of central Galilee and in the displacement of many more Arabs. The "cleansing of the Galilee" was the result of high-level policy rather than a random by-product of the war. Central Galilee contained a large number of Arab residents, including refugees from western and eastern Galilee. On 26 September, Ben-Gurion had told the cabinet that, should the fighting be renewed in the north, the Galilee would become "clean" and "empty" of Arabs.[43] In the event, it was Israel that renewed the fighting, and it was the IDF that carried out the expulsions. Four brigades were concentrated in the north for Operation Hiram. In four days of fighting they pushed the Syrians further east, caught Qawuqji's Arab Liberation Army in a pincer movement and knocked it out of the fight, and banished the Lebanese army from the Galilee. In hot pursuit of the retreating forces, the Carmeli Brigade crossed into Lebanon and captured fourteen villages which were later relinquished when the armistice agreement was signed. Thus, on the northern front, too, the tide turned dramatically and menacingly against the Arabs.

The third UN truce came into force on 31 October. On 22 December Israel once again broke the truce by launching a second offensive in the south. The objective of Operation Horev was to complete the destruction of the Egyptian forces, to drive them out of Palestine, and to compel the Egyptian government to negotiate an armistice. Conflict between the Arab states and lack of coordination between their armies in Palestine gave Israel the freedom to choose the time and place of the second offensive. Egypt appealed to its Arab allies for help but its appeals fell on deaf ears. Lebanon, Saudi Arabia, and the Yemen all promised assistance but failed to honor their promises. The Iraqis shelled a few Israeli villages near their front line as a token of solidarity with their embattled ally. Without exception the Arab states were either afraid to intervene or did not wish to intervene. The Israeli troops surged forward, expelled the Egyptians from the south-western flank of the Negev, and penetrated into Sinai to the outskirts of El-Arish. Operation Horev succeeded in compelling Egypt, the strongest Arab state with the best claim to lead the others, to open armistice negotiations with the State of Israel and thus to bring the war to an end. On 7 January 1949, the UN-decreed cease-fire went into force marking the formal end of the first Arab–Israeli war.

Conclusion

This survey of Israel's strategy and tactics in dealing with the Arab coalition in 1948 is not intended to belittle Israel's victory but to place it in its proper political and military context. And when one probes the politics of the war and not merely the military operations, the picture that emerges is not the familiar one of Israel standing alone against the combined might of the entire Arab world but rather one of a remarkable convergence between the interests of Israel and those of Transjordan against the other members of the Arab coalition, and especially against the Palestinians.

My purpose in writing this survey was not to pass moral judgment on Israel's conduct in 1948 or to delegitimize Zionism but to suggest that the traditional Zionist narrative of the birth of Israel and the first Arab–Israeli war is deeply flawed. The Zionist narrative, like all nationalist versions of history, is a curious mixture of fact and fiction. The new historiography has been denounced by its critics for being driven not by the scholarly search for truth about the past but by an anti-Israeli political agenda. Despite these criticisms, which are themselves politically inspired, the new historiography is essentially a cool attempt to use official documents in order to expose some of the fictions that have come to surround the birth of Israel. It offers a different perspective, an alternative way of looking at the momentous events of 1948. History is a process of demystification and the new historiography helps to demystify the birth of Israel, to give a fuller, more nuanced, and more complex picture of what is undoubtedly one of the great success stories of the twentieth century. That the debate between the traditional, pro-Zionist and the "new historians" should be so heated is hardly surprising. For the debate about the 1948 War cuts to the very core of Israel's image of itself.

Notes

1 Yehoshafat Harkabi, *Arab Attitudes to Israel* (Jerusalem, 1972), pp. 37–38.

2 See Avi Shlaim, "The Debate about 1948," *IJMES* 27 (1995) 287–304.

3 Walid Khalidi, *From Haven to Conquest: Readings in Zionism and the Palestine Problem Until 1948* (Beirut, 1971), pp. 858–71; Simha Flapan, *The Birth of Israel: Myths and Realities* (London, 1987), pp. 187–99; and Benny Morris, *1948 and After: Israel and the Palestinians* (Oxford, 1994), pp. 13–16.

4 Jacob Tsur, *Zionism: The Saga of a National Liberation Movement* (New York, 1977), pp. 88–89.

5 Zvi Elpeleg, *The Grand Mufti: Hajj Amin al-Hussaini, Founder of the Palestinian National Movement* (London, 1993), p. 86.

6 Flapan, *The Birth of Israel*, p. 130, quoting from a report by Michael Comay of a conversation with the British journalist Claire Hollingworth.

7 Muhammad Amin al-Husayni, *Haqa'iq 'an qadiyyat filastin* [Facts about the Palestine Question] (Cairo, 1956), p. 22.

8 Yezid Sayigh, *Armed Struggle and the Search for State: The Palestinian National Movement, 1949–1993* (Oxford, 1997), p. 14.

9 On the relations between 'Abdullah and the Zionists see Mary C. Wilson, *King 'Abdullah, Britain and the Making of Jordan* (Cambridge, 1987); Joseph Nevo, *King 'Abdullah and Palestine: A Territorial Ambition* (London, 1996); Yoav Gelber, *Jewish–Transjordan Relations, 1921–1948* (London, 1997); and Avi Shlaim, *Collusion across the Jordan: King 'Abdullah, the Zionist Movement, and the Partition of Palestine* (Oxford, 1988).

10 Ezra Danin, "Talk with 'Abdullah, 17 November 1947," S25/4004, and Elias Sasson to Moshe Shertok, 20 November 1947, S25/1699, Central Zionist Archives (CZA), Jerusalem. See also Shlaim, *Collusion across the Jordan*, pp. 110–117.

11 Interview with Yaacov Shimoni, 26 August 1982, Jerusalem.

12 Unsigned report, 16 March 1948, S25/3569, CZA.

13 David Ben-Gurion, *Yoman Ha-milhama, 1948–1949* [War Diary: The War of Independence, 1948–1949], 3 vols., Gershon Rivlin and Elhanan Orren, eds. (Tel Aviv, 1982), vol. I, p. 330.

14 Interview with Yehoshua Palmon, 31 May 1982, Jerusalem. See also Dan Kurzman, *Genesis 1948: The First Arab–Israeli War* (London, 1972), pp. 67–69; and Larry Collins and Dominique Lapierre, *O Jerusalem* (New York, 1972), pp. 269–270.

15 Kurzman, *Genesis 1948*, p. 137.

16 Government of Iraq, *Taqrir lajnat al-tahqiq al-niyabiyya fi qadiyyat filastin* [Report of the Parliamentary Committee of Enquiry into the Palestine Question] (Baghdad, 1949).

17 Golda Meir's verbal report to the thirteen-member Provisional State Council. Israel State Archives, *Provisional State Council: Protocols, 18 April–13 May 1948* (Jerusalem, 1978), pp. 40–44. See also Shlaim, *Collusion across the Jordan*, pp. 205–14.

18 Golda Meir, *My Life* (London, 1975), pp. 176–80.

19 For a comprehensive review of the literature and the debate see Avraham Sela, "Transjordan, Israel and the 1948 War: Myth, Historiography and Reality," *Middle Eastern Studies* 28 (1992) 623–88.

20 State of Israel, *Political and Diplomatic Documents, December 1947–May 1948* (Jerusalem, 1979), pp. 789–91.

21 Among the more revealing Arabic sources on the discord and deception inside the Arab coalition are Iraqi Parliament, *Taqrir Lajnat al-Tahqiq*; ʿAbdullah al-Tall, *Karithat filastin* [The Catastrophe of Palestine] (Cairo, 1959); Salih Saʾib al-Jubury, *Mihnat filastin wa-asraruha al-siyasiyya wa al-askariyya* [The Palestine Disaster and its Political and Military Secrets] (Beirut, 1970); and Muhammad Hasanayn Haykal, *Al-ʿUrush waʾl-juyush: kadhalik infajara al-siraʿa fi filastin* [Thrones and Armies: Thus Erupted the Struggle for Palestine] (Cairo, 1998). For two excellent reviews of Arabic sources and Arab historiography on the 1948 War, see Walid Khalidi, "The Arab Perspective," in Wm. Roger Louis and Robert W. Stookey, eds., *The End of the Palestine Mandate* (London, 1986), pp. 104–36: and Avraham Sela, "Arab Historiography of the 1948 War: The Quest for Legitimacy," in Laurence J. Silberstein, ed., *New Perspectives on Israeli History: The Early Years of the State* (New York, 1991), pp. 124–54.

22 King ʿAbdullah of Jordan, *My Memoirs Completed: "Al-Takmilah,"* translated from the Arabic by Harold W. Glidden (London, 1978), pp. 20–21.

23 Anita Shapira, "Politics and Collective Memory: The Debate over the 'New Historians' in Israel," *History and Memory* 7 (1995) 9–40.

24 Major ʿAbdullah al-Tall, who led the attack, reveals in his memoirs that he tricked Glubb Pasha into allowing him to rush reinforcements to another unit which was falsely reported to have fallen into a Jewish ambush in Kfar Etzion. See Tall, *Karithat filastin*, pp. 31–34.

25 John Bagot Glubb, *A Soldier with the Arabs* (London, 1957), p. 110.

26 Interview with Lieutenant-General Yigael Yadin, 19 August 1982, Jerusalem.

27 Interview with Major-General Moshe Carmel, 1 September 1983, Tel Aviv.

28 Uri Bar-Joseph, *The Best of Enemies: Israel and Transjordan in the War of 1948* (London, 1987).

29 Jubury, *Mihnat filastin*, pp. 189–90.

30 Ben-Gurion, *Yoman Ha-milhama*, vol. II, pp. 453–54.

31 Amitzur Ilan, *The Origins of the Arab–Israeli Arms Race: Arms, Embargo, Military Power and Decision in the 1948 Palestine War* (Basingstoke, 1996); and Robert Danin, "The Rise and Fall of Arms Control in the Middle East, 1947–1955: Great Power Consultation, Coordination, and Competition" (D.Phil. thesis, University of Oxford, 1999).

32 Folke Bernadotte, *To Jerusalem*, trans, Joan Bulman (London, 1951), pp. 163–64; 'Arif al-'Arif *al-Nakba* [The Catastrophe] 6 vols. (Beirut and Sidon, 1956–60), vol. III, p. 593; PRO, C. M. Pirie-Gordon to B. A. B. Burrows, 25 July 1948, FO 371/68822.

33 PRO, Sir Alec Kirkbride to FO, 6 August 1948, FO 371/68830.

34 Muhammad Mahdi Kubba, *Mudhakkirati* [My Memoirs] (Beirut, 1965), pp. 261–67.

35 Interview with Yehoshua Palmon, 31 May 1982, Jerusalem.

36 PRO, Glubb to Burrows, Secret and Personal, 22 September 1948, FO 371/68861.

37 Avi Shlaim, "The Rise and Fall of the All-Palestine Government in Gaza," *Journal of Palestine Studies* 20/1 (1990) 37–53.

38 Moshe Sharett, *Besha'ar Ha-umot, 1946–1949* [At the Gate of the Nations, 1946–1949] (Tel Aviv, 1958), pp. 307–9.

39 Interview with Yaacov Shimoni, 26 August 1982, Jerusalem.

40 Ben-Gurion, *Yoman Ha-milhama*, vol. III, p. 737, diary entry for 7 October 1948.

41 Glubb, *Soldier with the Arabs*, p. 192.

42 Glubb to Goldie, 16 October 1948. I am grateful to Colonel Goldie for giving me access to this letter.

43 Benny Morris, *The Birth of the Palestinian Refugee Problem, 1947–1949* (Cambridge, 1987), p. 218.

5   Jordan and 1948: the persistence of an official history

Eugene L. Rogan

The year 1948 was a defining one for the modern state of Jordan.[1] It was the year in which the government of King ʿAbdullah redefined its treaty relations with Britain and achieved greater independence from London's rule. It was the year in which the Arab Legion engaged in its first all-out war, and the people of Transjordan were mobilized behind the common Arab agenda of preserving Arab Palestine. It was the year in which the desert kingdom of Transjordan was transformed territorially and demographically into the Hashemite Kingdom of Jordan, through the integration of the West Bank and the absorption of a half-million Palestinian refugees. The events of 1948 isolated Jordan in inter-Arab politics, and were directly responsible for the assassination of King ʿAbdullah three years later. In effect, 1948 was a major turning point when the former British colony emerged as a sovereign actor and was caught up in the turmoil which has buffeted the region down to the present day.

The centrality of 1948 to the subsequent history of Jordan has given the events of that year particular importance in the foundation myths of the Hashemite kingdom. In essence, history has been employed to validate the course of action pursued by King ʿAbdullah and the state which he founded. Consequently, much of what has been published on the subject in Jordan has been limited to the memoirs of participants,[2] and a handful of works by nationalist historians who lived through the 1948 War and based their work primarily on the memoirs and documents of those who took part.[3] Uncritical and loyalist, these works constitute an official history of 1948 which portray the war very much in line with the Jordanian military and government's perspective.[4]

Almost since its inception, the "official history" has been challenged by a counter-history written by disaffected Jordanians, Palestinians who suspected that King ʿAbdullah colluded with the Jewish Agency at their expense for his own expansionist ends, and neighboring Arab states at ideological odds with the Hashemite kingdom.[5] Conspiratorial books on the "secrets of 1948" were published in Cairo and Beirut in the 1960s.[6]

These books were no less subjective than the Jordanian official history, reliant on personal perspectives and state-sanctioned truths – in this case of Jordan's enemies – and were dismissed as such by the proponents of the official history.

It was only after 1978, when archival sources became available to researchers in Britain and Israel, that a more objective history of 1948 could be written. The documents uncovered in the Israeli archives confirmed aspects which Jordanian historians have preferred to overlook, such as the extent of Jordanian contacts with leaders of the Yishuv before and after the 1948 War.[7] If they address this literature at all, the Jordanians have preferred to dismiss the British and Israeli documentation as the biased sources of their former colonial ruler and the Zionist enemy which naturally would be at variance with the Jordanian perspective.

The archival material exists within Jordan to present the Jordanian perspective on the history of 1948. The private and official papers of the Jordanian royal household, alternately referred to as the "Palace" or "Hashemite Archives," have never been opened to public use, though a narrow circle of Jordanian historians have been given some degree of access to these papers.[8] This privilege has been given only to loyal Jordanian historians, who have drawn selectively on the Hashemite papers to reinforce the Jordanian nationalist narrative. None to my knowledge has used these sources to address the claims of the archival-based histories published over the past decade.

Jordanian loyalism versus Arab nationalism

The first histories of Jordan's role in 1948 were published a decade after the end of the war. Two early texts set the parameters for radically divergent Jordanian and Arab nationalist narratives of the war. They were written by officers in the Arab Legion who had enjoyed the confidence of King 'Abdullah and played major roles in both the military campaigns and political negotiations behind the scenes. The authors were intimately acquainted with each other, though their relationship had deteriorated in the course of 1948 to the point of enmity by war's end. Each accused the other of working for two masters: General John Bagot Glubb was accused of putting the interests of his native Britain before those of Transjordan, while Colonel 'Abdullah al-Tall was accused of betraying his native Transjordan at the behest of his Egyptian paymasters.

Glubb Pasha was the commander of the Arab Legion. As a regular officer of the British Army, Glubb was sent to Iraq in 1920, where he resigned his commission to enter the service of the government of Iraq.

He was seconded to Transjordan in 1930 to create a desert patrol to secure the country's frontiers against Bedouin raids, and in 1939 he took command of the Arab Legion. While Glubb was first and foremost a British subject, he was avowedly loyal to King 'Abdullah and Transjordan. Glubb saw no contradiction between these loyalties, given his belief in the convergence of interests between Britain and Transjordan.[9]

Glubb wrote his memoirs of the 1948 War in the immediate aftermath of his dismissal from service by 'Abdullah's grandson, King Hussein, in February 1956. The politics of the day were still heavily influenced by the defeat of 1948. The loss of Palestine had given a common cause to Arab nationalists, led by Egyptian President Gamal 'Abd al-Nasir. 'Abd al-Nasir brought tremendous pressure to bear on those Arab states with Western leanings. Jordan, with its British military commander and support for the Western-sponsored regional alliance, the Baghdad Pact, became a particular target of attack. Glubb's dismissal took place against this background, and it influenced the tone of his book. In *A Soldier with the Arabs*, Glubb sought to clear his name and that of his adopted sovereign, King 'Abdullah, from the many accusations of treachery leveled against both in the aftermath of 1948.[10]

Colonel 'Abdullah al-Tall published his version of events one year after Glubb, in 1958. A promising young officer from a good family in the northern Jordanian town of Irbid, Tall enjoyed rapid promotion and the trust of King 'Abdullah. He was appointed military governor of Jerusalem after the Arab Legion secured its hold over the Old City in 1948. In this capacity, Tall met with his Jewish counterpart, Colonel Moshe Dayan, through United Nations intermediaries, which recommended him to act as a go-between for King 'Abdullah in his contacts with the Israeli government in the latter part of the war. Tall played an important role in Jordanian–Israeli negotiations from December 1948 through the spring of 1949. He subsequently fell out with the Jordanian state and resigned his commission in 1949 to enter the service of the Egyptian government. Tall effectively took political asylum in Cairo, and in March 1950 began to publish what he knew of 'Abdullah's negotiations with the Israelis.[11] In Glubb's words:

It appeared that Tell had opened the King's letters [to the Israelis] confided to his safe keeping and had taken photostatic copies, a fact that proved he was contemplating treachery even when he was high in the King's favour. The photostats of these letters Abdulla al Tell now presented to the Egyptian Press. He also gave interviews in which he stated that the British officers in the Arab Legion had prevented their units from fighting, in order to help the Jews, and that King Abdulla was a traitor to the Arab cause. He went so far as to say that King Abdulla was alone responsible for the loss of Palestine.[12]

Tall casts a very different light on his own actions. He portrays himself as a loyal soldier who struggled in vain to wrest his king from the influences of a British agent – Glubb Pasha.

Through my experiences in the army and in the government I was given the opportunity to learn about the political secrets which followed the Palestine War. From the very start of the war I was in rebellion against my commander Glubb. . . . Once the [situation] reached the extreme of treason, I began to collect evidence and record the history of the secrets behind the catastrophe. In those crucial days in which the treason was revealed to me, I did not deceive the king or his government; rather, I began tirelessly to give counsel and sincere, honourable opposition, and showed them the political obstacles towards which they were headed. . . . I wanted my king and his ministers not to bow their heads to Glubb, but they hardened against me and sided with Glubb.[13]

On the one hand, Tall sought to clear himself of the accusation that he had a part in the assassination of King 'Abdullah in 1951, for which he had been tried *in absentia* and sentenced to death. The tone and timing of the publication of Tall's memoirs, *The Catastrophe of Palestine*, were also directly linked to the anti-imperialism and Arab nationalism of Gamal 'Abd al-Nasir's Egypt. In the aftermath of the 1956 Suez Crisis, known in Arabic as the "tri-partite collusion" for the secret alliance of Britain, France, and Israel in the war, Tall was clearly playing to the anti-British gallery and his book sold well as a result.

These two books were to prove very influential in the subsequent accounts of Jordan's role in the 1948 War. Glubb's text formed the basis of the Jordanian loyalist account, and is extensively cited by subsequent Jordanian historians (though some are critical of the imperialist role played by the British officers in command of the Legion in 1948).[14] Glubb made two points central to the Jordanian telling of the story. He insisted that Transjordan acted at all times in accordance with the wishes of the people of Palestine, both in sending the Arab Legion into Palestine and in the subsequent unification of the West Bank with Transjordan, which he claimed reflected "the spontaneous and genuine desire of the Palestinian people."[15] And he argued that the Arab Legion held its lines against superior Jewish numbers despite depleted ammunition stores, no finances, and absolutely no cooperation from the other Arab forces. 'Abdullah al-Tall's memoirs, on the other hand, served the Arab nationalist telling of the story. In their public pronouncements, the Arab states had been dismissive of Jewish military preparation and overconfident of their ability to defeat the Zionist project. Arab public opinion was totally unprepared for the loss of Arab Palestine and the defeat of so many Arab armies. Tall's account provided an explanation based on imperialist conspiracies and of the ruler of an Arab state putting his narrow national interests before the interests of the broader Arab nation.

Both Glubb and Tall have left important texts for the historians of 1948. Subjective, apologetic, politically motivated, and diametrically opposed to each other, there is a great deal of truth to both narratives. Neither can be considered the *whole* truth. Both authors left out or glossed over inconvenient details. With the release of archival material in Israel and the United Kingdom, and the publication of a number of studies in the 1980s and 1990s based on these new materials by Israeli and Western scholars, as well as a number of Jordanian primary and secondary sources now in print, we now have contemporary documentary sources to reconcile the Jordanian loyalist and the Arab nationalist narratives. This essay makes an attempt at such reconciliation by reading the two historical narratives against each other, preserving what is most credible in each. However, rather than attempt a whole narrative of the war, this chapter will focus on the most controversial points in the history of 1948 to suggest a framework for a new Jordanian history of the war.

Towards a new Jordanian history of 1948

Shortly before his assassination in 1951, King 'Abdullah dictated the conclusion of his memoirs. It is a rambling document written in a cryptic style that aspired to candour. He sought to clear the air about a number of controversies unleashed by the Palestine War, though his brief treatment of "the Palestine Problem" set the tone of secrecy and self-justification which has marked the Jordanian writing of the history ever since.

I have already said that it is not seemly for me to go into certain confidential matters which should be kept hidden in the interest of the Arabs and of Arab brotherhood . . . Nevertheless it is my right to acquaint Arab public opinion . . . with matters which can be discussed openly. Among these are my relations with His Excellency Shukri al-Quwwatli and the events that transpired in Lydda and al-Ramlah, the happenings in Beersheba, the Egyptian withdrawal, the armistice at Rhodes, and the Triangle question.[16]

It seems only fitting that King 'Abdullah set the agenda for the issues to be addressed by a new Jordanian history of the 1948 War. However, it is essential to start with the one issue with which King 'Abdullah chose not to acquaint Arab public opinion. 'Abdullah's connections with the leaders of the Jewish Agency in Palestine before, during and after the war were most influential in Transjordan's political and military conduct, and yet they remain the great taboo among Jordanian historians.

The king and the Jews

King 'Abdullah's contacts with the Zionist movement date to the very beginning of his rule in Transjordan. Strapped for cash in his resource-poor state, 'Abdullah hoped to attract Jewish capital to aid in the development of Transjordan. He met with Chaim Weizmann in London in 1922 and received the chairman of the Zionist Executive, Colonel Frederick Kisch, in Amman in 1924. He encouraged Jewish investment in mining and electricity by Jewish financeers, with concessions to A. M. Novomeysky and Pinhas Rutenberg in the 1920s. The Jewish Agency approached the Hashemite amir to open Transjordan to Jewish settlement in the 1930s, and in 1932 bought an option from 'Abdullah to lease the lands of his estate in the Jordan Valley. His acquaintance with the Arabists in the Jewish Agency, especially Moshe Sharett and Elias Sasson, dated back to this period.[17]

In the aftermath of the second world war, contacts between King 'Abdullah and the Jewish Agency increased as the situation in Palestine deteriorated. Elias Sasson, head of the Arab Section of the Political Department of the Jewish Agency, had gained Egypt's provisional acceptance for a partition of Palestine, and sought 'Abdullah's support in August 1946, knowing that he had been alone among the Arab heads of state in supporting the Peel Commission's partition plan in 1937.[18] They met twice, in the king's Jordan Valley home in Shuna and found basic agreement in a partition plan which led to the creation of a Jewish state and the annexation of the Arab lands to Transjordan.[19] This was to remain Transjordan's undeclared policy through the remainder of 1947, though King 'Abdullah publicly followed the Arab League in its opposition to partition.[20] The Jewish Agency, concerned by 'Abdullah's public disavowal of partition in the lead-up to the United Nations debate, arranged another meeting with the Jordanian king, on 17 November 1947, at Pinhas Rutenberg's home in Naharayim on the Jordan River. The Jewish delegation was headed by Golda Meir acting on behalf of Sharett, with Elias Sasson and Ezra Danin. According to separate reports of the meeting by Sasson and Danin, the two sides struck agreement on a peaceful division of the territory of Palestine.[21] Common interest guided the Jewish Agency and Transjordan in their agreement. Partition held the prospect of statehood for the Yishuv, territorial expansion for Transjordan, and the abortion of a Palestinian Arab state that would inevitably be headed by their common enemy the mufti of Jerusalem, Hajj Amin al-Husayni.[22]

All that remained was to gain British acceptance of the agreement. On 7 February 1948, Transjordan's Prime Minister Tawfiq Abu al-Huda met in secret with Foreign Secretary Ernest Bevin in London. Glubb served as interpreter, and provided the only record of the exchange. Abu al-Huda claimed that the government of Transjordan had received many petitions from Palestinian notables asking for the protection of the Arab Legion upon the withdrawal of British troops.[23] "The Trans-Jordan government accordingly proposed to send the Arab Legion across the Jordan when the British mandate ended, and to occupy that part of Palestine awarded to the Arabs which was contiguous with the frontier of Trans-Jordan." Bevin is reported to have replied: "It seems the obvious thing to do . . . but do not go and invade the areas allotted to the Jews."[24]

The comings and goings of Jewish officials to Shuna and Amman had not gone un-noticed in Palestine or Transjordan.[25] The need for discretion combined with mounting concern over Jewish territorial gains in Haifa, Jaffa, and Tiberias, and horror over the massacre of Dayr Yassin, to lead to a break in communications between the Jewish Agency and King 'Abdullah, as well as a hardening of Transjordan's position to match the belligerence of the Arab League. The Arab Legion began to send troops into Palestine where they provided support to Arab irregulars fighting the Jewish forces and protection to strategic villages. Ben-Gurion and his advisers were concerned to avoid engaging the Arab Legion, recognized as the strongest of the Arab regular armies. Both the Jews and the Jordanians sought a final meeting before the British withdrawal on 15 May. Ben-Gurion sent Golda Meir, who was driven to Amman and met King 'Abdullah on the night of 10/11 May. Their meeting was cordial but inconclusive. According to Meir, 'Abdullah was no longer willing to abide by their earlier agreement and would only offer "a unitary state with autonomy for the Jewish parts."[26] A Jordanian witness, however, claimed that 'Abdullah promised that the Jordanian and Iraqi armies would not engage Israeli forces beyond the lines stipulated by the UN Partition Resolution.[27] It was no longer clear that the Arab Legion's entry to Palestine would be a peaceful one.

Relations with Shukri al-Quwwatli (and the Arab League generally)

The Arab heads of state suspected King 'Abdullah of supporting the UN partition plan opportunistically in the hopes of territorial expansion into Palestine. They were particularly concerned to prevent the entry of the Arab Legion into Palestine, and had decided to support the Palestine Arabs in their self-defense and to raise a volunteer army, the Arab Salvation Army, headed by Fawzi al-Qawuqji, in lieu of committing the regular armies of Arab League states. Transjordan went along with this plan and contributed 1,000 rifles and 500,000 rounds of ammunition, and some 350 Jordanian volunteers to the Salvation Army, which entered combat in Palestine in January 1948.[28] While the Salvation Army was roundly defeated in its engagements with Jewish forces, the League kept up appearances by circulating Qawuqji's audacious reports of victories in the Arab press. Indeed, Jordanian archives preserve copies of mendacious telegrams from Qawuqji claiming victory against the Jewish settlement of Mishmar-Haemek and claiming to have entered Jaffa and shelled Tel Aviv, inflicting "countless casualties" on its Jewish residents.[29] King 'Abdullah wrote in April to the Iraqi prime minister, Muhammad al-Sadr, complaining of the Salvation Army's short-comings, warning "the time remaining before 15 May is short for Arab preparations but long for the Jewish forces to secure the places set out for them in the Partition Resolution."[30]

In the aftermath of the massacre at Dayr Yasin in April, the Arab League recognized that it would have to commit regular troops to Palestine, and, over the objections of Hajj Amin al-Husayni and the Syrian government, accepted King 'Abdullah's offer to send in the Arab Legion. King 'Abdullah referred to this Syrian mistrust in his memoirs when he spoke of "my relations with His Excellency Shukri al-Quwwatli" quoted above. Arab suspicions were well founded, for there is no doubt that Transjordan *did* harbor territorial ambitions in Pa-lestine.[31] As already noted, 'Abdullah had shown a predisposition to partition since 1937, his meetings with officials from the Jewish Agency were an ill-kept secret, and his language was often oblique on Palestinian self-determination. In his telegrams to Arab heads of state following the entry of the Arab Legion into Palestine on 15 May, 'Abdullah spoke of "establishing order and security and the rights of the people and preventing a repetition of Dayr Yasin" but very little on preserving Palestine for the Palestinians. Only in response to a telegram from his old rival, Hajj Amin al-Husayni, did King 'Abdullah use the language of "purging Palestine and delivering it to its people."[32]

In fact, the Jordanian Arab Legion had far more grounds to complain of the vacillations of the Arab League than the League had of Trans-jordan's aims in the war. It is worth remembering that the Arab Legion had no intention of fighting a war in Palestine, but of occupying the "central and largest area of Palestine allotted to the Arabs by the 1947 partition."[33] This peaceful entry was scuttled by the decision of the Arab League two days before the end of the Mandate to send the armies of Egypt, Iraq, Syria, and Lebanon into Palestine along with the Arab Legion. While the size, equipment and discipline of the Legion recommended it for a peace-keeping mission, its 6,000 troops in May 1948 were insufficient to defeat the estimated 35,000 Jewish regulars and irregulars in an all-out war. Nor did the Arab states commit enough troops to shift the balance in their favor: 10,000 Egyptian troops, 3,000 Syrians, 3,000 Iraqis, and 1,000 Lebanese in addition to the 4,500 Legionnaires, or an estimated total of 21,500 Arab troops in May 1948.[34] Though King ʿAbdullah was designated commander-in-chief of the Arab forces, this was in name alone, as the national forces operated under their own commanders without overall coordination. And while the Arab League promised to free Transjordan from the budgetary constraints imposed on it by Great Britain, the League in fact only delivered £250,000 of a promised £3 million in financial assistance. Worse yet, Glubb's attempts to stockpile ammunition in advance of war were stymied when the Egyptian government confiscated a British arms shipment to Transjordan from Suez.[35] Against its wishes, Transjordan faced an all-out war with dubious allies, low levels of ammunition and supplies, and no budget to fight a war.[36]

Lydda and Ramla

Following the British withdrawal from Palestine, the Arab Legion entered Palestine on 15 May to take up positions in Janin, Nablus, and Ramallah.[37] The smooth occupation of the West Bank of the Jordan River for which Glubb Pasha and King ʿAbdullah had hoped, already complicated by the entry of the other Arab armies, was further disrupted by Jewish moves to occupy Jerusalem immediately after the British withdrawal. According to the UN Partition Resolution, Jerusalem was to remain an international zone independent of the Jewish and Arab states. Glubb, working within the strict limits agreed between Bevin and Abu al-Huda in their February meeting, hesitated to follow the Israelis in breach of international law. After three days of mounting pressures, King ʿAbdullah ordered the Arab Legion into Jerusalem. Glubb demurred another day before finally committing his troops on 19 May. "'If we move into Jerusalem,' I kept repeating, 'we shall use up half our army. Then we cannot hold the rest of the country.'"[38]

Nothing in the discussions held between King ʿAbdullah and the Jewish Agency had prepared Transjordan for the real battle the Arab Legion was forced to wage in Jerusalem.[39] Instead of a peace-keeping mission, Transjordan was at war with Israel. What is more, to win the battle in Jerusalem, the Legion had to control the strategic Tel-Aviv–Jerusalem road to prevent the resupply of Israeli troops in the Old City. In the first phase of the fighting, the Legion concentrated in Jerusalem and Latrun. After intense house-to-house fighting, the Legion occupied the Jewish Quarter on 28 May, thereby securing the Old City. The Legion held their positions in Latrun in the face of repeated heavy attacks, particularly from 25 May until the end of the first round of fighting on 11 June. Overstretched, the Jordanian army handed over their positions in Nablus and the northern half of the West Bank to Iraqi troops on 22 May. Yet four days before the truce took effect, the Legion extended its lines and sent 100 men to the town of Ramla to maximize the territory under its control to improve its bargaining position in the negotiations to follow under UN mediator Count Folke Bernadotte.

At the end of the first round of fighting, the Arab Legion had posted important gains. However, four weeks of war had taken a heavy toll. The Legion had suffered nearly 20 percent casualties and was running very low on ammunition with no prospect of resupply. Britain adhered to the arms embargo, and Transjordan had no alternate supplier.[40] There was no progress toward a peaceful resolution of the conflict. Bernadotte's proposals, which called for the annexation of Arab Palestine to Transjordan and a union between Transjordan and Israel, provoked both the Israelis and the other Arab states to adopt a bellicose stand. For the Arabs, Bernadotte's proposals stood to benefit Transjordan at their expense and that of Arab Palestine. The Israelis, on the other hand, had broken the arms embargo and succeeded in replenishing their arsenal. They aspired to statehood, not union with Transjordan, and they had the forces to realize their ambitions. Alone among the Arab states, Transjordan recognized the strategic advantage Israel enjoyed, and sought by all means to avoid renewing hostilities. In this, the Arab Legion's British commanders found themselves at odds with their Jordanian officers who, unaware of the limited engagement which Glubb and King ʿAbdullah had envisaged, were driven by the common Arab agenda of defeating the Zionist enemy and liberating Palestine.[41] Nor could the Jordanian government resist public pressures to execute the war to the certain victory over the Zionist enemy which was universally anticipated. With the Israelis and the other Arabs determined to continue the fight, Transjordan was drawn into the second round of the war, in which the Israelis redoubled their efforts to break Arab Legion positions on the Tel Aviv–Jerusalem road.

The Legion's positions in Lydda and Ramla, seized opportunistically before the truce, were untenable. Glubb claimed that the Transjordan government had recognized before 15 May that the two towns could not be secured, and that they did not feature in Transjordan's initial occupation plans.[42] Without troops to spare to reinforce the Legionnaires and volunteers sent to Lydda and Ramla, and unwilling to sacrifice men and matériel needlessly, Glubb ordered the withdrawal of troops from the two towns on the night of 11 July. The following morning, Lydda and Ramla were occupied by the Israelis.

The loss of these towns without a fight and the flood of outraged refugees into Arab Legion positions was equally demoralizing to soldiers and civilians. 'Arif al-'Arif described the situation in Ramallah to King 'Abdullah two days after the fall of Lydda and Ramla:

> Panic has spread, some are taking flight, and there is anger at all levels of society. The people have begun to say different things. Some blame the leaders of the fighting units – most though not all of them English – as incompetent and shortsighted, while others accuse them of ill intentions. . . . The only hope in this dangerous crisis is to undertake decisive action leading to a swift victory . . . for the people once thought and still think that there is a plan hatched to lead to acceptance of partition in the end.

'Arif went on to appeal for relief for the refugees, "most of whom are barefoot and naked without the means to protect themselves from the calamity of hunger and want."[43]

King 'Abdullah responded sharply to 'Arif's report. He defended the record of the Arab Legion, "which from the beginning of the crisis until today has made sacrifices and preserves what it can of the holy places, for which it deserves to be thanked." Moreover, he laid some of the blame for the fall of the two towns on the civilian defenders "who were expected to stand their ground and resist," and on the failure of the other Arab armies to come to their relief. He hinted that the *mufti*'s supporters were taking advantage of the situation to turn Palestinian opinion against Transjordan: "I know that there were pamphlets distributed in Nablus and Ramallah before the latest events and that there are agents based in Bir Zayt working to provoke trouble."[44] However, he did pledge relief funds for the refugees from the Jordanian government.

Arab public opinion was further incensed when British Foreign Secretary Bevin appealed in the immediate aftermath of the fall of the two towns for a renewed truce. No one believed the inhabitants of Lydda and Ramla were themselves to blame for the fall of their town. But the link between the British commander who ordered the withdrawal of Arab Legion troops, and the British foreign secretary who now sought to impose a truce which left Lydda and Ramla in Israeli hands, confirmed suspicions of imperialist conspiracies in which Transjordan was implicated.[45] For the first time since the start of the war, Transjordan and the Arab Legion were accused of failing rather than saving Palestine. Worse was yet to come.

Beersheba and the Egyptian withdrawal

The Arab Legion held its lines in Latrun and Jerusalem, against determined Israeli assaults and with ammunition and supplies dwindling to dangerously low levels, through the second round of fighting (9–18 July) and the "shooting truce" which lasted until October. The Israelis built up their troop numbers to an estimated 96,000 by 1 October, while the Arab armies did not quite reach half this number. The Iraqi and Egyptian forces were estimated at 15,000 men each, and the Arab Legion had managed to field a force of 10,000 through rapid recruitment and training.[46] The Israelis also enhanced their capabilities through arms purchases from Czechoslovakia, which reinforced their armor and air forces. When fighting resumed on 15 October, the Israelis concentrated their forces against Egyptian positions in the south of the country. Within one week, the Egyptian detachments had either been defeated or surrounded. Bi'r al-Sabi' [Beersheba] was taken by the Israelis on 21 October. The Egyptians turned to their brother Arab states for relief.

The Arab states were in no position to relieve the Egyptian troops. The Arab Salvation Army had been driven out of northern Palestine, the Lebanese had not only retreated but had surrendered a number of their own villages to the Israelis, and the Syrians were forced into retreat by the end of October. The Iraqis were overextended in the northern "triangle" of the West Bank and were in no position to contemplate sending a force big enough to make a difference to the besieged Egyptians. The nearest army to Egyptian positions was the Arab Legion. King Faruq was loath to admit his weakness and seek the assistance of his rival King 'Abdullah. The Egyptian Prime Minister Nuqrashi Pasha reportedly exclaimed to 'Abdullah in a meeting in Amman on 23 October, "the Egyptian Government has no need of anyone's assistance. But where are the royal Jordanian and Iraqi forces?"[47]

Relations between Egypt and Transjordan had deteriorated through the course of the crisis. As already noted, the Jordanians accused Egypt of commandeering a shipload of ammunition sent by the British for the Arab Legion at the start of the war. The Egyptians had refused to cooperate with King 'Abdullah in his capacity as commander of the combined Arab forces, refusing even to let him visit Egyptian positions. Communications between the two sides had been reduced to an exchange of propaganda with neither side presenting a full and honest account of the course of battle. The Egyptians accused the Jordanians of restraint, allowing the Israelis to concentrate their forces on the Egyptian front. Thus, it was bruited that the Jordanians allowed Lydda and

Ramla to fall in order to put pressure on the Egyptian right flank.[48] Now, after the fall of Bi'r al-Sabi', the Egyptians were trying to force the Jordanians and Iraqis to make diversionary attacks in Latrun or Jerusalem to draw Israeli troops away from the besieged Egyptian positions.

All that Glubb was willing to do was send a small detachment of 350 Arab Legion troops and an armored car unit to Hebron to reinforce the Egyptian soldiers there, now cut off from their lines of supply and communication by the Israelis. The Jordanians were seen to be extending the territory under their control, rather than coming to the relief of the Egyptian forces. Relations between the Jordanian and Egyptian soldiers were tense, marked by petty squabbles over the seniority of their respective flags.[49] The only assistance Glubb offered the Egyptian troops trapped in Faluja was to provide them with an insecure route of retreat. Glubb sent one of his officers, Major Geoffrey Lockett, to find a path from Legion positions in Hebron through Jewish lines to Faluja. Lockett reached the besieged Egyptians and presented them with Glubb's plan. They were to destroy their artillery and heavy weapons to prevent them falling into enemy hands. The Legion and the Iraqis would make a diversionary attack in the Bayt Jibrin area, and the Egyptians would follow Lockett's route through Jewish lines back to Hebron. This plan provoked the Egyptian commanders' suspicions that the Jordanians were disarming them and delivering them to the Israelis. Rather than face the humiliation of being taken prisoner, they rejected Glubb's plan and stood their ground.[50]

The Armistice at Rhodes: the Negev and the Triangle

Over the summer months of fighting, contacts between Israel and the Arabs were made in European capitals. Elias Sasson held meetings in London and Paris with Transjordan's minister to London, 'Abd al-Hamid Haydar, in August. The Israelis grew increasingly demanding with their successes on the battlefield.[51] After the Israelis leaked word of the negotiations to the press, King 'Abdullah sought to bring the talks more firmly under his control and to open a channel in Jerusalem through his ambitious military governor, Colonel 'Abdullah al-Tall.[52]

On 10 December, Colonel Tall was called by the head of the international observer force in Jerusalem for an urgent meeting with his Israeli opposite, Colonel Moshe Dayan. They met at the Hebron Gate, accompanied by an observer. Dayan said he had a very important letter from a high Israeli official to be delivered to King 'Abdullah. Tall took the letter, prised off the wax seal, and made a photostatic copy. It was a hand-written note from Elias Sasson to 'Abdullah asking the king to appoint a trustworthy agent to accompany Dr. Shawkat al-Sati, 'Abdullah's confidant and personal physician, to enter into discussions on his behalf leading towards a peaceful resolution of the conflict.[53] Unaware of the tampering with Sasson's letter, King 'Abdullah asked 'Abdullah al-Tall to serve as his interlocutor with the Israelis.

King 'Abdullah set out his position in writing for Sati and Tall to convey to Sasson. He sought Israeli recognition of the decisions taken by Palestinian notables in the Jericho Conference to unite the remainder of Arab Palestine with Transjordan.[54] He sought a return of Lydda and Ramla to Jordanian control, "as you know the troubles which we encountered after the withdrawal." He wanted to open negotiations on Jaffa's status, and suggested the Arab sector of Jerusalem, including the Old City, remain with the Arabs and the Jewish half with the Jews. The Negev, the Galilee, and the question of refugees were all to be opened to negotiation. And he warned Sasson that "any unacceptable results from these negotiations will bring trouble from our political enemies on the Arab side worse than you can imagine."[55]

King 'Abdullah's envoys met with Elias Sasson the next day. Tall was struck by the evident friendship between the two men, who lamented the turn of events which had drawn them into war. Sati put some of the blame on Golda Meir's poor skills as a negotiator in the prelude to war. "Golda Meir was dry during her interview with His Majesty before the troubles. If your excellency had visited yourself, it would have been possible to arrive at a better understanding."[56] This belief that optimal results would be had through direct meetings between reasonable *men* (Meir's gender was considered a real hindrance by many Jordanians) motivated the reopening of negotiations.

Secret negotiations between Transjordan and Israel opened at a sensitive moment, as the Israelis dealt the *coup de grâce* to the Egyptian army. On 22 December, the Israelis launched a new offensive against the Egyptians, driving the main body of Egyptian forces out of Palestine and encroaching on Egyptian territory, as they had done in Lebanon. Again Egypt appealed to Iraqi and Jordanian forces to put pressure on the Israelis to divert them from their attack on Egyptian positions. On 30 December, the Jordanian, Iraqi, and Egyptian commanders met to discuss means to relieve the Egyptian forces, to no avail.[57] King Faruq was forced to turn to Great Britain, invoking their 1936 Treaty, to request British assistance to preserve Egypt's territorial integrity against the Israeli onslaught. Britain and America interceded, and the Egyptian government quickly accepted a truce and entered bilateral negotiations with the Israelis on 13 January which led to an armistice agreement signed at Rhodes on 24 February. [58]

Transjordan stood to gain clear benefits from Egypt's defeat. In this regard, it is worth noting the difference in ʿAbdullah al-Tall's rhetoric when negotiating on Transjordan's behalf in 1948 and writing for an Egyptian audience a decade later. Elias Sasson recorded a conversation with Tall on 14 December when he asked what Transjordan's attitude would be to renewed Israeli hostilities with Egypt. Sasson quoted Tall as saying: "Strike the Egyptians as much as you can. Our attitude will be totally neutral."[59] By this action, two of King ʿAbdullah's rivals were eliminated: King Faruq, and the *mufti*, Hajj Amin al-Husayni, whose short-lived All-Palestine Government in Gaza was driven into exile with the retreating Egyptians. What is more, by entering into direct negotiations with the Israelis and signing an armistice, the Egyptians yielded the moral high ground to King ʿAbdullah, who could claim not to have been the first to come to terms *openly* with the Israelis.

Behind the scenes, negotiations between the Israelis and Transjordan continued without much progress through the early months of 1949. The defeat of Egypt, Lebanon, and Syria had strengthened Israel's position strategically, and Ben-Gurion was unwilling to commit his government to specific terms before he had achieved his territorial aims. Troubled by the change in position since his pre-war discussions with the Jewish Agency, King ʿAbdullah sought to accelerate negotiations by meeting with the Israelis in person in Shuna. Tall, who was present at the meeting of 16 January, was appalled by the king's manner with Sasson and Dayan and his attempt to play on old friendship with the enemy and to use moral suasion to obtain Transjordan's ends. "I had expected His Majesty to be clever and cautious, taking without giving, terrorizing without coveting. I almost melted with shame when His Majesty began to reveal his cards in a frightening way and speak in a servile and fatuous manner."[60] The truth of the matter was that the Israelis no longer placed the same value in their relationship with Transjordan as they had in the months before the outbreak of war. Moshe Shertok, now Sharett, wrote after meeting King ʿAbdullah on 30 January: "We [are] inclined [to] regard these contacts as mere public relations since he [i.e. King ʿAbdullah] is not master [of the] situation in relation either [to] Britain or his own government." Ben-Gurion was yet more dismissive of the king: "Obviously the man has no value."[61]

King ʿAbdullah had two objectives in this last phase of the war: to retain the territory under Arab Legion control, and to extend Transjordan's control over the northern "triangle" of the West Bank then held by the Iraqi army. The situation could not have been more delicate. ʿAbdullah was concerned to prevent any confrontation between frustrated Iraqi troops and the Israelis to forestall Israeli moves against territory in the West Bank. He met with an Iraqi delegation headed by the regent ʿAbd al-Illah on 2 February to negotiate a handover of Iraqi positions to the Arab Legion. The Iraqis ultimately went along with this plan, preferring to withdraw from Palestine without conceding defeat, without recognizing Israel, and without going to Rhodes to negotiate an armistice.

The armistice talks between Transjordan and Israel opened in Rhodes on 4 March. No progress was made for the first two weeks of talks as Ben-Gurion set in motion the conquest of the Negev Desert, assigned to Israel by the 1947 Partition Resolution but still under Transjordan's nominal control. The government of Transjordan made a formal complaint to the armistice commission on 7 March, claiming that Israeli troops had crossed into territory under Transjordan's control. On 9 March, the small Arab Legion detachment in the Negev engaged the Israeli column. The Israelis were concerned lest the British intervene on behalf of their ally Transjordan to prevent their occupation of the Negev. In the event, the British were unwilling to interfere outside the boundaries set by the Transjordan Mandate. Rather than take a futile stand against a vastly larger Israeli force, the Arab Legion detachment withdrew. The Israelis completed their occupation of the Negev on 10 March, and signed a cease-fire with Transjordan on the eleventh.[62] After Lydda and Ramla, this was the second instance of the Arab Legion ceding land without a fight. It provoked less reaction because the Negev was thinly populated and did not set off a flight of refugees.

Israeli negotiators now turned their attention to the Iraqi front. The Israelis were concerned for the security of the coastal plain to the north of Tel Aviv. Not only was the territory under Israeli control very narrow, but Iraqi positions dominated the high country overlooking the plain. While Israeli commanders argued for a military solution, the civilian leadership preferred to achieve their strategic objectives at the negotiating table to be legitimated through a UN-mediated armistice. They recognized that King ʿAbdullah was in a very weak bargaining position. He had Iraqi authorization to take over their lines, but needed Israeli acquiescence to effect the handover.[63] The Israelis set their price in a meeting between King ʿAbdullah, Moshe Dayan, and Yehoshafat Harkabi: "to turn over to Israel Wadi Ara and the ridge to its southeast, as well as the first line of hills sloping southward from Maʾanit to Budrus."[64]

The Israelis were very specific about their territorial minimum. It was an arc of land following the Iraqi line right to the Jordan river. In all, some 300 square kilometers of good farmland with an estimated 35,000 inhabitants were surrendered at the bargaining table to secure Israel's agreement for the Arab Legion to relieve Iraqi positions. The agreement included a number of empty promises concerning territorial compensation to Transjordan for the land conceded in the Triangle, and compensation for the displaced inhabitants, which the Jordanians and Israelis both acknowledged would never be honored. The Jordanians were particularly concerned to keep the agreement a secret for as long as possible.[65] Their hopes to contain Arab outrage by these measures were to prove in vain. The agreement was forwarded to the negotiating teams in Rhodes, who had been sidelined by the real negotiations in Shuna, and formed the basis of the armistice agreement signed between Israel and Transjordan on 3 April 1949. The agreement, once published, provoked a storm of criticism in Palestine and the Arab World.[66] For the third time in the war the Arab Legion had surrendered Palestinian territory without a fight and watched as helpless peasants were turned out as refugees.

Through tense negotiations King ʿAbdullah had won the West Bank but in the process he had alienated a large part of the Palestinians, many of whom had no choice but to seek refuge in the Hashemite Kingdom. Accused of self-interest and betrayal, the Jordanians have been unreconciled to their past ever since.

Conclusion

The passage of fifty years has not calmed the controversy surrounding the events of the Palestine War. The political significance of this history is magnified by the fact that 1948 turned Transjordan into a bi-national state of Palestinians and Jordanians, territorially through the annexation of the West Bank and demographically through the waves of refugees who settled in Transjordan and were granted citizenship. The historians of 1948 took on the heavy burden of attempting to write a narrative which would build consensus between Palestinians and Jordanians around a common national project of the Hashemite Kingdom of Jordan. The loss of Jerusalem and the West Bank in the 1967 War exacerbated matters, as the Hashemite monarchy's efforts to preserve its authority over Palestinians in the Occupied Territories was challenged with increasing success by the Palestine Liberation Organization. Even after King Hussein relinquished his country's claims to the West Bank on 31 July 1988, there was little scope for historical revisionism within Jordan itself, where it is widely believed that Jordanians of Palestinian origin represent a significant majority of the population (though the actual figures from the last decennial census remain a carefully guarded secret). In the aftermath of Jordan's 1994 peace with Israel, the scope for reexamination of the history of the Arab–Israeli conflict is held hostage to Israel's relations with the Palestinian Authority and its Arab neighbors. Jordanian public opinion remains unreconciled to peace with Israel. Fifty years on, the Jordanians still refuse to confront their past.

Stripped of their ideological inaccuracies, the Jordanian loyalist and the Arab nationalist narratives are not so difficult to reconcile. This is, in fact, what many of the new Israeli historians have achieved. While the material of the Israeli archives has largely supported the Arab nationalists' narrative of secret dealings between King 'Abdullah and the Israelis, the analysis of the new historians is far more appreciative of King 'Abdullah's pragmatism and political realism. Transjordan never adhered to the maximalist goals to which Arab nationalists aspired in 1948: it did not seek to defeat the Israelis, and it did not wish to see the creation of an independent Palestinian state. Like Egypt and Syria, Transjordan was guided not by Arab nationalist priorities but by its own narrower national interests. Motivated by these interests, Transjordan succeeded where the Arab states failed and prevented the Israelis from conquering the largest part of Arab Palestine. In the process, Palestinian self-determination was subordinated to Jordanian national interests. Given Jordan's sizable Palestinian majority, it is important that a more credible Jordanian history of 1948, that answers the challenge of 'Abdullah al-Tall's documentation and the Israeli archives, take the place of the official history.

Notes

1 The name "Transjordan" will be used throughout, except in reference to the country after the formal change of name in March 1950. However, the adjective "Jordanian" is used instead of "Transjordanian." The Amir 'Abdullah was crowned king on 25 May 1946 and is referred to consistently as King 'Abdullah in this text.

2 See, for example, Ma'n Abu Nuwar, *Fi sabil al-quds* [On the Road to Jerusalem] (Amman, 1968); Hazza' al-Majali, *Mudhakkirati* [My memoirs] (Amman, 1960); Mahmud al-Rusan, *Ma'arik Bab al-Wad* [The Battles of Bab al-Wad] (Amman, n.d. [1950?]).

3 Munib al-Madi and Sulayman Musa, *Tarikh al-urdunn fi'l-qarn al-'ishrin* [The History of Jordan in the Twentieth Century] (Amman, 1959); Sulayman Musa, *Ayyam la tunsa* [Unforgettable Days] (Amman, 1982, 2nd ed. 1997); Kamal Salibi, *A Modern History of Jordan* (London, 1993).

4 This point has been made by Avraham Sela, "Transjordan, Israel, and the 1948 War: Myth, Historiography and Reality," *Middle Eastern Studies* 28 (1992) 623–88.

5 Most notable among disaffected Jordanians is 'Abdullah al-Tall's *Karithat filastin* [The Catastrophe of Palestine] (Cairo, 1958). Among the works of

Palestinian historians, see in particular 'Arif al-'Arif's *al-Nakba* [The Catastrophe], 5 vols. (Beirut, 1956–61).

6 See, for example, Anis Sayigh, *al-Hashimiyun wa qadiyya filastin* [The Hashemites and the Palestine Problem] (Beirut, 1966); Salih Sa'ib al-Jubury, *Mihnat Filastin wa asraruha al-siyasiyya wa'l-askariyya* [The Palestine Disaster and its Political and Military Secrets] (Beirut, 1970); Muhammad Faysal 'Abd al-Mun'im, *Asrar 1948* [Secrets of 1948] (Cairo, 1968).

7 Books based on the British and Israeli archives include Sulayman Bashir, *Judhur al-wisaya al-urduniyya* [The Roots of the Jordanian Trusteeship] (Jerusalem, 1980); Mary C. Wilson, *King 'Abdullah, Britain and the Making of Jordan* (Cambridge, 1987); Uri Bar-Joseph, *The Best of Enemies: Israel and Transjordan in the War of 1948* (London, 1987); Ilan Pappé, *Britain and the Arab-Israeli Conflict, 1948–1951* (London, 1988); Avi Shlaim, *Collusion across the Jordan: King Abdullah, the Zionist Movement, and the Partition of Palestine* (Oxford, 1988); Joseph Nevo, *King 'Abdullah and Palestine: A Territorial Ambition* (London, 1996).

8 Muhammad 'Adnan al-Bakhit, Hind Abu al-Sha'ir, and Nawfan Raja al-Suwariyya, eds., *Al-Watha'iq al-Hashimiyya: awraq 'Abdullah bin al-Husayn* [The Hashemite Documents: The Papers of 'Abdullah bin al-Husayn], vol. V: Palestine, 1948 (Amman, 1995). Hereafter cited as *Hashemite Documents*.

9 John Bagot Glubb, *A Soldier with the Arabs* (London, 1957), p. 19; Shlaim, *Collusion*, p. 224.

10 Glubb, *Soldier with the Arabs*, p. 79.

11 Wilson, *King 'Abdullah*, p. 265, n. 53.

12 Glubb, *Soldier with the Arabs*, pp. 256–57.

13 Tall, *Karithat filastin*, from the introduction to the first edition (n.p.).

14 See, for example, al-Madi and Musa, *Tarikh al-urdunn*, and Musa, *Ayyam la tunsa*. For a critique of Britain's imperialist role c.f. Sadiq al-Shara'a, *Hurubuna ma' isra'il, 1947–1973* [Our Wars with Israel] (Amman, 1997), pp. 281–83.

15 Glubb, *Soldier with the Arabs*, pp. 97, 216–17.

16 King Abdullah, *My Memoirs Completed: "Al-Takmilah"* (London, 1978), p. 20.

17 Bar-Joseph, *Best of Enemies*, pp. 1–8; Bashir, *Judhur al-wisaya*, pp. 57–101; Yoav Gelber, *Jewish–Transjordanian Relations, 1921–1948* (London, 1997), pp. 7–22; Nevo, *King 'Abdullah and Palestine*, pp. 15–30; Shlaim, *Collusion*, pp. 41–69; Wilson, *King 'Abdullah*, pp. 103–11.

18 Wilson, *King 'Abdullah*, pp. 122–24.

19 Shlaim, *Collusion*, pp. 76–84. Glubb states quite explicitly: "We in Trans-Jordan produced our own solution. We favoured partition . . . Such parts of Palestine as were allotted to the Arabs would have been incorporated in the neighbouring Arab states." *Soldier with the Arabs*, p. 59.

20 Sulayman Musa, for example, draws on 'Abdullah's press statements in his discussion of the king's war aims, which were very much in line with the other Arab states, *Ayyam la tunsa*, pp. 131–34.

21 Bar-Joseph, *Best of Enemies*, pp. 8–11; Shlaim, *Collusion*, pp. 110–17.

22 Bar-Joseph, *Best of Enemies*, p. 3; Glubb, *Soldier with the Arabs*, p. 63; Nevo, *King Abdullah and Palestine*, p. 200. For a discussion of Hajj Amin al-Husayni's views of 'Abdullah cf. Philip Mattar, *The Mufti of Jerusalem: al-Hajj Amin al-Husayni and the Palestinian National Movement* (New York, 1988), pp. 79–81, 113–17.

23 Dozens of these petitions from the period before 15 May 1948 from all major Palestinian towns have been preserved in the papers of King 'Abdullah; cf. *Hashemite Documents*, pp. 29–98.

24 Glubb, *Soldier with the Arabs*, pp. 63–66; Madi and Musa, *Tarikh al-urdunn*, p. 469.

25 'Abdullah al-Tall, *Karithat filastin*, p. 64.

26 Bar-Joseph, *Best of Enemies*, pp. 47–50; Shlaim, *Collusion*, pp. 205–10.

27 Tall, *Karithat filastin*, pp. 66–67. Tall, who was not present at the meeting, quotes 'Abdullah's private secretary, Muhammad al-Dubati, in whose house the meeting took place.

28 Madi and Musa, *Tarikh al-urdunn*, pp. 466–67.

29 Qawuqji's letter of 9 April 1948 on Mishmar-Haemek and 'Abdullah's reply, *Hashemite Documents*, pp. 181–82; Qawuqji's telegram claiming entry into Jaffa of 29 April 1948 and 'Abdullah's reply, *Hashemite Documents*, pp. 191–92.

30 Letter of 14 April 1948, *Hashemite Documents*, pp. 200–01.

31 Wilson, *King 'Abdullah*, pp. 103–28, 151–67. This has been taken as the focus of Nevo's study, *King 'Abdullah and Palestine*, subtitled "a territorial ambition."

32 Telegrams to King Faruq, Shukri al-Quwwatli, and Bishara al-Khuri, 15 May 1948, and response to telegram from Hajj Amin al-Husayni, 16 May 1948, *Hashemite Documents*, pp. 220–23.

33 Glubb, *Soldier with the Arabs*, p. 96. Glubb makes oblique reference to agreements struck with the Jewish Agency, saying: "The Jews were most likely aware of this proposal and did not appear to object to it . . ."

34 Glubb, *Soldier with the Arabs*, p. 94; Madi and Musa, *Tarikh al-urdunn*, p. 472. British sources set the relative strength of Israeli and Arab forces on the eve of Britain's withdrawal at 74,000 and 19,200, respectively. Wilson, *King 'Abdullah*, p. 170.

35 Glubb, *Soldier with the Arabs*, pp. 91–92; King Abdullah, *Memoirs Completed*, p. 22.

36 Glubb, *Soldier with the Arabs*, pp. 85, 178. On the strategic shortcomings of the Arab participation in the war, cf. Shara'a, *Hurubuna ma' Isra'il*, pp. 263–67.

37 The text of King 'Abdullah's speech to the Arab Legion entering Palestine is reproduced in *Hashemite Documents*, pp. 217–18.

38 Glubb, *Soldier with the Arabs*, p. 101.

39 Sela, "Transjordan, Israel and the 1948 War," p. 627.

40 Glubb claimed Arab states refused to believe he was out of supplies. "The Arab Legion, they claimed, was commanded by British officers. King Abdulla was Britain's devoted ally. It was ridiculous to suppose that Britain would leave her ally exposed to attacks without ammunition. Hence . . . we were obviously lying." *Soldier with the Arabs*, p. 211.

41 See, for example, Glubb's efforts to restrain his officers in Jerusalem in October 1948 in Tall, *Karithat filastin*, p. 414.

42 Glubb, *Soldier with the Arabs*, p. 161.

43 'Arif al-'Arif to King 'Abdullah, Ramallah, 14 July 1948, in *Hashemite Documents*, pp. 271–72. This confirms Glubb's description of the public mood, *Soldier with the Arabs*, p. 163.

44 King 'Abdullah's reply to 'Arif, undated, in *Hashemite Documents*, pp. 272–73.

45 Tall, *Karithat filastin*, pp. 247–49.

46 Glubb, *Soldier with the Arabs*, p. 195.

47 King 'Abdullah, *Memoirs Completed*, p. 24.

48 Tall, *Karithat filastin*, pp. 247–48.

49 *Ibid.*, pp. 411–12.

50 Arab Legion plan for the withdrawal of Egyptian force in Faluja, 17 November 1948, in *Hashemite Documents*, p. 295; Glubb, *Soldier with the Arabs*, pp. 214–15; Tall, *Karithat filastin*, pp. 420–21.

51 Bar-Joseph, *Best of Enemies*, pp. 104–112; Shlaim, *Collusion*, pp. 279–86.

52 It is only here that Musa acknowledges secret contacts between Transjordan and Israel; while acknowledging these reached to the level of Prime Minister Abu al-Huda, he never mentions direct meetings between King 'Abdullah and the Israelis. *Ayyam la tunsa*, p. 423.

53 Among other things, the letter confirmed earlier contacts between Sasson and Haydar in Paris. Sasson to King 'Abdullah, 10 December 1948, photostatic copy reproduced in Tall, *Karithat filastin*, p. 439.

54 On the Jericho Conference cf. Wilson, *King 'Abdullah*, pp. 182–84.

55 Tall claimed to have edited these instructions to harden Transjordan's line before meeting with Sasson. *Karithat filastin*, pp. 440–42.

56 Tall, *Karithat filastin*, p. 442.

57 Memo from deputy chief of staff of the Jordanian Arab Legion, 30 December 1948, in *Hashemite Documents*, pp. 306–07.

58 See Fawaz Gerges' chapter in this collection.

59 Bar-Joseph, *Best of Enemies*, p. 149 n. 119.

60 Tall, *Karithat filastin*, p. 460.

61 Both quotes are from Bar-Joseph, *Best of Enemies*, p. 189.

62 Glubb, *Soldier with the Arabs*, pp. 229–34; Musa, *Ayyam la tunsa*, pp. 533–39; Shlaim, *Collusion*, pp. 400–05.

63 King 'Abdullah's letter to Walter Eitan confirming Iraqi permission for the Arab Legion to assume their positions dated 19 March 1949, cited by Bar-Joseph, *Best of Enemies*, pp. 216–17.

64 Bar-Joseph, *Best of Enemies*, p. 217.

65 *Ibid.*, pp. 221–31; Glubb, *Soldier with the Arabs*, pp. 233–37; Musa, *Ayyam la tunsa*, pp. 540–53; Tall, *Karithat filastin*, pp. 529–30; Shlaim, *Collusion*, pp. 410–28; Wilson, *King 'Abdullah*, pp. 188–89.

66 Glubb, *Soldier with the Arabs*, p. 241; Shlaim, *Collusion*, pp. 428–33.

6   Iraq and the 1948 War: mirror of Iraq's disorder

Charles Tripp

Iraq's role in the 1948 War was ambivalent. Its leaders were the first to advocate coordinated military intervention in Palestine by the armies of the Arab states. Yet its own army, despite being the largest single Arab force in Palestine by the end of the war, did little beyond occupying defensive positions in the hills of the West Bank. Similarly, Iraqi ministers called repeatedly for the imposition of an Arab oil and trade boycott of the Western powers supporting partition, yet did nothing to implement it. During the war itself, Iraq initially rejected all cease-fires, but failed to back this up with more effective military strategies. Following the fighting, the Iraqi government refused to participate in armistice talks and seemed intent simply on withdrawing its troops as rapidly as possible.

The marked disparity between the uncompromising rhetoric of successive Iraqi governments and the rather timid nature of their actions, has laid them open to charges of hypocrisy and double-dealing. This was so at the time, both in Iraq and in other parts of the Middle East. In February 1949 it led the prime minister of the day, Nuri al-Sa'id, to establish a parliamentary committee of enquiry into the war. This remarkable document – *Taqrir Lajnat al-Tahqiq al-Niyabiyya fi Qadiyyat Filastin* [Report of the Parliamentary Committee of Enquiry into the Palestine Question] – was published by the Iraqi government in September 1949. It provided an opportunity both for the public airing, but also for the public vindication of the records of successive Iraqi governments and military commanders in the years leading up to 1948 and during the war itself.

Presided over by 'Abdullah al-Damluji, the commission compiled a report and a dossier of appendices examining the question of Palestine from the London conference of 1939 onwards. It covered all the major meetings of the Arab League council and the recommendations of its political and military committees. Iraqi politicians, such as Nuri al-Sa'id himself, Salih Jabr, and Fadil al-Jamali, were generally placed in a favorable light, as was the Iraqi army and its commanders. This was set against a background of British perfidy, American hostility, Palestinian disunity, and the vacillation and weakness of the other Arab states, particularly Egypt and Saudi Arabia. Any faults ascribed to Iraqis were very minor by comparison with those of the other actors.[1] Silent on many aspects of the war and its background, the report nevertheless captures well the divergence of views, the rivalries, and disunity of the Arab states. Until the revolution of 1958 it remained the official Iraqi account of the 1948 war, conveying the impression that although this was by no means a glorious episode in Iraqi or Arab history, Iraqis had less to be ashamed of than most.

After 1958, other versions of these events emerged, forming part of the general indictment of the monarchical regime in Iraq and echoing similar charges leveled at the Syrian and Egyptian governments, respectively, by the young officers who had seized power in those countries. Thus the failure of the Iraqi governments of the time to act more effectively in defense of Arab Palestine, the subordination of Iraq's military contingent to the annexationist designs of King 'Abdullah of Transjordan and the Hashemite regime's subservience to its British patrons have figured in Iraqi accounts of the period published since the fall of the monarchy. Nevertheless, even in these accounts, something of the spirit of the 1949 parliamentary report survives. The Iraqi army in particular, but also some of Iraq's statesmen, generally emerge with honour, in marked contrast to those of the other Arab countries.[2]

These are all narratives in the service of power and, as power changed hands, so too did the narratives. However, the purpose remained much the same: to assign blame for the undeniable catastrophe in Palestine. Satisfying as recriminations may sometimes be, it seems to be ultimately more illuminating to see the ambiguities of successive Iraqi governments as indicative of the multiple nature of the Iraqi state itself, rather than simply as examples of bad faith. The tensions between the various aspects of that state are well brought out in the events of 1948. This does not absolve the individuals concerned of their responsibility as political actors. It does, however, demand that the context of their decisions should be taken seriously and, in this respect, the key context is that of the Iraqi state in whose name they were acting.

It is the contention of this chapter that the engagement of Iraq in the war of 1948 brings out the many ways in which that state can be characterized. The state of Iraq was formed by a number of elements which created the distinctive institutional and imaginative environment in which Iraqi state policy was formed. No state is monolithic, however much that image may be projected by its rulers. In this respect, the Iraqi state is no exception. It has always been a terrain of contestation for various forces trying to gain control of it as an apparatus of power and to incorporate it into a dominant narrative of their own choosing. These facets of the Iraqi state owe much to its history, as well as to the social forces which that history favored and the imaginative realms that they fostered.

In the first place, Iraq as a state was a creation of British imperialism. This was of enduring significance for those who wished to hold power within the state and could not be safely ignored. Second, Iraq was also constituted as a Hashemite state, ruled over by a dynasty initially imposed by the British but with its own concerns, within Iraq and beyond. Third, Iraq was an Arab state. This had resonance domestically since it raised the question of how Iraqis viewed the state and each other. Regionally, it raised the question of the part Iraq was expected to play as an Arab state and the degree to which there existed fundamental differences of opinion about the demands of Arab, as opposed to Iraqi nationalism.

Finally, the Iraqi state can be seen as a regime of power, sustaining a certain hegemony over a restive society. Those seeking to legitimate their command of the state needed to pay particular attention to the languages of power. Iraq's deeply inegalitarian society followed fault lines delineated by ethnic, sectarian, and socioeconomic difference, sometimes mutually reinforcing, but sometimes further fragmenting that society. By the 1940s widespread social protest in the new spaces created by the centralizing, urbanized state and by the emergence of mass politics led to the preoccupation of the ruling elites with questions of order and disorder. Furthermore, these preoccupations raised the question of the role of the armed forces, not simply as the state's instrument in the region, but as guarantor of a certain kind of political order within Iraq itself.

In the context of 1948, the significance of these aspects of the Iraqi state lay in the fact that the question of Palestine had the capacity to affect each of them in various ways. The cause of Palestine had long been a rallying point for both anti-British and anti-imperialist sentiment in Iraq, placing the political elite in a difficult position, given the continuing power of Great Britain in Iraq. Second, for the Hashemites, the question of Palestine, on a symbolic level, was linked to the memory of the Arab revolt and the disappointed hopes of that era. In terms of *Realpolitik*, it was connected to the ambitions of King ʿAbdullah of Transjordan which the Regent ʿAbd al-Ilah of Iraq tried to influence to his own advantage.

Palestine was not, of course, simply the preserve of the Hashemites. As a cause and as an example, it was central to pan-Arabism in Iraq. The position adopted on the question of Palestine helped to define the view of many about Iraq's Arab identity during the 1930s and the 1940s. This raised questions of the loyalty of various communities within Iraq, Arab and non-Arab, to the Iraqi state or to a particular conception of that state. The issue could thus sharpen differences between Kurds and Arabs, and between Shi'i and Sunni Arabs whose views were often at odds on the implications of Arabism for state policy. Most poignantly, the question of Palestine raised doubts about the future of Iraq's large and long-established Jewish community.

Finally, the cause of Palestine created the basis of a language of legitimation within Iraqi politics that politicians ignored at their peril. It was a language used frequently and often extravagantly, precisely because of its power to move significant sections of Iraqi society. It thus provided an opportunity for those in command of the state to create a following and to displace more radical languages of social revolution. However, its use clearly implied real consequences for state action. The policies that resulted, modest by contrast with the rhetoric, added to the disconcerting gap between the claims of those who ruled the Iraqi state and the actions of that state, contributing to the disillusionment of many.

During the 1930s, with the simultaneous heightening of tension in Palestine itself and the rise to prominence in Iraq of army officers and politicians fired by a pan-Arab vision, the cause of Palestine had come to the forefront of Iraqi public life. The politics of the *Muthanna* Club, the work of the Committee for the Defense of Palestine, the activities of individuals like the Iraqi army officer Fawzi al-Qawuqji (later commander of the Arab Liberation Army in 1948) and others, as well as the influence of men like Arab nationalist Sati' al-Husri and a large cohort of Palestinian teachers in the educational sector left their mark. With the arrival in Baghdad in 1939 of the exiled Mufti of Palestine, Hajj Amin al-Husayni, and his inclusion in the circles of power surrounding Rashid 'Ali al-Kaylani, concern with Palestinian issues appeared to be overwhelming.[3] However, these developments also brought out the tensions within the Iraqi state – and contributed to the British decision to intervene in 1941. British intervention dispersed the main players, but it could not dissolve the concerns which had led to Iraqi engagement with Palestinian issues. In the wake of the Second World War, these features reasserted themselves, shaping and, to some degree, limiting the actions of the Iraqi state during the year of 1948.

Prelude to war: 1946–1947

During this period, as the partition of Palestine became more likely, Iraqi statesmen consistently called upon the Arab countries to prepare for a military campaign and Iraqi generals drew up the necessary plans. However, encouragement of the military option, while appearing radical and uncompromising, was also a way of retaining control of the situation. This feature appealed strongly to Iraqi governments. They sought thereby to check the activities and the ambitions of both 'Abdullah of Transjordan and Hajj Amin al-Husayni of Palestine, whilst positioning Iraq to ensure that no other Arab state gained unilateral advantage in Palestine. At the same time they ensured that the cause of Palestine could not be taken up by the opposition to serve as a pretext for disorder in Iraq itself. In all these calculations, the idea of an independent Palestine played very little part.

In 1946 Tawfiq al-Suwaydi's liberalizing measures had encouraged the re-emergence of a contentious public life, where resentments at long-established inequalities and immediate concerns about unemployment and inflation were given powerful voice. The Iraqi Communist Party (ICP) became active, trades unions revived and strikes were organized. In the Kurdish areas, a more radical strand of Kurdish nationalism and social protest emerged.[4] Faced by an apparently inexorable tide of disorder, the regent and many of the prime minister's colleagues took fright. Al-Suwaydi was dismissed and repression ensued, organized first by the rather inept premier Arshad al-'Umari and, from November 1946, by the much more skilful and effective Nuri al-Sa'id.

Nuri threw the opposition into confusion, dealt a severe blow to the ICP through the arrest of much of its leadership and prepared the way for elections that would reassert his power and that of his allies. The causes of unrest did not disappear, but under Nuri's mixture of patronage and repression the strikes and demonstrations of the previous year largely vanished. This allowed Nuri to step back and to ensure that his protégé, Salih Jabr, became prime minister in March 1947. Jabr was the first Shi'i prime minister of Iraq and his appointment disconcerted some who took Sunni domination of the state for granted. Others, however, were encouraged by this apparent new beginning and initially gave Jabr the benefit of the doubt, despite his known association with Nuri.

It is against this political background that the familiar sequence of events concerning Palestine unfolded, demanding responses from all Arab governments, including that of Iraq. In organizing Iraq's response,

Jabr, Nuri, and others kept one eye firmly on the possibility of domestic disorder. However, they also needed to focus on the behavior of the other Arab states, where the recent formation of the Arab League could scarcely conceal the absence of any agreed ordering of relations between Arab countries. This dual focus led to a variety of responses. Successive Iraqi administrations tried to retain control, risking little and seeking to limit the capacity of the Palestine issue to make the governance of Iraq more precarious, whilst ensuring that Iraq's regional interests were not placed in jeopardy. These concerns, in which the future of Palestine itself was only a part – and often a rather small part – of the government's calculations, formed the foundation for Iraq's behavior as a state in the critical year of 1948.

Two narratives were at work. On a symbolic level, the leading statesmen of Iraq publicly voiced radical and uncompromising views on the future of Palestine. During the first half of 1946, with Nuri al-Sa'id's encouragement, the Iraqi parliament passed a series of strong resolutions on the Palestine issue, recalling criticism of the 1939 White Paper. Nuri was, in fact, a known supporter of the White Paper. Nevertheless, his intervention set the tone for the debate. Fadil al-Jamali (director-general of the Iraqi Ministry of Foreign Affairs until May 1946, when he became minister of foreign affairs), moved from a position where he had defended Iraq's interest in Palestine before the Anglo-American Commission of Inquiry (AACOI) on largely pragmatic and strategic grounds, to a notably more radical stance at the Arab League meeting in Bludan in June 1946.[5] He called for sanctions and an oil boycott of both the United States and Great Britain – and denounced Saudi Arabia and Egypt when their representatives dissented. The secret decisions of Bludan which threatened economic reprisals against American and British commercial interests if their governments tried to implement the AACOI recommendations merely made a gesture in this direction.[6]

Similarly, at the December 1946 meeting of the Arab League the Iraqi delegation raised for the first time the possibility of sending a joint Arab armed force to Palestine. They did, however, acknowledge that any such proposal would require British approval and suggested that if this were not forthcoming, the Arab states should arm the Arabs of Palestine.[7] Following the breakdown of the London talks on Palestine and of Bevin's referral of the issue to the UN in February 1947, Nuri al-Sa'id used the Iraqi parliament once again to pass a series of resolutions, urging the Arab states to unite in declaring Palestine an independent Arab state, threatening the United States and Great Britain with economic sanctions and proclaiming an embargo on raw materials to

Zionist factories in Palestine. Although not specified, it seemed that the Iraqi government might deny oil to the Haifa refinery.[8]

In September 1947, at Sofar, Salih Jabr strongly attacked the partition proposals and committed Iraq to an oil boycott of the Western powers if Saudi Arabia would do likewise. He also called for the Arab armies to prepare for coordinated military intervention. The other Arab states were willing at least to consider this possibility, but the imposition of trade and oil sanctions was too radical. This helped to shape the discussions at the meeting of the Arab League at Aley in October 1947. The Iraqi delegation persuaded the Arab League to set up a Military Committee, headed by the Iraqi assistant chief of staff, General Isma'il Safwat, to look into the military situation in Palestine. Safwat's preliminary report of 9 October 1947 urged the recruitment and training of volunteers to fight in Palestine, as well as the supply of arms to the Palestinians. He also recommended that the Arab states concentrate their armies on the borders of Palestine, that a unified Arab military command be set up and that the Arab air forces prepare to attack the Zionists' supply lines.[9]

The UN vote on the partition of Palestine in November 1947 and the British declaration that they would be withdrawing in May 1948 heightened the sense of crisis. Demonstrations of protest erupted in Iraq and the government and its critics vied with each other to ensure that these served their own purposes. In large part, Salih Jabr succeeded in ensuring that his administration did not become the main target – a matter of extreme and justified concern, as the events of January 1948 were to prove. Anxious to be seen to be doing something, Jabr asked King 'Abdullah of Transjordan to allow a battalion of Iraqi troops to be sent to the frontier of Palestine. 'Abdullah refused and Jabr had to find other symbolic ways of emphasising his public commitment to preventing the partition of Palestine.[10]

This became apparent at the Cairo meeting of the Arab League in December 1947 when Jabr attacked the other Arab states for their inaction and reproached them for failing to take up the various Iraqi proposals. Nevertheless, he declared that it was not too late to act and urged both the immediate implementation of the secret Bludan agreements, as well as the implementation of the recommendations contained in the second report of Safwat's Military Committee. This had called on the Arab states to commit themselves to the immediate formation of a joint command and planning staff to organize possible collective military action on behalf of the Arabs of Palestine.[11] Only such a move, Jabr stated, could prevent the establishment of a Jewish state.

Nuri al-Sa'id, who was sent to Cairo at the behest of the British to exercise a moderating influence on Jabr, backed him instead and criticized the other Arab states for doing so little to help the Palestinians. He also took the opportunity to embarrass the Saudi government by asking them to join an oil boycott and to use their special relationship to put pressure on the United States. The other Arab states, more cautious in their public approach and unwilling to commit themselves to radical economic sanctions or to military action, found themselves outflanked by Iraq. Although they were willing for General Safwat to continue to study the military situation, they rejected his main recommendations. Instead, they agreed merely to increase financial aid and small arms supplies to the Palestinian Arabs and to the rapidly forming Arab volunteer forces. [12]

These symbolic moves to enhance Jabr's and Nuri's reputations, by apparently committing Iraq to a vigorous strategy designed to prevent the establishment of a Jewish state in Palestine, can also be seen in another light. Despite the Iraqi government's rhetoric and despite their reiteration of Iraq's right to act unilaterally in defense of the Palestinians, neither on the economic nor the military fronts did Iraq take any initiative that might have had irreversible consequences. Nor was the government of Salih Jabr at all eager for a confrontation with Great Britain at a time when he was trying to negotiate a revised Anglo-Iraqi Treaty which he believed would be to Iraq's advantage – and would enhance his own political standing.

Consequently, whilst the public, symbolic face of the Iraqi state corresponded to the most pan-Arab interpretation of its obligations, other important aspects of that state were making themselves felt with greater weight. Nuri and Jabr had linked Zionism with communism to prevent their domestic critics from using the Palestine question and its anti-imperialist overtones to mobilize opposition to their regime. This had been accompanied by a repressive campaign designed to disrupt the organization of the ICP and to throw into confusion their many fellow-travellers. In this respect, they sought to insulate the Iraqi state as hierarchy and structured inequality from the radicalizing effect of campaigns in support of Palestine. [13]

This identification was easier to make once the Soviet Union had come out in support of the partition of Palestine and the establishment of a Jewish state. Furthermore, the re-emergence of the question of partition in 1947 was also significant for two other aspects of the Iraqi state: as a Hashemite state and as Great Britain's ally. As far as the Hashemite aspect was concerned, Transjordan and Iraq had signed a general treaty of friendship and alliance in April 1947. King 'Abdullah was pressing the Iraqi government to make this an effective bilateral agreement that could lead to the establishment of a federal state, effectively uniting the two countries. The Iraqi government and the regent were more circumspect and did not want to see themselves dragged along in the wake of 'Abdullah's schemes. However, by 1947 they were already willing to support the idea of a joint Iraqi–Transjordanian military occupation of Palestine. At the same time that Jabr was advocating the intervention of all the Arab armies, if the partition plan were implemented, he was privately telling British officials that he was in favor of cooperating with 'Abdullah in the take-over of Palestine.[14]

It could be argued that this was due to a fairly realistic assumption on the part of the Iraqi leadership that the two Arab armies most likely to cooperate well were those of Iraq and Transjordan. However, there were other considerations at work. Chief of these was the common hostility not only of the Hashemites in both countries, but of most of the Iraqi and Transjordanian political establishments to Hajj Amin al-Husayni, proposed by some as the putative leader of a future Palestinian state. The Transjordanian and the Iraqi governments were as one in their refusal to allow al-Husayni to play any part in the deliberations of the Arab League and, partly as a result, the League failed to decide on a future Arab government of Palestine when it met in Cairo in December 1947.[15] At the same time, the Arab volunteer forces were placed under two Iraqis, Fawzi al-Qawuqji as commander of the Arab Liberation Army (ALA) in the field and General Taha al-Hashimi as inspector-general in charge of recruitment. Although this was largely the work of the Syrian president, Shukri al-Quwwatli, and was not designed to enhance Hashemite influence – rather the reverse – the effect was equally harmful to Hajj Amin al-Husayni's interests.[16]

Nuri al-Sa'id had by this stage become convinced that the British were unwilling to countenance the take-over of the whole of Palestine by the armed forces of Iraq and Transjordan, as he had once hoped. Furthermore, he saw little chance that the Arab states, individually or collectively, could deflect the United States from its chosen course of supporting the partition of Palestine and the establishment of a Jewish state. He seemed therefore to accept that partition would take place and put his energies into trying to persuade the British to withdraw sooner than planned in order to deprive the Zionist forces of the advantages they enjoyed in the developing civil war. He also tried to convince the British of the need to send increased military supplies to Iraq, within the context of the renegotiated Anglo-Iraqi Treaty.[17]

Nuri's efforts were unsuccessful, but it was the question of the treaty, embodying the British connection with the Iraqi state, which was the major preoccupation of Salih Jabr's government, overshadowing the question of Palestine. The negotiations proceeded in secret during 1947, during which it became apparent that Jabr stood on the threshhold of negotiating the final withdrawal of British forces from Iraqi territory. This process meant that the Iraqi government was unwilling to do anything to alienate Great Britain. However, there was a convergence of British and Iraqi thinking on Palestine. In December 1947, Jabr and Nuri visited Amman on their way back from London and told King 'Abdullah that Great Britain not only favored partition, but was also in favor of Transjordan taking over the Arab areas of Palestine. They also pledged Iraqi support for such a move. Wary as they were of the Arab world's reaction to more permanent annexation by Transjordan, they were cooler about King 'Abdullah's suggestion that Iraq and Transjordan should immediately form a federal union. The king evidently hoped that this would provide the military and political backing needed for his plans in Palestine.[18]

It was at this point, however, that the Iraqi government's attempt to renegotiate Iraq's relations with Great Britain came to a violent and abrupt end in the events known as *al-Wathba* [the leap] which brought down Jabr's government. In January 1948 most Iraqis learnt, to their surprise, that their government had been secretly negotiating a new Anglo-Iraqi treaty, the terms of which became known publicly only with its signature at Portsmouth in January 1948. Great Britain was to withdraw all its forces from Iraq and hand over the RAF's two air bases to Iraqi control. However, a joint defense board of British and Iraqi officials would oversee Iraq's military planning, Great Britain would remain Iraq's principal military supplier and would be allowed to take over the air bases again in time of war. Furthermore, this treaty would last until 1973, fifteen years beyond the expiry date of the treaty it superseded.

The reaction in Iraq was one of outrage, mixed with political opportunism since most of the government were in Great Britain for the signing ceremony. Protest marches and demonstrations erupted on the streets of Baghdad and soon spread to the other cities of Iraq. Although initially organized against the Portsmouth Treaty, the processions and demonstrations were used to protest against many features of the Iraqi political establishment. Slogans were raised against the monarchy, against the political figures associated with the status quo, against the landlords and other representatives of the unequal economic order of Iraq, as well as against the obvious targets of Great Britain and the forces of imperialism. The passions that were released confirmed for much of the political establishment their worst fears about the latent potential for serious political disorder and the police intervened with great violence. The regent, who had initially supported the Portsmouth Treaty, took fright and now declared that he would refuse to endorse it. This signaled the end of Jabr's government. He was replaced by Muhammad al-Sadr who presided over a government composed of Jabr's political rivals but who was largely concerned to re-establish order in Iraq's disturbed political life.[19]

The effect of the *Wathba* was to cause both the British and the Iraqi governments to keep at arms' length from each other.[20] Whilst the Iraqi government concentrated on domestic problems, chiefly the economy, political order, and the forthcoming elections, the British government's chief links in Iraq were with the Regent 'Abd al-Ilah. This was particularly the case on the question of Palestine. To a large degree, therefore, during these critical months of 1948, Iraqi political initiatives on Palestine were in the hands of the regent and his circle. He began to take a more active role, personifying in many respects the Hashemite aspect of the Iraqi state with marked consequences for Iraqi state policies in the war of 1948.

The year of war: 1948

In the first half of 1948, as the plight of the Arab population of Palestine became ever more desperate and the Arab irregular forces proved themselves to be no match for the Haganah, it became harder for the governments of the Arab states to resist the mounting call within their own countries for military intervention in Palestine. This seemed to vindicate the stance of successive Iraqi governments during the previous couple of years, endorsed repeatedly by General Safwat's Military Committee. However, the context in which this occurred and the shape it took in Iraq reflected once more the multiple character of the Iraqi state.

Hamdi al-Pachachi, the new Iraqi minister of foreign affairs, took part in the Cairo meeting of the Arab League in early February 1948. A pan-Arab nationalist, he was nevertheless conscious of the regent's sensibilities, particularly on relations with Transjordan and on the role of Hajj Amin al-Husayni. Like his predecessors, he supported General Safwat's attempt to persuade the Arab states to set up an effective joint military command to prepare for the possibility of intervention on the expiry of the British Mandate. Like other pan-Arab Iraqis, however, he was also conscious of the fact that Iraq could only participate militarily in Palestine on terms largely set by King 'Abdullah of Transjordan. Paradoxically, this dampened the enthusiasm of many in the Iraqi government for Iraqi military intervention since they feared that it would largely be used to serve the purposes of King 'Abdullah. In some respects, this fear was to be justified by events.

Faced by the caution of the other Arab states and aware that King 'Abdullah was preparing to intervene, the Regent 'Abd al-Ilah began actively to advocate Iraq's military intervention and to involve the other Arab states. He thus drew closer to General Safwat and to the senior army commanders, increasing his own popularity in the officer corps. The regent could see the need both to play a prominent role on the Palestine issue and to cement his own following within the Iraqi armed forces, whose centrality as the guarantor of political order in Iraq had been underlined in the preceding few months. He was also counting on active intervention by the Arab states' armies to preclude any decisive role being assigned to the depleted forces of Hajj Amin al-Husayni. In addition, such intervention would have the advantage of implicating all the Arab states in the outcome of military action in Palestine. Since it seemed increasingly likely to the regent and to those closest to him that partition would indeed come about, it was better that it should not be seen solely as the responsibility of the Hashemites.[21]

Consequently, in early April 1948 the regent urged King 'Abdullah to take over the Arab-designated areas of Palestine and promised Iraqi forces as garrisons in Transjordan. 'Abdullah was understandably unenthusiastic. Jordanian premier Tawfiq Abu al-Huda's meeting with Ernest Bevin in London the previous month had already confirmed British approval of his plans for the occupation of the areas assigned to the Arab state in the partition of Palestine. 'Abdullah was more concerned, therefore, that other Arab armies might seize this moment to act against Transjordan. In this respect, he could not preclude the opportunism of Iraq itself and tried to guard his country's eastern and southern approaches by urging the regent to concentrate the Iraqi army around Basra as a deterrent to Saudi Arabia.[22]

By this stage, however, the military situation was developing rapidly in Palestine itself as the Haganah and Palmach prepared for the offensive that would lead to the capture of Tiberias, Jaffa, Safad, and Haifa by the end of April 1948, as well as opening up the corridor linking west Jerusalem to the concentration of forces around Tel Aviv. These events finally led the Arab League to take seriously the possibility of military intervention. Transjordan announced that the Arab Legion would enter Palestine on the expiry of the Mandate and won Arab League approval, on condition that the entry of Arab armies did not lead to permanent annexation. King Faruq made a similar pledge on behalf of Egypt, although the Egyptian government was more non-committal. Since war was now inevitable, King 'Abdullah agreed with the regent that Iraqi troops should enter Transjordanian territory.[23] The regent left promptly for Cairo where he convinced the Egyptian authorities to commit Egypt's regular forces to intervene on the expiry of the Mandate. His initiatives did not have the explicit approval of the Iraqi government, but once he had succeeded in winning round both King 'Abdullah and King Faruq to the idea of Iraqi military participation the Iraqi government could hardly fail to authorize the despatch of the initial Iraqi contribution of 3,000 troops to Transjordan.[24]

These moves led to the Arab League's approval in early May of the formation of a joint command for all the Arab forces, to be headed by Iraqi General Nur al-Din Mahmud, with General Isma'il Safwat as his chief of staff. King 'Abdullah, however, persuaded the Arab League to appoint him supreme commander of the Arab forces, with General Nur al-Din Mahmud as his deputy. Thus, King 'Abdullah became nominal commander of the only coordinated Arab forces taking part in the war. However, it became a force that served chiefly the interests of King 'Abdullah, thereby creating the very impression which the Iraqi regent had tried to avoid: the cooperation of the two branches of the Hashemite dynasty to annex the Arab areas of Palestine. This was both the military and the political reality – a reality which, once its foundations had been laid, largely determined the role of the Iraqi armed forces during the fighting of 1948. It was left to the regent and other politicians thereafter to try to reconcile this with the symbolic aspects of Iraqi engagement that they had taken so much care to cultivate in the previous years.

The Iraqi military intervention took place in two phases. In the brief initial phase, on 15 May, half of the rather modest initial contingent of Iraqi troops tried to capture Kibbutz Gesher and to secure a crossing of the river Jordan opposite the town of Beisan. This attack, which was conducted in full view of the regent who was visiting the front, seems to have been ill thought out.[25] It is uncertain that it could have achieved much in military terms even had it succeeded in securing the crossing since there were still too few Iraqi forces in reserve to exploit any opening. It may be that it was more symbolic in character – intended by the regent and by those officers who sought his favor to impress upon the Transjordanians and others the valor of the Iraqi troops and to have a quick military victory at the outset of the campaign to publicize at home.

In the event, the attack was repulsed and there was no such good news to transmit to Baghdad. The failure was not important in military terms, but it did underline the subordinate position of the Iraqi forces vis-à-vis the high command of King 'Abdullah and his military advisors, principally Brigadier Glubb. Engaged as he was in the key battle for

Jerusalem, Glubb recommended that the Iraqi forces relieve the Arab Legion garrisons in Nablus and Jenin. From his perspective, this had the dual advantage of freeing more Arab Legion troops for the defense of Jerusalem and guarding their northern flank against Israeli attack.[26]

On 22 May 1948 the Iraqi Expeditionary Force (IEF), commanded by General Nur al-Din Mahmud, took over from the Arab Legion in Nablus and subsequently occupied the entire northern sector of the West Bank, reinforced by fresh troops from Iraq. They arrived in time to organize a successful defense of Jenin in the first week of June and thereafter consolidated their positions. In theory, the IEF was supposed to play its part in a coordinated campaign, the plans for which had been drawn up initially in late 1947 under the auspices of General Safwat's committee. In essence, the plan envisaged the capture of Haifa and the splitting of the Jewish forces in Galilee from those on the coastal plain. In accordance with Safwat's estimates of the strength of the Haganah, the Arab states were required to make very substantial military commitments. The implication was that if they were serious about seeking a military solution to the problem of Palestine, the Arab governments must take their military obligations seriously.[27]

In the event, the Arab states only committed about half of the forces deemed necessary by General Safwat. There was little or no coordination and no sign that Safwat's plan was being followed. General al-Jubury (chief of staff of the Iraqi army at the time) has claimed that when he confronted King 'Abdullah with his suspicion that the plan had been scrapped, the king denied this, but then proceeded to devote his own forces to the capture and defense of Jerusalem. The Iraqi contingent was assigned a purely defensive role and no attacks were authorized against the Israeli positions in the coastal plain or the Galilee (areas designated as part of the Jewish state by the UN).[28] Such a role accorded with King 'Abdullah's larger plan for the 1948 war and it is unlikely that the Iraqi high command was unaware of this. These realities were harder for some of the junior officers to accept. They may have believed in the slogans under which the IEF was despatched and the declared objectives of the Arab states in the campaign of 1948. They were soon disillusioned and it was not long before they were blaming the political leadership and particularly both branches of the Hashemite house for the Arab losses in Palestine.[29]

After the failed Israeli attack on Jenin in June 1948, the Iraqi forces were left unmolested. The Israelis had more urgent strategic goals and no interest in provoking the Iraqis. Since the latter had no orders to go on the offensive, they maintained their occupation of their static defensive positions and awaited the outcome of the war. This period was characterized by the phrase *Maku awamir* ["no orders"] repeated by embittered returning soldiers and by the critics of Iraqi government policy. It seemed baffling to many that, as the IEF grew in size (it numbered about 18,000 men by the autumn of 1948) its operations virtually ceased. This was happening at a time when the truces of June and July allowed the Israeli forces to regroup and re-arm, facilitating their successful campaigns to occupy Lydda and Ramleh in July and their breaking of the Egyptian line in the Negev in October. On neither occasion did the Iraqi forces act to relieve the pressure on the other Arab armies.

These developments and the small role played by the Iraqi army were not generally known in Iraq itself. As early as April 1948, when it seemed that war was inevitable in Palestine, the Iraqi government had taken the precaution of declaring martial law. This allowed them to censor all news relating to the situation in Palestine, as well as all criticism of Iraqi policy. It had the added advantage for Sadr's government of bringing to an abrupt end the strikes and demonstrations that had continued during the spring of 1948. It was under these conditions that the promised general elections took place, returning a parliament in which, as ever, the supporters of the regent, Nuri al-Sa'id, and the political establishment predominated. In June a new government was formed, led by the conservative but rather weak Muzahim al-Pachachi.

Aware of the demands of the regent and the sensibilities of the British, Pachachi reverted to the policy of combining rhetorical radicalism on Palestine with inaction regarding the *de facto* partition of the country. Thus, in June and July the Iraqi delegation stood out from the other Arab delegates in rejecting the two cease-fires arranged by the UN – but then declared that they were forced to accept them since Iraq was not strong enough to stand on its own. At the same time, Pachachi was careful to reassure the British that Iraq was willing to accept the emerging status quo. In the parliamentary debates, he and Nuri al-Sa'id tried to persuade others to accept this state of affairs by asserting that because world opinion and the great powers favored partition and the establishment of a Jewish state there was little that could be done by the Arab states, let alone by Iraq on its own. Pachachi was thus trying to absolve himself of responsibility for a situation which, to be fair, he had largely inherited.[30]

Similar motives played a part in the Iraqi government's otherwise rather surprising and belated recognition of Hajj Amin al-Husayni's All-Palestine Government in Gaza, established at the time under Egyptian auspices. This did not signify any fundamental change in the Iraqi position since it made no material difference to the role of the IEF in effectively allowing King 'Abdullah to proceed with the consolidation of his control over the West Bank. Symbolically, however, it was a move which acknowledged the recriminations that might flow from the general realization that most of Iraq's diplomatic energies had been geared to preventing the emergence of an independent Palestinian state, in however truncated a form, under the rule of Hajj Amin al-Husayni. In recognizing the enfeebled All-Palestine Government, the Iraqi government was trying retrospectively to alter the historical record, once it was clear that such recognition would have little effect.[31]

The same could be said of the major parliamentary debate on Palestine in November 1948, after the defeat of the Egyptian army in the Negev and the attempt by the Egyptian government to place some of the blame on Iraqi inaction. Pachachi, Salih Jabr, and Nuri al-Sa'id argued that only Iraq had advocated a serious pan-Arab military campaign and only Iraq had called for an oil embargo against the Western states. Jabr acknowledged that Transjordan had taken Iraq's military plan seriously, but he accused the other Arab states of rejecting Iraq's military and economic strategies. Countering the Egyptian accusation of Iraq's unwillingness to help, Pachachi blamed Egypt not only for its own misfortunes, but also for effectively sabotaging Iraq's plan for coordinated Arab action. A series of resolutions were then passed which bore so little relationship to the situation on the ground in Palestine as to verge on the fantastic. They also did nothing to prepare the Iraqi public and its armed forces for an acceptance of the true scale of the disaster that had befallen the Arab population of Palestine.[32]

As the parliamentary debate demonstrated, Nuri al-Sa'id, Salih Jabr, and many others in the political elite, including the regent, were satisfied that no other Arab state had come well out of the affair. The enemies of the Hashemites had not performed particularly creditably and there was little sense, therefore, that Iraq, as a Hashemite state, could be singled out for particular blame. Nor had a Palestinian state emerged that might have acted as a platform for dissent and a reproach for the failures of the Arab states. Transjordan was in a strong position on the ground in Palestine and in the Arab world to ensure the eventual annexation of those parts of Palestine occupied by the Arab Legion. Neither the regent, nor Nuri, nor much of the political establishment in Iraq had any significant objection to this. Indeed, for the regent and his circle it seemed to be a positive advantage that King 'Abdullah should become preoccupied with Palestine since this might distract him from his plans for Syria – the focus of the regent's own developing ambitions.[33]

The Jewish community in Iraq and 1948

The relative inactivity of Iraq during 1948 had suited many in the political elite, but it had clearly not suited all. In particular, Sadiq al-Bassam, the minister of defense in Pachachi's government, found that there was little for him to do, other than to administer martial law. He used this opportunity, therefore, to prosecute his own war-time strategy, targeting the Jewish community in Iraq itself. This may partly have been due to his own formation in the pan-Arabism of the 1930s which had portrayed Iraqi Jews as a potential fifth column. However, Bassam was merely the most powerful representative for a time of the trend within Iraq that made the position of Jewish Iraqis increasingly untenable. In this sense, he represented the Iraqi side of an equation in which there was less and less space for the existence of a Jewish Arab Iraqi identity. The other side of the equation, which exerted a correspondingly powerful force on the Iraqi Jews, was the Zionist movement itself which set out not simply to protect, but also to "save" them by encouraging their mass immigration to Israel. The mass exodus of Iraqi Jews was not to take place until 1950–51 when about 120,000 arrived in Israel. However, in 1948 it was becoming clear that their position as a community had become precarious.[34]

The Iraqi government was aware of the dangers to the security of the Jewish community and made every effort to prevent the kind of violence against Jews associated with the *Farhud* of 1941.[35] Martial law made this relatively easy. However, since late 1947 Iraqi governments had themselves introduced discriminatory legislation against Iraqi Jews, restricting their freedom of movement and requiring them to put up bonds if they wished to leave the country. With the introduction of martial law, these restrictions were tightened and it became apparent that the rules were being used in a variety of ways to arrest and fine members of the Jewish community, ostensibly on suspicion of links with Zionism, but often for reasons of extortion.

Under the new government of June 1948, discrimination against the Jews became more systematic and public. In July the Jewish members of parliament were asked to absent themselves when the Palestine issue was debated.[36] Later in the same month, parliament passed legislation criminalizing Zionism and stating that the sworn testimony of two Muslim witnesses would now suffice to incriminate any Jew. Numerous arrests of Jews followed. In August, the Iraqi government declared that all Jews who had left Iraq for Palestine would now be considered criminals and restrictions were placed on three of the major Jewish owned banks in Iraq. At the same time, the minister of defense instructed the authorities at the port of Basra to dismiss all their Jewish employees (constituting nearly 25 percent of the administrative and clerical staff) and similar instructions were sent to other state concerns, such as the railways and the telegraphs.[37]

However, Bassam overstepped the mark when he authorized the arrest and trial in September of a prominent Iraqi Jewish businessman, Shafiq Ades, charged with purchasing military surplus equipment and sending it to Israel. The fact that the government allowed the trial and authorized Ades' public execution under very dubious circumstances indicated that Pachachi was willing to sanction the discriminatory policies being pursued by his minister of defense. The international outcry that followed, as well as the protests within Iraq, not simply from the Jewish community, led Pachachi to dismiss Bassam and to use the occasion to deny that his government was anti-Jewish, insisting on the distinction between Zionism and Judaism. He reiterated the claim that under Iraqi law and under the Shari'a, Iraqi Jews were to be considered full Iraqi citizens with the same rights as all Iraqis – but the legislative record of his government and the actions of his security services clearly belied this claim, as was to be demonstrated over subsequent months.[38]

During this time, the Iraqi Jewish community became increasingly fearful – fears exploited by representatives of the Zionist organizations, more concerned with the immigration of the Iraqi Jews to Israel than with their continued existence as a long-established part of Iraqi society. This situation had not been created by the war of 1948, but the same forces that contributed to that war also spelt the destruction of the Iraqi Jewish community. Assisting in this was part of the symbolic repertoire of those in authority in Iraq, designed to placate a demand that something should be done to curb the power of the Zionist enemy. However, in practical terms, the effect was the excision of a key element of Iraq's metropolitan society and culture.

Disengagement and withdrawal: 1949

The ambiguity of the Iraqi government between its symbolic claims and its actual dispositions was to have serious consequences for the Iraqi state conceived of as an apparatus of power. The officer corps had been intimately involved in the Palestine issue, both emotionally, given the power of pan-Arabism within these circles, and materially or professionally as soldiers in 1948. The effects of dissonance between these two roles were not immediate. There were reports of disaffection at the time, but these were characteristically mixed with more specific, professional concerns about promotion, pay and equipment. In so far as the junior officers were concerned, there appears to have been as much criticism of the lack of professionalism of the senior officers as there was criticism of the political establishment for committing them to a war which they could not win – and possibly were not supposed to.[39]

Trying to reconcile these varying claims was too daunting for Pachachi. By December, he realized that he had no answer to the most pressing question of how to disengage militarily from the conflict whilst keeping control of the political repercussions of such a move. The Iraqi public was unprepared for so sharp a disappointment of their expectations and increasingly violent demonstrations marked the latter part of 1948. Claiming that he now realized that his policy was a failure, Pachachi resigned the premiership.[40] This allowed the regent to appoint a more forceful and capable figure to handle the Iraqi military disengagement, with all that this implied for the authority and the control of the government responsible. It was scarcely surprising that he should have turned to Nuri al-Saʿid once more. He was seen as the man who could both address the key question of order within the Iraqi state, and guide Iraq safely through the inevitable recriminations that would follow the defeat. In particular, Nuri would have to dispel the dangerous perception that the only parties that seemed to have gained from 1948 were the Zionists and the Hashemites.

Accepting the premiership in January 1949, Nuri al-Saʿid immediately addressed both principal aspects of his mission with his characteristic ruthlessness and despatch. Following the widespread protest demonstrations of the closing months of 1948, Nuri used his powers under martial law to order hundreds of arrests. He concentrated mainly on the leftists, especially the ICP, since he saw their involvement and their alliance with the pan-Arabists as holding the greatest danger for the dominant order. Nuri sought to drive a wedge between these two factions by making much of the Soviet Union's support for Israel, effectively accusing the ICP of supporting Zionism. The communists' leaders, including Comrade Fahd, who had been in prison since 1946, were brought before a military court and charged with organizing subversion. They were found guilty, sentenced to death and executed within a matter of days. The campaign did little to change the opposition's attitude to the Iraqi government, but it effectively demoralized and intimidated them.

Nuri now turned his attention to the pressing question of disengagement from Palestine. In January he tried, for a short time, to obtain both Arab and great power agreement to a four-point plan in which Jerusalem was to remain under Arab rule, Israel would be disarmed and its frontiers guarded by the UN, all refugees would return to their homes

and the port of Haifa was to be placed under international administration. Quite apart from the impossibility of making this plan even
minimally acceptable to Israel, the Arab states' rejection of the plan was
assured by the recognition it seemed to give to the partition of Palestine
between Israel and Transjordan. Nor were the great powers interested in
proposals that were so obviously unacceptable to the main parties
involved.[41]

It is difficult to say whether Nuri intended these proposals to be taken
seriously. Given the limited number of options for practical policy by
this stage, the temptation to return to the realm of symbolic politics in
which posture was all important must have been overwhelming. Nuri
and others had already acknowledged that there was no military solution
to the problem of Palestine. Nor could the Arab states make much
headway against the kind of diplomatic support enjoyed by Israel. Nuri
occasionally spoke of economic sanctions as a means of at least putting
pressure on Israel, if not undermining its very existence – the aspect
emphasized depended on the audience he was addressing. In practical
terms, he resisted continuing British pressure to reopen the Haifa
pipeline, which the Iraqi government had closed in April 1948.
However, apart from the trade boycott of Israel itself, the Arab states
had little leverage in this regard either.[42]

Nuri also took a number of measures intended to suggest to the
Iraqi public in general and to the Arab world at large that the Iraqi
government had behaved creditably throughout the whole Palestine
episode. In February 1949, as mentioned at the outset of this chapter,
Nuri set up the parliamentary commission of inquiry to look into the
course of events which had led to the war and defeat in Palestine.
Faced by King 'Abdullah's *de facto* annexation of the West Bank, after
the Jericho conference of December 1948, Iraq remained non-committal. Its official recognition of the All-Palestine Government was still
on record, but Nuri knew that this would soon lapse and recognition
of King 'Abdullah's gains would eventually follow. In the meantime, he
ensured that Iraq kept its distance from Transjordan and advised the
regent similarly to distance himself from the Transjordanian Hashemites. This was relatively easy to achieve. The regent himself was
far less eager now to associate himself with the course of events in
Palestine. More interesting for him were developments in Syria,
particularly after the *coup d'état* of Colonel Husni Za'im in March
1949.[43]

Nuri continued to maintain an unrelenting stance publicly on the
links between the Jews of Iraq and the Zionist movement. At one stage
he suggested that Jewish inhabitants of Iraq might be exchanged for a

similar number of Arab refugees from Palestine – with the property of the Jews being used to compensate the Palestinians for what they had lost in Palestine. Meanwhile, the Iraqi security services uncovered a Zionist network in Iraq which was helping Iraqi Jews emigrate to Israel. This led in turn to extensive arrests in the Jewish community and to increased suspicion, effectively barring young Iraqi Jews from state employment and from the professions, reinforcing the impression for many that there was now no future for them in Iraq itself.[44] Nuri would assert periodically that he had no wish to discriminate against Iraqi Jews, but the actions of his government belied his words.

Symbolic politics also seems to have been to the fore in Nuri's decision that Iraq should take no part in the armistice talks on Rhodes. The refusal to recognize Israel as an interlocutor or to commit Iraq to signing a truce with Israel appeared to place Iraq in the most uncompromising of lights. Fadil al-Jamali, Nuri's foreign minister, did say that Iraq would accept the agreements reached by the four Arab states bordering Israel, but would not be a party to this process itself despite the fact that its own forces were still confronting those of Israel along a substantial part of the latter's border. There was clearly no intention of using these troops to launch any military initiative against Israel and, indeed, in February, the Iraqi government announced that it would be withdrawing the IEF.

By this stage, Egypt, Syria, and Lebanon were all negotiating armistice agreements with Israel. Jordan was also involved, but could not negotiate on behalf of Iraq. It did reach an agreement with the Iraqi government that the Arab Legion should start taking over from the IEF in March. However, the failure of Iraq to negotiate directly with Israel meant that the latter could apply increasing pressure simply by refusing to recognize any agreement between Iraq and Jordan, raising the possibility that Israel might occupy the territory vacated by Iraqi troops. Israel used this leverage to some purpose, eventually agreeing to accept the Iraqi forces' hand-over to the Arab Legion if Israel were allowed to occupy a strip of land 2–3 kilometers deep along the entire 180 kilometer front with the IEF. Jordan was in no position to refuse and the Iraqis were evidently not going to make a stand. As a result, Jordan signed an armistice with Israel on 3 April and on 12 April the Arab Legion completed the take-over from the IEF. Iraq's determination not to be seen to be dealing directly with the Zionist enemy had effectively given Israel a further 400 or so square kilometers of territory.[45]

In symbolic terms, this stance was felt to be important by the Iraqi government. However, it did little to strengthen the material position of the Arab Legion and was clearly disastrous for the Palestinian villagers who suddenly found their lands occupied not by Iraqi soldiers but by the state of Israel. Nuri al-Sa'id was aware of the political dangers of the return of an army that had scarcely seen any action, and had thereby contributed to the larger defeat. Consequently, the IEF was withdrawn rapidly from the West Bank, but was only allowed to return to Iraq itself in phased groups over a period of four months. By August all the troops had returned to Iraq and Nuri had succeeded in avoiding serious clashes between officers of the IEF and soldiers of the Arab Legion whom many regarded as being no better than agents of the British. He and his defense minister had also succeeded in avoiding any immediate repercussion in the form of attempted coups or mutinies by the officer corps. Army salaries had been exempted from the otherwise general pay cuts imposed at the time and officers with known records of dissent had been judiciously posted around the country away from their units and their friends.[46]

Conclusion

The events surrounding 1948 illustrate the disjunctures between the rhetorical and the material aspects of Iraqi politics. Radical statements were rarely followed by actions as dramatic or as forceful as the language suggested. Even the deployment of substantial military forces by the Iraqi state can be seen partly as a strategy of control and partly as a theatrical display, rather than as an attempt materially to prevent the establishment of the state of Israel. The ideal of an independent Arab Palestine to which successive Iraqi governments pledged themselves, was outweighed in reality by fear of the implications of a Palestinian state dominated by a regime hostile to the Hashemites. This prospect was a powerful influence on the ways in which the resources of the Iraqi state were actually deployed. It was not the only influence at work, but it did much to further the view within Iraq and in the region that the Hashemite dynasty, in Iraq and in Transjordan, was responsible for the failure of an independent Palestinian state to emerge in 1948.

However, this was a development of which Iraqi statesmen such as Nuri al-Sa'id were fully aware. They had pursued the policies they chose not because of their ignorance of the alternatives or because they underestimated the kinds of reaction they might provoke. On the contrary, throughout this period there is clear evidence that the Iraqis of the old order were sensitive, sometimes exaggeratedly so, to the threats they faced, of which the question of Palestine and its baneful influence was but one element. Their handling of that question, as borne out by the events of 1946–49, should therefore be seen in the context of their preoccupations with the competing demands of the state which they sought to direct and to dominate.

In this regard, it can be argued that they emerged relatively successfully from the turmoil of those years. Their techniques of control, of cooptation, and selective repression, their use of patronage and their understanding of regional dynamics, as well as the importance they attached to the symbolic power of "Iraq alone" served them well. Of course, there were grumbles of dissent in the officer corps of the armed forces and more vociferous criticism from other quarters in Iraqi political society. These, however, were often tied to more general social criticism and to opposition which fed off stronger causes than mere resentment of the inconsistent policies pursued by the monarchical regime towards Palestine.

The overthrow of the monarchy in 1958 was, therefore, not a direct and uncomplicated outcome of 1948, although this has figured large in the self-justifications of some of the army officers involved in those events. Nuri and his colleagues were obviously aware of the danger – and events in Syria and in Egypt in the years following 1948 would serve as powerful reminders. Part of their mistake may have been that, having successfully pre-empted the short-term consequences of disgust with the conduct of the Iraqi leadership, they may have underestimated some of the longer-term repercussions. These flowed not so much from the war itself, but from the multiple and conflicting forces at work in the Iraqi polity – and which had shaped Iraqi government policies in relation to Palestine in 1948, just as they were to do in relation to other issues in the 1950s.

Iraq's role in the events surrounding 1948 is interesting, therefore, for a number of reasons. It sheds a particular light, generated by the tensions of Iraqi politics, on the historical trajectory of events. In doing so, it throws into question assumptions about what Iraq was doing and what its leaders were seeking to achieve in 1948. It can also tell us much about the centrality of the competing narratives of Iraqi politics, their logic, and the often conflicting forces associated with them. Thus, Iraq as a British creation, still tied in a variety of ways to the reality of British power, placed constraints upon the state as an actor and helped to shape the imaginative world in which the governments of the state acted. Equally, the Hashemite and the Arab aspects of Iraq's political history were not simply potent imaginative constructs, but also had material effects on the forms of interaction between Iraq and other Arab states. At the same time, these contested markers of identity, with their implied social and political conventions, colored and could exacerbate inter-communal relations within Iraq, as well as affecting the hierarchies of the Iraqi political order.

It was in this respect that those who directed Iraq's foreign and defense policies showed that they were acutely aware of changing attitudes towards the dominant order, as new ideas and new possibilities of social upheaval and reform took hold among the growing political public. A preoccupation with questions of order led them to stress forms of communal solidarity with pledges which they then found difficult in practice to redeem. It also led them to place increasing reliance on the armed forces as the instrument that would guarantee their position, despite social upheavals and lapses in credibility. In the event, their assumption that they could retain overall control proved to be fatally flawed.

The events of 1948 did not generate this weakness. Rather, they were symptomatic of the way it played itself out in Iraqi politics. For some in Iraq, the year 1948 took on iconic significance – although, with characteristic ambiguity, it is uncertain whether this was because of the Palestine catastrophe or the events of the *Wathba*. Nevertheless, when combined with other perceived failures of the old order, the visible failure in Palestine was seen as one of the shortcomings of an elite that had forfeited its right to dominate the Iraqi state. This did not change the multiple character of the Iraqi state, but it did show that increasing ingenuity and ruthlessness were needed to manage its potentially contradictory aspects – a lesson not lost on subsequent rulers of Iraq.

Notes

1 *Taqrir lajnat al-tahqiq al-niyabiyya fi qadiyyat filastin* [Report of the Parlia-mentary Committee of Enquiry into the Palestine Question] (Baghdad, 1949), pp. 1–2, 42–46.
2 See Salih Sa'ib al-Jubury, *Mihnat filastin wa-asraruha al-siyasiyya wa-l-'askariyya* [The Palestine Disaster and its Political and Military Secrets] (Beirut, 1970); Khalil Sa'id, *Ta'rikh al-jaysh al-'Iraqi fi filastin 1948–1949* [History of the Iraqi Army in Palestine] (Baghdad, 1969); Fawzi Ahmad, *'Abd al-Salam Muhammad 'Arif* (Baghdad, 1989), pp. 23–25.
3 See Michael Eppel, *The Palestine Conflict in the History of Modern Iraq* (London, 1984), pp. 30–106.
4 Hanna Batatu, *The Old Social Classes and the Revolutionary Movements of Iraq* (Princeton NJ, 1982), pp. 530–32; David McDowall, *A Modern History of the Kurds* (London, 1996) pp. 293–98.
5 Al-Jamali had argued before the AACOI that Iraq had a legitimate interest in

Palestine because of the centrality of the port of Haifa to its own economic security, both as a port and as the terminal for Iraq's major oil pipeline; cf. Mouayad Ibrahim K. al-Windawi, "Anglo-Iraqi Relations 1945–1958" (Ph.D. dissertation, University of Reading, 1989), pp. 112–13.

6 *Taqrir lajnat al-tahqiq*, pp. 14, 55–61; Windawi, "Anglo-Iraqi Relations," pp. 113–14.

7 Eppel, *Palestine Conflict*, pp. 156–57.

8 'Abd al-Razzaq al-Hasani, *Tarikh al-wizarat al-'iraqiyya* [History of the Iraqi Cabinets] (Beirut, 1982), vol VII, pp. 155–56.

9 *Taqrir lajnat al-tahqiq*, pp. 20–21 (Aley meeting); pp. 123–25 (principal recommendations of Military Committee's 1st report); pp. 132–33 (text of the Military Committee's 1st report).

10 PRO, Kirkbride (Amman) to Burrows, 8 December 1947, enclosing the translation of a letter from King 'Abdullah to the Regent 'Abd al-Ilah, FO 371/61580 E12009.

11 *Taqrir lajnat al-tahqiq* pp. 23–29 (position adopted by Jabr at the Cairo meeting); pp. 125–28 (principal recommendations of the Military Committee's 2nd report); pp. 140–45 (Text of the Military Committee's 2nd report).

12 Windawi, "Anglo-Iraqi Relations," pp. 120–22; Walid Khalidi, "The Arab Perspective," in Wm. Roger Louis and Robert W. Stookey, eds., *The End of the Palestine Mandate* (London, 1986) pp. 121–23.

13 Batatu, *Old Social Classes*, pp. 597–603.

14 Eppel, *Palestine Conflict*, p. 165.

15 PRO, Kirkbride (Amman) to Foreign Office, 21 December 1947, FO 371/61583 E12132.

16 Khalidi, "The Arab Perspective," p. 122.

17 Windawi, "Anglo-Iraqi Relations," p. 122.

18 PRO, Kirkbride (Amman) to Foreign Office, 20 December 1947, FO 371/61583 E12130.

19 Batatu, *Old Social Classes*, pp. 545–66.

20 Windawi, "Anglo-Iraqi Relations," pp. 124–25.

21 Eppel, *Palestine Conflict*, pp. 181–88.

22 PRO, Kirkbride (Amman) to Foreign Office, 5 April 1948, FO 371/68448 E4324; Avi Shlaim, *The Politics of Partition* (Oxford, 1998) pp. 112–13.

23 Eppel, *Palestine Conflict*, p. 184.

24 Windawi, "Anglo-Iraqi Relations," pp. 127–29.

25 Jubury, *Mihnat filastin*, pp. 173–82; Eppel, *Palestine Question*, p. 190.

26 John Bagot Glubb, *A Soldier with the Arabs* (London, 1957), p. 130; Eppel, *Palestine Conflict*, pp. 187–91.

27 *Taqrir lajnat al-tahqiq*, pp. 128–31, 151–58; Shlaim, *Politics of Partition*, pp. 154–56; Juburi, *Mihnat filastin*, pp. 131–33.

28 Jubury, *Mihnat filastin*, pp. 169–93.

29 PRO, Pirie-Gordon (Amman) to Foreign Office, 29 July 1948, FO 371/68471 E10179; Richmond (Baghdad) to Walker, 24 August 1948, FO 371/68451 E11431.

30 PRO, Chancery (Baghdad) to Eastern Department, 27 July 1948, FO 371/68451 E 10024.

31 Windawi, "Anglo-Iraqi Relations," pp. 135–37; Avi Shlaim, "The Rise and Fall of the All-Palestine Government in Gaza," *Journal of Palestine Studies,* 20/1 (1990) 45–50.

32 PRO, Mack (Baghdad) to Bevin, 6 December 1948, FO 371/68453. The Iraqi parliament called on the Arab League to draw up a unified military plan for the defense of Palestine and to devise a policy that would defeat the attempt to create a Jewish state in Palestine. It declared that urgent action on both plans should begin immediately to "clear Palestine of Jewish bands and especially the whole city of Jerusalem."

33 Jubury, *Mihnat filastin*, pp. 356–80.

34 Moshe Gat, *The Jewish Exodus from Iraq 1948–1951* (London, 1996), pp. 1–35.

35 The *Farhud* refers to the violence against the Jews of Baghdad in June 1941 following the collapse of Rashid ʿAli al-Kaylani's government and before the British forces entered the city; cf. Elie Kedourie, "The Sack of Basra and the *Farhud* in Baghdad," in *Arabic Political Memoirs and Other Studies* (London, 1974), pp. 283–91.

36 PRO, Chancery (Baghdad) to Eastern Department, 27 July 1948, FO 371/68451 E10024.

37 PRO, Richmond (Baghdad) to Burrows, 1 September 1948, FO 371/68451 E11708; Gat, *Jewish Exodus*, pp. 36–38.

38 PRO, Mack (Baghdad) to Foreign Office, 30 September 1948, FO 371/68452 E13085; Gat, *Jewish Exodus*, pp. 38–45.

39 PRO, Richmond (Baghdad) to Walker, 24 August 1948, FO 371/68451 E11431; British military attaché (Baghdad) to Mack, Report on the Iraqi Army for 1949, 27 February 1950, FO 371/82450.

40 PRO, Mack (Baghdad) to Foreign Office, 8 December 1948, FO 371/68453 E15650.

41 PRO, Mack (Baghdad) to Bevin, 17 May 1949, FO 371/75129 E6601.

42 Windawi, "Anglo-Iraqi Relations," pp. 141–47.

43 Patrick Seale, *The Struggle for Syria: A Study of Post-War Arab Politics, 1945–1958* (London, 1986), pp. 73–83; Matthew Elliot, *'Independent Iraq': The Monarchy and British Influence 1941–1958* (London, 1996), pp. 75–79.

44 Gat, *Jewish Exodus*, pp. 51–67; Elie Kedourie, "The Break Between Muslims and Jews in Iraq," in M. R. Cohen and A. R. Udovitch, eds., *Jews Among Arabs: Contacts and Boundaries* (Princeton NJ, 1989) pp. 21–63.

45 Glubb, *Soldier with the Arabs*, pp. 227–37; Shlaim, *Politics of Partition*, pp. 288–89; Eppel, *Palestine Conflict*, p. 192.

46 PRO, British military attaché (Baghdad) to Mack, Report on the Iraqi Army for 1949, 27 February 1950, FO 371/82450.

7   Egypt and the 1948 War: internal conflict and regional ambition

Fawaz A. Gerges

This chapter examines Arab historiography on Egypt's role in the 1948 Palestine War in order to disentangle myth from reality. Most Arab writers allocate the largest share of the blame for defeat in Palestine to the old regimes and marshal arguments and evidence to prove their incompetence, corruption, and treachery. Had the Arab world been ruled by more determined and nationalist leaders, so the argument runs, the war would have been won and the state of Israel would not have been born. Arab historiography called into question the very legitimacy of the old political order in Egypt, Iraq, Syria, Lebanon, and Transjordan. The defeat of the Arab states in 1948 represented one of the final nails in the coffin of the old ruling social and political classes. Intentionally or not, Arab writers played an important part in legitimizing the new men on horseback, who began to seize power since the late 1940s, and who promised to redeem Arab honor and prepare for a second round with Israel. Indeed, the institutionalization of militarism in the Arab world owes a great deal to the discrediting of the old regimes. Egypt was a classic case. Egyptian and Arab societies in general are still paying the price of this revolutionary transformation in Arab politics.

Egypt's decision to intervene in the Palestine War was influenced by political and tactical considerations. King Faruq decided to enter the 1948 War against the advice of his prime minister, Mahmud Nuqrashi, the army, and the major political parties. Despite the skepticism of the members of parliament and their questioning of the wisdom of intervention, they, like the king, were influenced by public sentiment and the logic of inter-Arab politics and supported Faruq's decision to enter the war.

The ruling political establishment did not take the war in Palestine seriously and did not plan, prepare, or put Egyptian society on a war footing, either before or during the course of hostilities. The Egyptian military had major shortcomings in training, weapons, ammunition, and transport. The army also had no intelligence on Jewish armed forces and was indirectly dependent on Britain for logistics. The decision to intervene in Palestine was thus a classic case of a breakdown in the decision-making process, where narrow political calculations and inflated regional ambitions superseded strategic thinking.

The ambivalence and improvisation of the political elite had a long-term damaging effect on military–civilian relations. Egyptian rulers ignored the views of their military chiefs and involved them in a costly armed adventure without adequate consultation and preparation. Army officers resented the fact that their views were not taken into account and that they consequently suffered a humiliating defeat. The deep wounds inflicted on the Egyptian military in 1948 poisoned its relationship with the ruling civilian establishment and expanded their political appetite. The seeds of *coups d'état* were sowed in Egypt and several Arab states as well.

The ambivalence of the ruling elite also manifested itself in the way Egypt interacted with the other Arab states before, during, and immediately after the end of the war. The conventional wisdom stipulates that the Arab states were united in their hatred of the Jewish state and had common aims to destroy it. This version does not take into account the tensions within the Arab world. Mistrust and suspicion characterized Egypt's interactions with its Arab partners during the Palestine crisis. Arab leaders were deeply divided in their assessment and response to the creation of Israel and had differing political objectives. Thus, the Arab coalition was fragmented. Egypt and the other Arab states had their own parochial interests to advance. There was no shared vision to unify Arab ranks in the fight against Israel, and the Arabs lacked both a political and military strategy to deal with Israel. Inter-Arab rivalries played a critical role in the calculations of Arab leaders to intervene directly in Palestine and the manner in which they executed the war.

Arab-Egyptian historiography and the 1948 War

The story of Egypt and the Palestine War cannot be understood except within the context of Arab historiography and its differing and competing interpretations. This story is highly contested in Egypt and the rest of the Arab world. Many Egyptian and other Arabic sources reveal a sense of disarray and fragmentation within Arab ranks. No unity of purpose existed on how best to deal with the newly established Jewish state. Although Arab historiography may be classified into two basic modes – apologetic and self-critical – it proffers three broad explanations for the Arab defeat in 1948. The first claims that the war against the newly created Jewish state would have been easily won had it not been for the selfishness, corruption, and betrayal of Arab leaders. According to this view, the Arabs were united in their determination to prevent the Jews from establishing a political homeland in Palestine. Arab writers who take this view place the blame for defeat squarely on the shoulders of their rulers, particularly King 'Abdullah of Transjordan and King Faruq of Egypt, who are said to have sold out Palestine to further their narrow provincial interests.[1]

A second explanation views the war as a diversionary tactic by the old ruling elite to pacify rising sociopolitical expectations and maintain domestic control. Dedicated Arab armies are portrayed as having been let down by political leaders who sent them to the battlefield unprepared, under-armed, and under-fed in order to divert attention from dismal political conditions at home. Thus, the purpose of military intervention in Palestine was not to fight and win the war but to dupe the masses and absorb the shocks of their political frustration.[2]

A third school of Arab historiography asserts that the main reason for the Arab defeat lies in the collusion between Arab rulers and foreign powers – Britain and the United States. Arab and Egyptian writers, with few exceptions, point to the decisive role played by the British officers, who commanded the Arab Legion, and who allegedly subordinated Arab interests to those of their mother country. Arab writers accuse the Hashemites, King Faruq of Egypt, and King Sa'ud ibn 'Abd al-'Aziz of Saudi Arabia of being subservient to Britain and serving its imperial designs in the region. In particular, King 'Abdullah is denounced as an imperialist stooge and collaborator with the Zionists.[3]

Why did Egypt intervene in Palestine?

From the outset, the army, Premier Nuqrashi, and the major political parties expressed their doubts about the wisdom of sending the regular army to fight in Palestine. In addition to being unprepared militarily for war, Egypt was engaged in the revision of its treaty with Britain.[4] During the Arab League meeting at Aley, Lebanon, in October 1947, Nuqrashi bluntly informed his colleagues that Egypt could not intervene directly in the war because of its problems with Britain.[5] On the popular level, however, the 1947 United Nations decision to partition Palestine enraged the Arab masses. Student protest exploded in many Egyptian cities, and they called on the Egyptian government to take all necessary actions to save Palestine. As student demonstrations intensified, the interior ministry instructed the police to ban them. Defying the government's restriction, the students' rallying cry – "give us weapons Nuqrashi" – echoed loudly and threateningly.[6]

As the fighting intensified in Palestine in 1948 and as the situation of Palestinians deteriorated, the Egyptian public increased its pressure on the government to intervene directly in the war. Egyptians of all political persuasions volunteered to fight in Palestine. Adding pressure on the government to act, the Muslim Brothers sent many of their followers to fight alongside the Palestinians.[7] The public's anger and frustration appeared to have played a critical role in nudging the king to intervene in Palestine. Although Premier Nuqrashi was against intervention, he said he was swayed by public opinion that "was all in favour of the war, and considered anyone who refused to fight as a traitor."[8]

Other Arab states also recognized the need to participate directly in the war. On 11 May 1948, the secretary general of the Arab League, 'Abd al-Rahman 'Azzam, warned the Egyptian government that Arab rulers would find it difficult not to intervene directly in the Palestine War, and that Egypt could find itself isolated unless it made up its mind. 'Azzam added that King 'Abdullah had decided to move his forces into Palestine on 15 May regardless of what the other Arabs did and that if the Arab armies did not participate in the war, 'Abdullah could occupy the Arab part of Palestine and blame the other Arab states for failure. 'Azzam pointed out that Iraq, Syria, and Lebanon had decided to intervene because they could not afford to remain disengaged, and that he hoped that Egypt would join its Arab sisters. The Egyptian minister of war, Muhammad Haydar Pasha, asserted subsequently that Egypt did not want to intervene in the Palestine War but submitted to the Arab League's wishes out of solidarity.[9]

Initially, the government responded to public pressure by encouraging soldiers and activists individually, including the Muslim Brothers, to volunteer for the war.[10] But as the fighting escalated and public restiveness deepened, King Faruq found it difficult to remain aloof. To a certain extent, the king's hands were fettered by internal political considerations.[11] In 1948, public opinion played a decisive role in influencing Egypt's foreign policy. This was a classic case of how an ambivalent leadership was forced to take action because of internal dynamics.

Another important consideration for the king was the logic of inter-Arab politics. Since its establishment in 1945, the Arab League was split into two blocs, one combining Egypt, Saudi Arabia, Syria, and Lebanon, and a Hashemite bloc comprising Transjordan, and Iraq. The kings of Egypt, Transjordan and Saudi Arabia had dynastic ambitions. Each wanted to play a leadership role. Faruq feared 'Abdullah's regional ambitions, particularly his designs on greater Syria, which included Lebanon and Arab Palestine. In fact, one of the major reasons behind

Faruq's intervention in the 1948 War was his desire to contain 'Abdullah and prevent him from gaining further influence and power in the Arab arena. Following in the footsteps of his father, Faruq also wished to become the undisputed leader of the Muslim world and gain public support inside Egypt after his reputation had been tarnished by personal scandals.[12]

As the slide to war escalated in late April–early May, the Arab League met in Syria on 12 May and decided to commit the Arab armies in Palestine. On 11 May, four days before the war, Faruq ordered his minister of war, Haydar, to prepare the army to enter Palestine without even informing Nuqrashi, who had been adamantly opposed to Egypt's participation.[13] Although Egypt was woefully unprepared for war and although the cabinet, the parliament, and the army were aware of the dismal conditions of the military, Faruq overruled all of them and drove Egypt into war.[14]

Many Egyptian and other Arab politicians failed to appreciate the strength of the Jewish armed forces – dismissively referred to as "the Zionist gangs" – despite the existence of strong evidence. Cultural misperceptions and racist attitudes toward Jews in general blinded and entrapped Arabs. As one senior Iraqi officer put it: "Arab propaganda underestimated the Zionists' strength and considered their leadership a criminal gang that ruled through terrorism. Arabs believed that at the first opportunity Jews would rebel against their leaders who were forcing them to fight."[15]

Indeed, Arab politicians listened to the misleading accounts of 'Azzam, secretary general of the Arab League, and Hajj Amin al-Husayni, the grand mufti of Palestine and chair of the Arab Higher Committee. They were both away from Palestine and ignorant of internal conditions there, and overestimated Arab strength, claiming that all "the Arabs needed was three or four thousand fighters to throw Jews in the sea."[16]

After he had received orders to send the army to Palestine, the minister of war, Haydar, told the Cabinet: "the Egyptian military is capable on its own of occupying Tel Aviv, the capital of Jews in fifteen days, without assistance from the other Arab states."[17] In two closed meeting in the parliament and senate three days before the onset of hostilities, Nuqrashi shifted his stance in favor of intervention and reassured skeptical members that "the Egyptian army had plenty of arms and ammunition and was well prepared."[18]

However, neither Faruq nor Nuqrashi took war seriously. In a meeting with the chiefs of the armed forces on 10 May 1948, Nuqrashi assured some army officers that the fighting in Palestine would be "a political demonstration", not a real military action, and that the conflict would be politically and swiftly resolved by the United Nations. Earlier, Nuqrashi had put it bluntly to his Arab colleagues in a meeting in ʿAley, Lebanon, in October 1947: "I want you to know that if Egypt agrees to participate in this military demonstration, it is unprepared to go beyond that."[19] Furthermore, Faruq told Nuqrashi, when the latter objected to direct intervention, that British forces, which were stationed in Egypt, would prevent Egyptian troops from crossing into Palestine, thus enabling him to pin the blame on the British for not participating in the war.[20] In his memoirs, President Gamal ʿAbd al-Nasir confirmed this sentiment: "Officers felt by listening to the government's statements that it was a political war . . . How could such a thing be called a war with no troops mobilized, no preparation for weapons and ammunition, and no plans and information for the officers in the theatre of operation. Thus it was just a political war – a stalemate."[21]

The ruling political establishment did not take the war in Palestine seriously and did not plan, prepare, or put Arab societies on a war footing either before or during the course of hostilities. Between the period of partition and Britain's decision to withdraw, the Iraqi Parliamentary Commission of Enquiry noted that Arab states did not plan strategically or tactically for the impending hostilities.[22] Given such complacent attitudes, Arab armies' capabilities were not adequately assessed. For example, the Egyptian military had major shortcomings in training, weapons, ammunition, and transportation. Also, the army had no intelligence on the Jewish armed forces and was indirectly dependent on Britain for logistics. Britain exercised considerable influence over Egypt and its army through its military mission. Between 1931 and 1947 the Egyptian army did not have a single military exercise that would have prepared it for a major war.[23] As the commander of Egyptian forces in Palestine put it, "The army almost lost its military spirit."[24] Another senior officer acknowledged that "we were surprised by the Palestine campaign because we were unprepared. I opposed the war for lack of military supplies but they [politicians] forced us to fight . . . I almost had a stroke when they ignored my opinion."[25] In his memoirs ʿAbd al-Nasir said that after he was ordered to join a unit that was being deployed into Palestine, he went to the war headquarters only to find them silent and empty: "When I found the chief officer in charge, he was preparing dinner."[26]

Until the 1948 war, the Egyptian army was used primarily to maintain internal stability. This fact explains the reluctance of Egyptian authorities to send more than a small proportion of the army – around 10,000 troops – to Palestine.[27] The Egyptian government also used the cover of its intervention to declare emergency laws inside Egypt and to curtail personal freedoms and suppress the opposition.[28]

Despite the skepticism of the members of parliament and their questioning of the wisdom of intervention, they were influenced by public sentiment and the logic of inter-Arab politics and supported the king's decision to enter the war. In this context, the decision to intervene in Palestine was a classic case of a terribly flawed decision-making process, where narrow political calculations and inflated regional ambitions superseded strategic thinking. British documents clearly show that Egypt and the other Arab states seemed to be more concerned with internal politics and jockeying for power and advantage over each other than with the proposed new Jewish government.[29]

Military–civilian relations

As early as October and November 1947, Safwat submitted two reports that were categorical in their warnings to Arab leaders of the impending military disaster unless they ensured superiority in numbers and material and acted with maximal speed. On balance, before intervention and during the war itself, most of the military chiefs' recommendations appeared to have fallen on deaf ears. Far from being integrated, the military and political apparatus remained separate. Politics and state interest played a critical role in the calculations and deliberations of Arab rulers.[30]

Take, for example, the appointment of 'Abdullah as commander of all Arab forces. As one historian convincingly put it, "although Arab rulers put King 'Abdullah in charge of the military, his appointment was symbolic. They did not trust each other. They [Arab leaders] questioned his intentions and even more so the head of his army, Glubb Pasha."[31] Not only did Arab political leaders ignore the views of their military chiefs but they also involved them in a costly adventure without adequate preparation or a unified command. The tensions and conflicts between the civilian–military leadership during the Palestine War were partly responsible for the armed *coups d'etat* that shook the Arab world to its core after 1949.

This reality is not to absolve the military from historical responsibility for its dismal performance in Palestine. Arab historiography does just that by pinning the blame on the ruling political establishment and portraying the Arab armies as helpless victims in that complex struggle. While the conduct of the old regimes has been critically scrutinized, no such exercise has been applied to the military's performance. For example, the military chiefs denounced their civilian superiors for failing to unify the Arab command structure, and most Arab historians echo this criticism. According to Nuqrashi, however, Egyptian military chiefs had never suggested that the Arab states should unify their command, a clear rebuttal of the army's criticism.[32]

A case in point is General Safwat, a former Iraqi chief of staff, whom Walid Khalidi praised for his "professional credentials and integrity." Safwat was a typical officer who did not possess any operational experience and who was promoted by seniority, not qualifications, as was the case in most Arab states.[33] Many battles were lost and units were wiped out as a direct result of mistakes and miscalculations made by army officers. The military failed dismally to collect intelligence on the enemy before and during the course of hostilities. Like their civilian superiors, Arab military officers exhibited similar tendencies of pettiness and jealousy toward each other. This conduct affected their ability to cooperate on the battlefield. One writer has argued further that in contrast to their Jewish counterparts, some senior Arab officers did not put a high premium on their soldiers' lives.[34]

In their memoirs, Ahmad 'Ali al-Muwawi, who was a field commander, and 'Abd al-Nasir, then a junior officer, acknowledged that some of the officers who led Egyptian troops were inexperienced, having rushed through the military academy to go to Palestine before they had completed their training course. 'Abd al-Nasir was himself one of these officers.[35] Muwawi gives a disturbing account of incompetent and lethargic officers, who were neither well trained nor well motivated. The Egyptian field commander also gives a sketch of foot soldiers, who were poorly trained, dressed, and fed.[36] It is worth noting that neither Faruq, commander-in-chief of Egyptian troops, nor his war minister, Haydar, were knowledgeable about military strategy and tactics. Haydar spent most of his career as director of prisons in Egypt. Other senior Arab officers were more traditional than creative in their military thinking.[37]

Arab historians tend to be silent when it comes to assessing the military's role in Palestine, while being highly critical of the civilian leadership. This undifferentiated view had critical implications for military–civilian relations in Arab societies. One of the major results of the 1948 war was the discrediting of the old social and political classes and the legitimizing of the men on horseback as saviours and redeemers. In this context, Arab historians of 1948 contributed considerably to the popularity of this simplistic dichotomy.

The first round of fighting, 15 May – 10 June

The Egyptian army aimed to advance from Rafah on the Egyptian border toward the north and ultimately toward Tel Aviv and occupy all

Jewish settlements on the way. Three days before intervention, King Faruq had a meeting with his minister of war and a team of officers, who were being sent to Palestine. Faruq said that "Egypt was obliged to enter the war with the rest of the Arab states even though we are not fully prepared." Faruq added: "King 'Abdullah and the Iraqi regent 'Abd al-Ilah promised me that their armies would do most of the fighting. Egyptian forces would march toward Tel Aviv and when the Arab Legion enters the city, we will advance and help the Legion occupy it." Faruq concluded his pep talk by warning his officers against engaging in any battle where enemy forces were superior in numbers. Faruq seemed not to appreciate the gravity of his decision because he gave the impression that Egypt's participation was symbolic rather than real.[38] In other words, the Egyptian leadership did not specify to its military chiefs the strategic objective behind intervention.[39]

King 'Abdullah had a different perception from that of his Egyptian counterpart. On 13 May, the same Egyptian military team traveled to Amman to put the final touches on the military plans with the other four Arab countries. King 'Abdullah made a telling remark that other delegates heard: "The Arab League appointed me as the commander-in-chief of the Arab armies. Should not this honour be conferred on Egypt, the largest of the Arab states? Or is the real purpose behind this appointment to pin the blame and responsibility on us in case of failure?"[40] From the outset, confusion abounded about the military functions of each country. Arab rulers neither trusted each other nor rationally coordinated their military strategy. Egypt and Transjordan, in particular, had differing objectives.[41] To simplify, 'Abdullah's aim was to annex the Arab part of Palestine to his kingdom, and Faruq's main aim was to prevent 'Abdullah's territorial aggrandizement.

This lack of inter-Arab coordination was compounded by an absence of strategic planning by the separate Arab states. In the case of Egypt, political calculations, not military strategy or tactics, marked Cairo's military campaign. The Egyptian regime had no appreciation of the complexity and danger of its military adventure, and it saw intervention as a "military demonstration" and a police action to punish "the Zionist gangs." Some Egyptian officials believed that the Zionist gangs would flee as soon as the Egyptian forces approached. This was a classic case of how cultural misperceptions blinded officials and distorted their analysis.

On 15 May, to the surprise of many Arabs, the Egyptian army entered Palestine. The first official report announced that "operations in Palestine are just designed to discipline the Zionist gangs."[42] Egyptian units, numbering fewer than 10,000 soldiers, with no strategic plan, raced through Sinai in order to occupy the Gaza coastline first and then advance north and join forces with the Arab Legion which they did on 24 May. Unable to occupy the well-defended Jewish settlements, the Egyptian army did not exert itself, preferring to march forward leaving them behind. Egyptian troops overextended themselves in the process and established stationary, fixed positions in contrast to the more flexible and mobile Jewish forces. Egyptian lines of supply, transportation, and communication became vulnerable to attacks by Jewish units.[43] Gamal ʿAbd al-Nasir, a brigade major in the Palestine war, noted: "We did not fight as an army, but we acted as separate units spread over a large territory. The result was that the enemy succeeded in keeping us fixed in our positions and reserved for itself the freedom of action."[44]

Politics and public relations played an important role in the way the Egyptian army conducted military operations, and sometimes interference by the political leadership in Cairo hindered rational planning. The political leadership in Cairo used to contact the field commanders and instruct them on tactical objectives by telephone. On 21 May, for example, while Egyptian units were busy planning an operation, Cairo sent them an urgent message: "we want al-Majdal today."[45] Egyptian leaders seemed to be interested in achieving a symbolic military victory to score political gains at home. They assumed that the further their army advanced in Palestine, the weaker Jewish resistance would become. Again, this thinking reveals the depth of cultural, political, and strategic ignorance that characterized the Arab conduct of the war.

On 29 May the United Nations passed a resolution calling for a truce. Israel and Transjordan accepted the UN resolution, and Transjordan ordered its military forces to cease firing on 2 June. Egypt also implicitly accepted the cease-fire. Initially, Iraq, Syria, and Lebanon did not adhere to the truce and fighting continued until 11 June. After much acrimonious debate in the Arab League, the four Arab countries separately informed the UN of their acceptance of the truce; so did the secretary general of the Arab League. The bickering and disagreement among the Arab states over the UN decision is revealing. On its own, and without prior consultation with its allies, Transjordan broke ranks with them. Far from acting cohesively, the Arab coalition, with its differing war aims, began to fracture.[46]

At the time the first truce was declared, on 11 June, the Egyptian army had taken positions on the coastal strip to about 14 miles north of Gaza. Its position was far from secure, however. The Egyptian field commander complained bitterly to his superiors in Cairo about shortages of men and equipment and warned of the danger of over-extension. Egyptian forces, he stressed, could not advance one step further without endangering their entire strategic position and he could not therefore be responsible for any disaster that might befall Egyptian troops. The Egyptian field commander also reminded his superiors that Egypt's political objectives should be consistent with its military means.[47]

From the outset, Egyptian officers were opposed to participation in the Palestine war. Both the minister of war, Haydar, and his chief of staff, 'Uthman al-Mahdi Pasha declared they were against intervention. As the latter put it: "I opposed entering the war but they forced us to fight."[48] The first round of fighting reinforced their belief that the army, with its meager resources, was unprepared to fight a major battle. In particular, many of the junior officers who fought in the war felt betrayed and neglected by their political masters in Cairo. As the war dragged on and some units were encircled, their junior officers, many of whom later would belong to the Free Officers organization, held the royal regime responsible for the army's humiliation and defeat. The king and his men were accused of corruption and of stabbing the military in the back by procuring obsolete and deficient weapons and ammunition.[49] Egyptian officers' discourse was not only designed to expose the incompetent political leadership but also to protest their innocence and rationalize defeat.[50] Their fear was that the civilian leadership might try to pin the blame for the defeat on them. There were signs pointing in that direction after Muwawi and other senior officers were detained and interrogated at the war's end.[51]

Arab historians echo the grievances of the Free Officers and contrast their noble sacrifice with the selfish behavior of the ruling elite. Some authors claim that the reason for the defeat of the Egyptian army lay in the faulty weapons that were purchased by King Faruq and his corrupt men.[52] It is in this sense that Arab historians indirectly contributed to the discrediting of the old order and to the legitimizing of militarism in the Arab world.

The second round of fighting, 9 July – 18 July

Israel fully exploited the first cease-fire to regroup its forces and import heavy armaments from abroad, thus tipping the military balance decisively in its favor. In the first round of fighting, Israel did not have heavy armaments and equipment. While Israel successfully used the truce to compensate for that shortcoming from private arms merchants, the Arab states encountered difficulties in acquiring desperately needed ammunition and heavy weapons. It also seems that Arab leaders did not take the war seriously or plan for a prolonged confrontation.[53] According to Israeli historians, the UN arms embargo, which resulted in a critical shortage of ammunition and spare parts on the Arab side, substantially aided the Israeli war effort.[54]

When the second round of fighting started on 9 July, Israel was fully prepared and launched devastating counter-offensives, gaining the upper hand on the battlefield. On 12 July, Israel occupied Lydda and Ramla, two important Palestinian towns along the main road from Tel Aviv to Jerusalem, and expelled a large number of their inhabitants. This breakthrough had devastating psychological ramifications for Palestinians as well as for the balance of power between Israel and its Arab neighbors. The fall of Lydda and Ramla led to bitter recriminations between Transjordan and Egypt. Arab writers accused ʿAbdullah and the British commander of his army of treachery for failing to defend the two towns, even though Glubb had warned that these towns could not possibly be held in the event of fighting being resumed.[55]

Some writers claimed further that ʿAbdullah in collusion with the Zionists and British officers turned the other way, while Zionist forces occupied the two towns and expelled their Palestinian residents. One writer asserted that "King ʿAbdullah agreed to meet and negotiate with the enemy. Thus he recognized Israel's existence. As the supreme commander of Arab forces, he stabbed his army and nation in the back, and he inserted a wedge in Arab ranks that benefited the enemy and that led to the destruction of the Arab coalition."[56]

In the second round of fighting, far from coordinating their activities, the Arab armies operated separately because neither the Jordanians nor the Egyptians trusted each other.[57] After the fall of Lydda and Ramla, the Egyptian field commander complained to his superiors in Cairo about the lack of coordination among the various Arab armies and asked for a clear delineation of operational lines for his troops.[58] Israel succeeded in delivering major blows to the Arab armies, particularly that of Egypt. As an Israeli "new historian" argued, "after July 1948, the first Arab–Israeli war devolved into an Israeli–Egyptian struggle, with Transjordan (and Lebanon, Iraq, and Syria) merely looking on from the sidelines."[59]

On 18 July, the day a second truce was agreed to, the Egyptian field commander summarized the military situation in very gloomy terms. Muwawi's blunt report reflected the deterioration of the Egyptian strategic position since the resumption of fighting on 9 July. The report reiterated the army's shortages of tanks and other heavy equipment, of dangerously low levels of ammunition, and lack of coordination among the Arab armies. The report also lamented the lack of internal organization, strategic reserves, and competent training of regular troops that resulted in costly blunders on the battlefield. Although the report implicitly referred to the low morale among Egyptian soldiers, other sources give this factor more prominence.[60] The field commander stressed that his forces had overextended themselves without having sufficient strategic reserves on which to rely. The report also warned that the strategic position of Egyptian troops had been weakened because they could no longer adequately defend their long lines of supplies and transportation. Unless Egyptian leaders were prepared to remedy these serious military problems, the report concluded by explicitly calling on the leadership in Cairo to find a political solution to the crisis.[61]

Not only did the Arab states not coordinate military strategy but they also bickered over how to respond to the UN cease-fire resolution on 15 July. Although on 16 July the Arab League's Political Committee agreed to a cease-fire in Jerusalem only, two days later the secretary general of the Arab League reversed course and agreed to a general truce. Again, this shift in the Political Committee's stance had to do with Transjordan and Egypt's preference for a truce. King 'Abdullah told Lebanese Prime Minister Riad al-Sulh that Transjordan could not continue to fight because of its lack of ammunition. Iraq followed suit. Whether Transjordan had adequate ammunition or not – Sulh believed that the lack of ammunition argument masked a lack of political will to fight – its decision to cease fire left Egypt at the mercy of an Israeli offensive. Egypt itself had no stomach for further fighting.[62] Political strains within the Arab coalition were tearing it apart.[63] Psychologically, the disagreement and bickering over the cease-fire weakened the resolve of Arab soldiers and made them reluctant to endanger their lives.[64]

The second truce, 19 July – 14 October

When on 18 July the second cease-fire was finally concluded, it was assumed that this truce would be of indefinite duration. Israel used this truce to consolidate its superior position by harassing and attacking Egyptian forces. Israeli forces struck at will the scattered and lightly defended Egyptian positions which assumed a stationary posture without having sufficient resources and reserve units.

Instead of coordinating their military strategy, Arab leaders started quarreling among themselves in the Arab League and blamed each other for the poor showing on the battlefield. Defeat exacerbated divisions within Arab ranks. Mistrust between Egypt and Transjordan reached new heights. When King 'Abdullah visited Egypt in June 1948 during the first truce, as commander-in-chief of Arab forces, he requested to visit the Egyptian military headquarters in Palestine. His wish was not granted. 'Abdullah wrote that the visit did not achieve any positive result because his command remained purely symbolic.[65]

Time and again, Faruq and 'Abdullah bickered over the size of each other's flag in their territories in Palestine. Faruq complained bitterly to UN mediators that the Jordanian flag in one of the towns controlled by Cairo was a few centimeters larger than the Egyptian flag. Tensions and infighting also marked relations between Egyptian and Jordanian units on the battlefield. Moreover, hardly anything is written about friction and strife between Arab military forces and local Palestinians. For example, Egyptian troops mistreated and mistrusted Palestinians whom they accused of treachery. Conflict between Egyptian units and locals intensified after the former attempted to disarm Palestinian fighters.[66]

Neither Faruq nor 'Abdullah seemed to appreciate the seriousness of the war against Israel. They appeared to be more concerned about their respective strategic positions than that of Israel. At the Alexandria meeting of the Arab League on 8 September, Egypt proposed the creation of an "all-Palestine government" in Gaza, a radical departure from the League's previous position. Egypt thus in theory recognized the Palestinians' right to self-determination. Egypt's defeat on the battlefield brought about this reorientation of its policy. Its sponsorship of the All-Palestine Government, however, had more to do with inter-Arab rivalries and local politics than heightened opposition to Israel.[67] The immediate purpose of the proposed Arab government in Palestine was to "provide a focal point of opposition to 'Abdullah and serve as an instrument for frustrating his ambition to federate the Arab regions of Palestine with Transjordan."[68] In this context, Nuqrashi made it clear to UN mediators that any settlement that resulted in Transjordan's annexation of Arab Palestine would destroy the Arab balance of power.[69] 'Abdullah was furious, and he perceived the Egyptian move as directed specifically against his regional ambition. The Jordanian delegation walked out of the Alexandria meeting, and Transjordan clearly stated that it would "contest" the legitimacy of this government.[70] The establishment of the All-Palestine Government in Gaza served as a magnet for rivalry between Egypt and Transjordan and deepened suspicion and mistrust within Arab ranks during the war and afterwards.[71]

The third round of fighting, 15 October – 5 November

While Egypt and Transjordan were quarreling with each other, Israel was consolidating its strategic position. In mid-October, Israel broke the truce and singled out the Egyptian forces for an all-out offensive in the south. Israeli forces neutralized the small Egyptian airforce and encircled land units in several theatres. This round of fighting witnessed an intensification of Israel's air raids on Egyptian positions. Israel dominated the skies and delivered painful blows to Egyptian troops. This new development dramatically changed the strategic configuration of forces between Israel and its Arab neighbors, a testament to Israel's ability to use the cease-fire to build up offensive capability and to plan strategically to win the war.

Encircled and cut off in the Negev, the field commander of the Egyptian forces requested that ammunition be delivered by small planes. They also requested the immediate intervention of Jordanian and Iraqi forces to reduce pressure on their front. When the UN Security Council called for a cease-fire on 22 October, Egypt lost control over the entire Negev and its forces were isolated into three separate, unconnected positions. Egypt had all but lost the war. Without an immediate, coordinated rescue operation by the Arab armies, Israel could readily deliver a crushing blow to Egypt.[72]

Given the differing aims of the Arab states and their deep-seated suspicion of each other, a collective Arab response did not materialize. A day after the Security Council's cease-fire resolution, Nuqrashi visited Amman to attend the Arab prime ministers' meeting to discuss ways and means of dealing with Israel's attack on the Egyptian forces in the Negev. When King ʿAbdullah inquired about the real conditions of the Egyptian army, Naqrashi responded calmly and defensively by claiming that "the Egyptian army is in a good position and that there is no need to take Zionist propaganda seriously." When, in the afternoon, members of the Political Committee and prime ministers met again, ʿAbdullah inquired what the Arab states could do to assist the Egyptian army in the Negev. Nuqrashi retorted that "the Egyptian government does not ask help from anyone. I came here to know why the other Arab states have not attacked so far to relieve pressure on the Egyptian army. Where is the Iraqi army and where is the Arab Legion?" At that point, King ʿAbdullah left the meeting without responding to Nuqrashi. In the evening a third meeting took place in which it was agreed that the Iraqi, Jordanian, and Syrian armies would develop a plan to assist the besieged Egyptian forces in Faluja. However, such a plan never materialized due to mutual suspicions and mistrust.[73] Nuqrashi returned to Cairo empty-handed. The war in Palestine became a private war rather than an Arab–Israeli war.

In the meantime, the conditions of besieged Egyptian troops in Faluja – a third of the Egyptian army according to Nasir – were deteriorating rapidly, with no relief in sight. Although the overall strength and numbers of Egyptian forces increased substantially between 15 May 1948 and October 1948 – from 10,000 to about 45,000 – they were still no match for the better armed and better trained Jewish defense forces, who also outnumbered their Arab enemies. So despondent and desperate was the Egyptian field commander that he asked his government to find a political solution to the conflict.[74]

One of the intriguing questions is why Transjordan did not come to the aid of Egypt? Egyptians believed that they were stabbed in the back. They blamed King ʿAbdullah for endangering the security of the Egyptian army by evacuating the towns of Ramla and Lydda as well as for his inaction in the face of the Israeli assault on the encircled Egyptian forces. In a closed meeting of the Egyptian parliament, on 30 November 1948, the Egyptian minister of war claimed that "if the Arab armies do not fight, I have to state here that Egypt will fight by its own and on its own."[75] Similarly, Nuqrashi told the parliament, that, unlike the other Arab states, Egypt did respond to Transjordan's requests for military assistance. He also said that the Jewish forces would have occupied Jerusalem if it was not for Egypt's support of the Jordanian army.[76]

The findings of the Iraqi Parliamentary Commission of Enquiry contest Nuqrashi's account. Time and again, Iraqis asserted, Egypt procrastinated and did not respond to their requests for military collaboration. From the outset, Egypt, the Commission argues, refused to unify military ranks with the Arab states.[77] But the Commission's conclusion is disputed by some Iraqi officers who served in Palestine, and by many Arab historians, who assert that neither the Jordanians nor the Iraqis did much to help ease the pressure on the besieged Egyptian forces. Transjordan and Iraq appeared to have turned deaf ears to the pleas of Egyptian forces. King ʿAbdullah was reportedly pleased by Israel's humbling of his principal Arab rival – Egypt. Arab writers accuse ʿAbdullah and the British chief of his army, Glubb Pasha, of collusion with Jewish forces to expel Egyptian troops from Palestine and divide the land between them. On the whole, Arab historiography does not give much credence to ʿAbdullah and Glubb's protestation that Transjordan was fully engaged in the war and could not divert or mobilize new forces to assist Egypt effectively. ʿAbdullah and his British masters are found guilty of conspiring against the Arab nation.[78]

The final round, December 1948 – January 1949

Israel had the upper hand during the final round of war. It kept up the pressure on the besieged Egyptian forces in Faluja to surrender, thus delivering a crushing psychological shock to Egypt and forcing Cairo to sue for peace. When Arab and Egyptian officials complained to General Riley, the senior observer of the UN in Palestine, about Israel's violations of the cease-fire, he bluntly told them that the current truce was unviable because of Israeli military dominance. General Riley advised Arab officials to negotiate a permanent truce with Israel.

Between 10 and 12 November, Arab military chiefs met in Cairo to assess the military situation and submitted one of the most comprehensive reports to the Political Committee of the Arab League. The report compared the balance of power between Israeli and Arab forces and concluded that the latter had a strategic edge over all Arab states. The military chiefs warned that the current defensive posture of the Arab armies was bound to lead ultimately to defeat in the Palestine war. The report listed four reasons for the poor performance of the Arab armies: (1) Arab armies had not been prepared to fight a prolonged war; (2) the Arab states had failed to mobilize sufficient forces and resources and use them effectively to win the war; (3) no unified command was established to manage and coordinate the various Arab armies; and (4) unlike Israel, the Arab states did not use the two truces to make up for their military shortages.[79]

The military chiefs' recommendations focused primarily on the need to allow the armies to fight the war professionally without being hindered by political considerations. Before taking any military decision, the report urged politicians to keep their military chiefs informed on political objectives. Finally, the military commanders called on their civilian superiors to mobilize all the Arab nations' resources to obtain the needed men and material to win this war.[80]

Again, like other previous reports, this one was not translated into action. Arab rulers still could not coordinate their military strategy and agree on a tentative plan to relieve the encircled Egyptian units in Faluja. Deep cleavages within the Arab coalition precluded any meaningful military cooperation. By the end of 1948, Egyptian officials appeared to recognize this fact and hoped to find a political solution that would enable them to withdraw their troops from Faluja in an honorable manner.[81] Despite this belated awareness, Egyptian leaders would not accept the UN Security Council's cease-fire resolution of 16 November unless a solution was found to the encircled Faluja brigade.

On 22 December Israel's leaders – knowing that 'Abdullah would not go out of his way to support Egypt militarily – seized the opportunity to launch a second offensive against Egypt. They succeeded in throwing the Egyptian forces back across the international border. Once again, the Arab League remained passive and could not take collective Arab action to counterbalance Israel's new offensive. Desperate to stop the Israeli push into Egyptian territory, Cairo appealed to London and Washington for assistance. Britain saw in Israel's threat to Egyptian sovereignty an opportunity to apply the terms of the 1936 Treaty and impress their estranged ally by drawing red lines for Israel's expansion.[82] Arab historians are silent about Britain's intercession on Egypt's behalf. To give the British any credit for stopping Israel's advance deep into Egyptian territory would conflict with Arab historians' portrayal of Britain as an active supporter of the Zionists. One writer claimed that "perhaps Britain encouraged the Arabs to enter the war, knowing full well that they could not win because of the weakness of their armies. The destruction of the Arab armies would keep them dependent and thus preserve British influence in the region."[83] Another put it more bluntly, "in the final analysis, the British were the source of evil."[84]

Britain also wanted, according to two Arab writers, to prove to the world that Egypt could not defend the Suez Canal, which required the presence of British forces there.[85] The irony is that both conventional Zionist and Arab historiography share a parallel view of Britain as the enemy. Britain's Palestine policy was a difficult balancing act, torn between imperial interests and the imperative of its alliance with the United States. By the end of 1948, Britain was so concerned about the fragmentation and weakening of the Arab position and the likelihood of "a peace imposed by Israel" that it attempted unsuccessfully to mediate between Egypt and Transjordan. Israel brilliantly exploited the divide between both countries to its own advantage.[86]

Once Israel's forces crossed the international border between Palestine and Egypt, Britain and the United States worked actively for an end to hostilities. The UN proposed a cease-fire that was accepted by Egypt and Israel in early January 1949. King Faruq decided to disengage from the Palestine imbroglio. On 13 January, bilateral negotiations between Egypt and Israel got under way with the help of the UN acting mediator, Ralph Bunche, on the island of Rhodes, and an armistice agreement was signed six weeks later, on 24 February. This agreement formally terminated the state of belligerency between Israel and Egypt. The other Arab states followed suit by signing separate bilateral agreements with Israel: Lebanon on 23 March; Transjordan on 3 April; and Syria on 20 July.

Although in Rhodes Egyptian negotiators asked for major territorial concessions in the Negev, they wanted to cut their losses and find an honorable way out of the Palestine imbroglio. In the late 1940s, as in the late 1970s, Egypt felt embittered, unappreciated by the other Arab states, and was the first one to officially break ranks with them. Egypt preferred bilateral negotiations with Israel in order to secure a better deal in Rhodes than the other Arab parties. Israel agreed to an Egyptian military presence in the Gaza Strip, to the release of the Egyptian brigade from Faluja, and to the demilitarization of al-Awja. Israel easily could have captured the Gaza Strip and given it to King 'Abdullah. However, Egypt wanted to keep the Gaza Strip because it did not wish Transjordan to make additional territorial gains and share a border with Egypt. Faruq made political and military concessions to Israel to prevent that from happening.

Arab historiography is silent on the informal discussions that were held in Paris in late 1948 between Kamal Riad, Faruq's emissary, and Israeli officials, particularly Elias Sasson, that dealt with broader political questions. These included Israel's relations with Egypt and the other Arab states. Israel did everything in its power to sow discord in Arab ranks. In this context, David Ben-Gurion regarded the signature of the armistice agreement with Egypt, the largest Arab state, as the greatest event in a year of momentous events, after the establishment of the state of Israel and its subsequent victories on the battlefield.

Political consequences

Internally, military defeat complicated the Egyptian government's ability to deal with the unstable internal political-economic situation. The government intensified its repression of the Muslim Brotherhood and finally dissolved it in December after one of its armed factions unleashed political violence and terrorism.[87] Less than a month later, Nuqrashi was assassinated. The Muslim Brother assassin bluntly told an Egyptian court that he killed Nuqrashi because the latter had collaborated with the Jews.[88] The stage was set for future blood feuds between the state and the Muslim Brothers.

Tensions between the royal regime and the embittered military officers who fought in Palestine were heightened. Terrified that its defeated army could rebel, the government did not allow the units from Palestine to return to their bases in Cairo. It forced them to remain for a while in Isma'iliyya. Some Free Officers were questioned and even accused of collusion with the Muslim Brothers to foment instability.[89] The monarchy was so weakened by the Palestine War that it became only a matter of time before the military would step in and seize power.[90] Time and again, political actions produced the opposite of expected results. Faruq intervened in Palestine partly to consolidate his authority by appealing to Egyptians' nationalist sentiments. The result was that intervention weakened Faruq considerably and led ultimately to his downfall.

Egypt was not the only Arab state to undergo dramatic transformation after the war. The defeat in 1948 had rippling effects throughout the Arab lands. In country after country, the old regimes became vulnerable to ideological currents that ultimately swept them away. A coup in Syria in 1949 overthrew President Shukri al-Quwwatli and established a pattern of military intervention in Arab politics. King 'Abdullah was assassinated in 1951, and Egypt entered a period of political instability that culminated in the Free Officers' revolution in July 1952. In other words, the defeat in 1948 led to the militarization of Arab politics.

Furthermore, the war and its aftermath exacerbated inter-Arab rivalries, and the high hopes pinned on the Arab League vanished. Egypt, the largest and strongest Arab country, was humiliated by its defeat at the hands of the young Jewish state. The Palestine war played an important role in poisoning inter-Arab interactions. Although by the end of the 1950s and 1960s the old order had collapsed, the new radical regimes that seized power continued to bicker and quarrel among themselves more intensely than before. Separate state interests persisted regardless of the form of the regime in power.

Moreover, the Arab defeat and its historiography had critically affected relations between civil societies and their governments. By pinning the blame on the corruption and treachery of the ruling political establishment, Arab writers unwittingly reinforced and deepened the conspiratorial thread in Arab political culture. Many Arabs were convinced that the war against the small Jewish state could have been won had it not been for the collusion of Arab leaders with foreign powers. The war was lost not only because of the inherent weaknesses in the Arab coalition but also because Arab politics was inherently corrupt. Citizens no longer had any trust in their governments, and political institutions could not be consolidated in the absence of trust and civility between state and society.

Many Arabs had hoped that the end of colonialism would usher in a new dawn of liberal-democratic politics in the Arab world, in a new relationship between governments and their citizens. The Arab defeat and the subsequent assigning of blame shattered all that. In the aftermath of defeat, Arab politics became infected with conspiracies. The quest for political redemption would await the arrival of a new messiah, who abolished politics altogether. After 1948, the new men on horseback, who stepped forward and seized power in Egypt, Iraq, and Syria, promised to do just that. The new knights not only failed to redeem Arab honor but their costly military adventures intensified Arab disenchantment and widened the gap further between the ruled and the ruling elite.

Fu'ad Saraj al-Din, an outspoken senator, questioned the Arab leaders' intentions and their conduct of the war before a closed session of the Egyptian Senate on 30 November 1948. He accused the Arab regimes, including Egypt, of political hypocrisy and expediency on account of their failure to inform their citizens about the real situation in Palestine. Saraj al-Din noted that Arab governments, while squandering human and material resources on the war, had implicitly accepted the UN decision to divide Palestine. He challenged them to either fight the war and win or stop the costly charade and inform the people that Israel was there to stay.[91] Saraj al-Din's indictment captures Arab states' ambivalence and vacillation in the Palestine War. No consensus on Israel existed within the Arab world. Far from intervening to defend the Palestinians and destroy Israel, Egypt's intervention was a classic case of internal conflict and regional ambition.

Notes

1 Gamal ʿAbd al-Nasir, *Falsafat al-thawra* [The Philosophy of the Revolution] (Cairo, n.d.), p. 12; Government of Iraq, *Taqrir lajnat al-tahqiq al-niyabiya fi qadiyyat filastin* [Report of the Parliamentary Committee of Enquiry into the Palestine Question] (Baghdad, 1949), p. 18; Muhammad Faysal ʿAbd al-Munʿim, *Asrar 1948* [Secrets of 1948] (Cairo, 1968), pp. 195–96, 669; Falih Khalid ʿAli, *al-Harb al-ʿarabiyya al-israʾiliyya, 1948–1949, wa taʾsis israʾil* [The Arab–Israeli War, 1948–1949, and the Establishment of Israel] (Beirut, 1982), pp. 65, 105, 248–50, 410–11; Ibrahim ʿAbd al-Satar, *Karithat al-ʿarab fi filastin* [The Arab Disaster in Palestine] (n.p., n.d.), pp. 56–57; ʿArif al-ʿArif, *al-Nakba* [The Catastrophe], 5 vols. (Sidon and Beirut, 1956–61), vol. IV, pp. 787–89.

2 ʿAbd al-Nasir, *Falsafat*, pp. 12, 14–15; ʿAbd al-Munʿim, *Asrar 1948*, pp. 194–95; *Mudhakkirat ʿAbd al-Nasir ʿan harb filastin ʿam 1948* [ʿAbd al-Nasir's Memoirs of the 1948 Palestine War] (Paris, n.d.); ʿAli, *al-Harb*, pp. 61, 65, 414–15; ʿArif, *al-Nakba*, vol. I, p. 178.

3 See his lengthy testimony in Muhammad Hasanayn Haykal, *al-ʿUrush waʾl-juyush: kadhalik infajara al-siraʿ fi filastin* [Thrones and Armies: Thus Erupted the Struggle in Palestine] (Cairo, 1998), pp. 440–46; ʿAbd al-Munʿim, *Asrar 1948*, pp. 193–94, 196–97, 200, 201, 249; ʿAli, *al-Harb*, pp. 62, 103, 195–96, 228, 410–11, 414–17; ʿAbdullah al-Tall, *Karithat filastin* [The Catastrophe of Palestine] (Cairo, 1959), pp. 21, 27, 35–6, 65–73, 100, 232, 344–45, 432, 437–42, 473–79; ʿArif, *al-Nakba*, vol. I, p. 109 and vol. II, pp. 339–40, 653; Salah al-ʿAqqad, *Qadiyyat filastin: al-marhala al-harija, 1945–1956* [The Palestine Question: The Difficult

Phase] (Cairo, 1968), pp. 61–62; ʿAbd al-Satar, *Karithat al-arab*, pp. 56–57. Hajj Amin al-Husayni also subscribed to this position; see his *Haqaʾiq ʿan qadiyyat filastin* [Truths About the Palestine Question] (Cairo, 1956).

4 ʿAbd al-Munʿim, *Asrar 1948*, pp. 190–96, 688; *Akhir Saʿa* [Cairo daily newspaper], 20 May 1952; Walid Khalidi, "The Arab Perspective," in Wm. Roger Louis and Robert W. Stookey, eds., *The End of the Palestine Mandate* (London, 1986), p. 109; Haykal, *al-ʿUrush*, pp. 48–49.

5 Khalidi, "Arab Perspective," p. 119.

6 *Al-Ahram* [Cairo daily newspaper], 15 December 1947.

7 Kamil Ismaʿil al-Sharif, *al-Ikhwan al-Muslimun fi harb filastin* [The Muslim Brothers in the Palestine War] (Cairo, 1951); ʿAli, *al-Harb*, pp. 142–43; ʿArif, *al-Nakba*, vol. II, pp. 398–99.

8 Muhammad Hasanayn Haykal in *Al-Ahram*, 29 September 1952; *Al-Ahram*, 12 January 1948. Nuqrashi also told Arab League Secretary General ʿAbd al-Rahman ʿAzzam of domestic imperatives; see ʿAzzam's testimony to Haykal, *al-ʿUrush*, pp. 450–51; ʿArif, *al-Nakba*, vol. II, pp. 341, 398; ʿAli, *al-Harb*, pp. 32, 109; Muhammad Hasanayn Haykal, *al-Mufawadat al-siriyya bayna al-ʿarab wa israʾil* [Secret Negotiations between the Arabs and Israel] (Cairo, 1996), p. 248.

9 Ibrahim Shakib, *Harb filastin, 1948, ruʾiya masriyya* [The Palestine War, 1948: An Egyptian Perspective] (Cairo, 1986), pp. 123–24; ʿAbd al-Munʿim, *Asrar 1948*, p. 190.

10 Shakib, *Harb filastin*, p. 116; ʿAli, *al-Harb*, p. 90; ʿArif, *al-Nakba*, vol. II, p. 341; ʿAbd al-Munʿim, *Asrar 1948*, p. 190; al-Sharif, *al-Ikhwan*, p. 47; Haykal, *al-ʿUrush* pp. 49–50, 53.

11 ʿArif, *al-Nakba*, vol. II, pp. 340, 382; ʿAqqad, *Qadiyat filastin*, p. 60; Haykal, *al-ʿUrush*, pp. 47, 72.

12 Muhammad Hussein Heikal, *Mudhakkirat fiʾl-siyasa al-misriyya* [Memoirs in Egyptian Politics] (Cairo, 1978), p. 30; ʿArif, *al-Nakba*, vol. III, pp. 663–64; Khalidi, "Arab Perspective," p. 109. Muhammad Hasanayn Haykal simplifies a great deal by asserting that Faruq's rhetoric and actions represent an ideological, nationalist shift. Haykal, a pan-Arab writer, ascribes too much rationality and agency to the ruling elite in Cairo. Egypt, asserts Haykal, was not just fighting for Palestine and Palestinians but also to avoid being isolated from its natural Arab environment. Haykal simplistically portrays Faruq and his royal men as die-hard nationalists, see his *al-Mufawadat al-siriyya*, pp. 211–14, 272–73; Haykal, *al-ʿUrush*, pp. 25–30, 34–35, 45–7, 75–77; ʿAbd al-Munʿim, *Asrar 1948*, pp. 163, 169, 693; ʿAli, *al-Harb*, p. 33.

13 Muhammad Naguib in *Al-Masaʾ* [Cairo daily newspaper], 2 June 1974.

14 *Al-Ahram*, 3 June 1951; *al-Musawwar* [Cairo weekly magazine], No. 968, 13 May 1953; Haytham al-Kilani, *al-Istratijiyat al-askariyya liʾl-hurub al-ʿarabiyya al-israʾiliyya, 1948–1988* [Military Strategies of the Arab–Israeli Wars, 1948–1988] (Beirut, 1999), p. 127; Shakib, *Harb filastin*, p. 127; ʿAbd al-Munʿim, *Asrar 1948*, pp. 191–93, 345, 688; ʿArif, *al-Nakba*, vol. II, p. 382; ʿAqqad, *Qadiyyat filastin*, p. 59.

15 Khalil Saʿid, *Tarikh al-jaysh al-iraqi fi filastin, 1948–1949* [History of the Iraqi Army in Palestine, 1948–1949] (Baghdad, 1969); ʿAbd al-Munʿim, *Asrar 1948*, pp. 331, 671; ʿArif, *al-Nakba*, vol. III, pp. 655–56.

16 Ahmed Faraj Tayi, *Safahat matwiya 'an filastin* [Forgotten Pages on Palestine] (Cairo, 1967), p. 5.

17 Shakib, *Harb filastin*, p. 127; Heikal, *Mudhakkirat*, p. 3. Heikal, not to be confused with Muhammad Hasanayn Haykal, the seasoned pan-Arab journalist, was chairman of the Egyptian Senate.

18 For the minutes of the parliament and Senate secret meetings, see Haykal, *al-'Urush*, pp. 78–85. Some Arab politicians also believed that "the Zionist gangs" would surrender or run for cover as soon as the Arab armies entered Palestine. King Sa'ud viewed Palestine as a "small village" that was not worth much investment, and, more than once, his Jordanian counterpart King 'Abdullah declared that "the Arab Legion will occupy Jerusalem in 48 hours and march forward toward the head of the snake – Tel Aviv." 'Abd al-Mun'im, *Asrar 1948*, p. 671.

19 *Akhir Sa'a*, 13 May 1953; 'Abd al-Mun'im, *Asrar 1948*, pp. 193, 671; 'Arif, *al-Nakba*, vol. IV, p. 853.

20 Shakib, *Harb filastin*, pp. 124–25; Haykal, *al-'Urush*, p. 48.

21 Gamal 'Abd al-Nasir in *Akhir Sa'a*, 10 March 1965.

22 Musa al-'Alami, *Ibrat filastin* [Lessons from Palestine] (Beirut, 1949), pp. 24–5; Khalidi, "Arab Perspective," p. 108; Kilani, *al-Istratijiyat*, pp. 121–23, 140.

23 Anon., *al-'Amaliyat al-harbiyya bi filastin 'am 1948* [Military Operations in Palestine, 1948] (Cairo, 1961), part 1; *Al-Musawwar*, No. 968, 13 May 1953; Hasan al-Badri, *Al-Harb fi ard al-salam: al-jawla al-'arabiyya al-isra'iliyya, 1947–1949* [War in the Land of Peace: The First Arab–Israeli Round, 1947–1949] (Beirut, 1976), p. 113; Shakib, *Harb filastin*, pp. 126, 156–58, 170–76, 422; 'Abd al-Mun'im, *Asrar 1948*, pp. 235–39, 688–89; 'Ali, *al-Harb*, p. 109; Kilani, *al-Istratijiyat*, pp. 108–09, 132; Steven Green, *Taking Sides: America's Secret Relations with a Militant Israel* (New York, 1984), p. 25; Edgar O'Ballance, *The Arab-Israeli War, 1948* (London, 1956), p. 36; 'Arif, *al-Nakba*, vol. IV, pp. 848–53.

24 *Akhir Sa'a*, 13 May 1953.

25 *Al-Ahram*, 24 March 1953.

26 "Memoirs of President Gamal 'Abd al-Nasir in Palestine," *Akhir Sa'a*, 9 and 10 March 1955.

27 Shakib, *Harb filastin*, pp. 126, 156–58, 170–76, 422; Kilani, *al-Istratijiyat*, p. 108; 'Aqqad, *Qadiyat filastin*, pp. 81, 85.

28 Shakib, *Harb filastin*, pp. 127–28, 132; 'Ali, *al-Harb*, p. 65.

29 For a sample of British documents, see PRO, Sir R. Campbell to Mr. Bevin, 6 July 1948, FO 371/68857; Cairo to Foreign Office, 6 October 1948, FO 371/68642; Cairo to FO, 8 October 1948, FO 371/68642; Cairo to FO, 8 October 1948, FO 371/68642; Cairo to Bevin, 16 October 1998, FO 371/68862; Cairo to FO, 9 November 1948, FO 371/68643; Amman to FO, 14 December 1948, FO 371/68862; Cairo to FO, 16 December 1948, FO 371/68644; Cairo to FO, 18 December 1948, FO 371/68644; Cairo to FO, 16 December 1948, FO 371/68364.

30 See Safwat's reports in *Taqrir lajna al-tahqiq*, pp. 30–33, 123–58. For an English version of Safwat's reports, see Walid Khalidi, "Selected Documents on the 1948 Palestine War," *Journal of Palestine Studies*, 27/3 (1998),

118–22; Khalidi, "Arab Perspective," pp. 121–22; 'Arif, *al-Nakba*, vol. I, pp. 21, 100, 178; Kilani, *al-Istratijiyat*, pp. 112–13, 133; 'Ali, *al-Harb*, p. 36; O'Ballance, *The Arab-Israeli War*, p. 40.

31 'Arif, *al-Nakba*, vol. III, pp. 664–65. See also Haykal, *al-Mufawadat*, p. 249.

32 Shakib, *Harb filastin*, pp. 376–77.

33 Haykal, *al-Mufawadat*, pp. 249–50.

34 'Ali, *al-Harb*, p. 224; 'Abd al-Mun'im, *Asrar 1948*, p. 674; Kilani, *al-Istratijiyat*, p. 117; 'Arif, *al-Nakba*, vol. III, pp. 719–20, 730; 'Aqqad, *Qadiyat filastin*, pp. 64, 72; 'Abd al-Satar, *Karithat al-'arab*, p. 20. David Ben-Gurion sarcastically noted that the composition of Arab armies reflected the social structure of their societies: "Officers were overweight and soldiers too slim." David Ben-Gurion, *Rebirth and Destiny of Israel* (New York, 1954), p. 244. See also 'Arif, *al-Nakba*, vol. IV, pp. 849–50.

35 *Al-Musawwar*, no. 968, 13 May 1953; *Akhir Sa'a*, No. 1063, 9 April 1955; 'Arif, al-Nakba, vol. IV, p. 849.

36 See his lengthy testimony to Haykal, *al-'Urush*, pp. 453–58.

37 Haykal, *al-'Urush*, pp. 104–06.

38 Shakib, *Harb filastin*, p. 161.

39 Haykal, *al-Mufawadat*, pp. 273–74.

40 Shakib, *Harb filastin*, p. 163.

41 *Taqrir lajnat al-tahqiq*, pp. 42, 122–23, 192.

42 'Arif, *al-Nakba*, vol. II, p. 381; 'Ali, *al-Harb*, p. 108.

43 'Abd al-Mun'im, *Asrar 1948*, pp. 685–86; 'Arif, *al-Nakba*, vol. II, p. 386; Kilani, *al-Istratijiyat*, pp. 120, 143–44; 'Aqqad, *Qadiyyat filastin*, pp. 88–89; Haykal, *al-Mufawadat*, p. 274.

44 *Mudhakkirat 'Abd al-Nasir*.

45 Haykal, *al-'Urush*, p. 156; Shakib, *Harb filastin*, pp. 223, 425; 'Abd al-Mun'im, *Asrar 1948*, pp. 350, 352, 677; Kilani, *al-Istratijiyat*, pp. 143, 152–53.

46 See the letter by Riad Sulh, Lebanese prime minister, to his Iraqi counterpart Mazahim al-Pachachi in August 1948 in *Al-Nida'* (Cairo daily newspaper), 31 August 1948; *Taqrir lajnat al-tahqiq*, p. 38; 'Abd al-Mun'im, *Asrar 1948*, pp. 179–89; 'Arif, *al-Nakba*, vol. II, pp. 550–51; 'Aqqad, *Qadiyyat filastin*, pp. 94–95.

47 Shakib, *Harb filastin*, pp. 241–43; 'Abd al-Mun'im, *Asrar 1948*, p. 394; Haykal, *al-'Urush*, pp. 253–54.

48 *Al-Ahram*, 24 March 1953; 'Abd al-Mun'im, *Asrar 1948*, pp. 190–93; 'Ali, *al-Harb*, p. 108; 'Arif, *al-Nakba*, vol. II, p. 341.

49 As a junior officer in the Egyptian army, 'Abd al-Nasir's critical views of how the war was conducted reflected those of most of his comrades. See his *Falsafat al-thawra* and *Mudhakkirat*. See also 'Ali, *al-Harb*, p. 110.

50 Kilani, *al-Istratijiyat*, p. 154.

51 'Arif, *al-Nakba*, vol. III, pp. 718, 743.

52 'Ali, *al-Harb*, pp. 249–50; 'Arif, *al-Nakba*, vol. IV, pp. 850–51. For more details about the debate surrounding these allegations, see the articles by Ihsan 'Abd al-Qudus in *Ruz al-Yusif* (Cairo weekly magazine), 13, 20, and 27 June 1950.

53 Muhammad 'Izzat Darwaza, *al-Qadiyya al-filastiniyya fi mukhtalaf mara-hiliha* [The Palestine Question in all its Facets] (Beirut, 1959), pp. 175–77; Tall, *Karithat filastin*, pp. 203, 277–78; 'Abd al-Mun'im, *Asrar 1948*, p. 439; 'Ali, *al-Harb*, p. 213; 'Arif, *al-Nakba*, vol. III, pp. 566–67.

54 Amitzur Ilan, *The Origins of the Arab–Israeli Arms Race: Arms, Embargo, Military Power and Decision in the 1948 Palestine War* (London, 1996), pp. 221, 234. Benny Morris, "Refabricating 1948," *Journal of Palestine Studies*, 27/2 (Winter 1998), 92–3.

55 Avi Shlaim, *Collusion across the Jordan: King Abdullah, the Zionist Movement, and the Partition of Palestine* (Oxford, 1988), pp. 262–63; 'Abd al-Mun'im, *Asrar 1948*, pp. 200, 443, 450–51, 453–54; Ali, *al-Harb*, p. 411; 'Aqqad, *Qadiyyat filastin*, pp. 96–97; Haykal, *al-'Urush*, pp. 257, 327. Even the Iraqi Parliamentary Commission of Inquiry, which was not unfriendly to Trans-jordan, implies that the two towns were surrendered without a fight. See *Taqrir lajnat al-tahqiq*, pp. 209, 211.

56 'Ali, *al-Harb*, p. 416. However, 'Abdullah blamed Egypt and other Arab governments for the loss of Lydda and Ramla; 'Abdullah ibn al-Husayn, "*al-Takmila,*" [Completion] in 'Umar al-Madani, ed., *al-Athar al-kamila li'l-Malik 'Abdullah ibn al-Husayn* [The Complete works of King 'Abdullah ibn al-Husayn] (Amman, 1979), p. 261; Hazza' al-Majali, *Mudhakkirati* [My Memoirs] (Amman, 1960), pp. 77–79.

57 'Abd al-Mun'im, *Asrar 1948*, pp. 404–05.

58 Shakib, *Harb filastin*, pp. 278–79.

59 Morris, "Refabricating 1948," p. 90.

60 Shakib, *Harb filastin*, p. 430.

61 *Ibid.*, pp. 291–94.

62 Riad al-Sulh's secret memo was published by *Al-Hayat* (Beirut daily newspaper), 16 August 1952. See also PRO, Cairo to FO, 31 August 1948, FO 371/68376; Mamduh al-Rusan, *'Iraq wa qadaya al-sharq al-'arabi al-qawmiyya* [Iraq and the Nationalist Causes of the Arab East] (Beirut, 1979), pp. 268–71; letter from Lebanese Prime Minister Riyad Sulh to Iraqi Prime Minister Mazahim al-Pachachi, 14 August 1948, cited by Qasri, *Harb filastin*, pp. 205–06; Kilani, *al-Istratijiyat*, p. 128; Shakib, *Harb filastin*, p. 291.

63 *Taqrir lajnat al-tahqiq*, p. 42.

64 Kilani, *al-Istratijiyat*, p. 129.

65 Sulayman Musa, *Ayyam la tunsa* [Unforgettable Days] (Amman, 1982), p. 313; Kilani, *al-Istratijiyat*, p. 134; 'Aqqad, *Qadiyat filastin*, p. 96.

66 'Arif, *al-Nakba*, vol. II, pp. 397, 400, 652; vol. III, p. 728; PRO, Sir R. Campbell (Cairo) to Mr. Bevin (FO), 6 July 1948, FO 371/68857.

67 'Ali, *al-Harb*, pp. 236–38; *Awraq hukumat 'umum filastin* [Documents of the All-Palestine Government] (Beirut: PLO Research Center, n.d.). It is also reported that Egypt confiscated an arms shipment sent by Britain to Transjordan. This action poisoned Egyptian–Jordanian relations further. See 'Arif, *al-Nakba*, vol. II, pp. 452, 594; Avi Shlaim, "The Rise and Fall of the All-Palestine Government in Gaza," *Journal of Palestine Studies*, 20/1 (1990), 39–40.

68 Shlaim, "All-Palestine Government," p. 40.

69 ʿArif, *al-Nakba*, vol. III, p. 675.

70 PRO, E 12817, FO 371/68642, n.d..

71 *Taqrir lajnat al-tahqiq*, p. 44; Shakib, *Harb filastin*, p. 309; ʿAqqad, *Qadiyat filastin*, pp. 104–05; Haykal, *al-Mufawadat*, pp. 290–93; Haykal, *al-ʿUrush*, p. 328; Shlaim, "All-Palestine Government," p. 43. The issue of an independent Palestinian government continued to poison relations between Jordan and Egypt long after 1948. See *Madbatat al-jalsa al-ula min dawr al-ijtimaʿ al-ʿadi al-thani ʿashar* [Minutes of the First Meeting of the 12th Ordinary Session of the Arab League Council], 25 March 1950; Minutes of the Second Meeting . . . of the Arab League Council, 27 March 1950; Minutes of the Third Meeting . . . of the Arab League Council], 29 March 1950; Minutes of the Fourth Meeting. . .of the Arab League Council, 1 April 1950; Minutes of the Fifth Meeting . . . of the Arab League Council, 8 April 1950.

72 Shakib, *Harb filastin*, p. 322; Kilani, *al-Istratijiyat*, p. 137; ʿAli, *al-Harb*, pp. 244–45.

73 Shakib, *Harb filastin*, pp. 225–26; ʿArif, *al-Nakba*, vol. III, pp. 749–51; Badri, *al-Harb*, pp. 410–12; Kilani, *al-Istratijiyat*, p. 137.

74 Shakib, *Harb filastin*, pp. 235–42; ʿAbd al-Munʿim, *Asrar 1948*, p. 506; ʿArif, *al-Nakba*, vol. IV, p. 801.

75 Shakib, *Harb filastin*, pp. 364, 374.

76 *Ibid.*, p. 378.

77 *Taqrir lajnat al-tahqiq*, pp. 213–15.

78 Tall, *Karithat filastin*, pp. 243–67; ʿArif, *al-Nakba*, vol. III, pp. 611, 659–60, 744–45; vol. IV, pp. 799, 820–22, 839–40, 890–96; ʿAbd al-Munʿim, *Asrar 1948*, pp. 541–43, 686–87; ʿAqqad, *Qadiyyat filastin*, p. 102; ʿAbd al-Satar, *Karithat filastin*, p. 56; Haykal, *al-Mufawadat*, p. 306. The Iraqi Parliamentary Commission of Enquiry gave a different account from the dominant Arab discourse. The Commission asserted that despite Iraq's repeated attempts to assist besieged Egyptian forces, Cairo did not coordinate its military activities with Baghdad because of political differences with and suspicions of the Hashemites. *Taqrir lajnat al-tahqiq*, pp. 45–46.

79 *Taqrir lajnat al-tahqiq*, pp. 218–20; ʿAbd al-Munʿim, *Asrar 1948*, pp. 574–75; Shakib, *Harb filastin*, p. 348; ʿAli, *Al-Harb*, pp. 252–54; ʿArif, *al-Nakba*, vol. III, pp. 754–57.

80 *Taqrir lajnat al-tahqiq*, pp. 218–20; ʿAbd al-Munʿim, *Asrar 1948*, p. 575; ʿArif, *al-Nakba*, vol. III, pp. 754–57. Some Arab historians maintain that the Jewish leadership knew about the secret findings of this gathering through the Jordanian leadership and the British, who allegedly collaborated with the Jewish Agency. ʿArif, *al-Nakba*, vol. III, p. 756; ʿAli, *al-Harb*, p. 254; Shakib, *Harb filastin*, pp. 249–53.

81 Shakib, *Harb filastin*, pp. 354–57, 382.

82 PRO, Cairo to FO, 29 December 1948, FO 371/69289; Shakib, *Harb filastin*, pp. 400, 407. Desperate to stop Israel's push into Egyptian territory, King Faruq met with the US ambassador and sent an urgent message to President Harry Truman pressing him to intervene personally to halt Israeli advances. Haykal, *al-Mufawadat*, p. 300.

83 'Abd al-Mun'im, *Asrar 1948*, pp. 193–94, 196–97, 694; Haykal, *al-Mu-fawadat*, p. 274.

84 'Arif, *al-Nakba*, vol. III, p. 665.

85 'Abd al-Mun'im, *Asrar 1948*, pp. 694–95; Haykal, *al-'Urush*, pp. 103–04.

86 PRO, Cairo to FO, 20 December 1948, FO 371/68644; FO to Washington, 22 December 1948, FO 371/75344; Sir R. Campbell to FO, 27 December 1948, FO 371/68644; Cairo to FO, 31 December 1948, FO 371/68603.

87 Shakib, *Harb filastin*, p. 16; 'Aqqad, *Qadiyyat filastin*, pp. 112–12; George Kirk, *The Middle East, 1945–1950* (London, 1954), p. 291. 'Arif argues that it was King Faruq who initiated the suppression of the Muslim Brothers because he resented their impressive performance in Palestine and feared that they could challenge his rule after the war; 'Arif, *al-Nakba*, vol. IV, pp. 844–45.

88 'Arif, *al-Nakba*, vol. IV, pp. 845, 913.

89 Shakib, *Harb filastin*, p. 435.

90 'Arif, *al-Nakba*, vol. IV, pp. 851–52.

91 Shakib, *Harb filastin*, pp. 375–76.

Joshua Landis

Recent scholarship on the 1948 War has concentrated on Israeli concerns. Central to revisionist studies of the last two decades has been the importance of the Zionist–Transjordanian alliance that emerged during the 1930s and 1940s.[1] The opening of the Israeli archives has determined this line of inquiry, which presents the balance of power in the region in an entirely new light.[2] The Yishuv, the Jewish community in Palestine, was not David fighting an Arab Goliath, we have learned. In part, this reflected the military balance of power, but it was also due to the political understandings reached among Zionist leaders, King 'Abdullah and the British. We now have a much clearer understanding of how disunited the Arabs were, how little reason the Yishuv had to fear the Arab Legion, and how close the Zionists came to avoiding war with the Arab states altogether.[3] The "new historians" have focused on Israel and Jordan at the expense of the other Arab states, about which we know relatively little. The Arab states, not surprisingly, were also influenced by the Amman–Tel Aviv secret dialogue, and the threat it posed.

For Syria, the danger of King 'Abdullah's dialogue with the Jewish Agency was not so much the likelihood that it would help the Yishuv to become a state, which most believed to be quite small. The real danger was the prospect that it would allow the Hashemites to become the dominant power in the region. From the outset of the war, the primary concern of the Arab states was the inter-Arab conflict.[4] Certainly, all Arab leaders wished they could defeat the Zionists and preserve Palestine for the Arabs – they all made bellicose pronouncements and postured as if it were in their power to defeat the Jews – but they had neither the battle plans nor the ability to do so. From the beginning, the fight was over the balance of power in the region and the future of the Arab world; this was not a war waged to destroy the Jewish state.[5]

That the conflict was an inter-Arab struggle was particularly apparent in Damascus. During the 1948 War in Palestine, President Shukri al-Quwwatli fought to protect his country's independence. In Quwwatli's estimation, Syria faced its greatest threat from King 'Abdullah of

Jordan and not from the Yishuv. After becoming the ruler of Transjordan, King 'Abdullah made no secret of his ambition to unite the central Arab lands of Greater Syria, which included Palestine, Syria, Lebanon, and Jordan. The ultimate object of his desire was a throne in Damascus. King 'Abdullah was determined to transform his small desert kingdom into the dominant state in the Levant. Ever since gaining independence, Syria and Jordan had waged a war of words over the greater Syria issue. Once the French left Syria in 1946, 'Abdullah promoted his project by fomenting rebellion in Syria, encouraging dissent within the Syrian army, and forming alliances with Syria's neighbors. Shukri al-Quwwatli lived in constant fear that King 'Abdullah would exploit the conflict to carry out his Greater Syria project, first by expanding his kingdom over the Arab portions of Palestine and then by striking at Damascus itself. From President Quwwatli's perspective, the war in Palestine offered 'Abdullah the ideal opportunity to bring down Syria's republican regime and to push forward his ambition to reestablish Hashemite rule in Damascus. Each stage of Syrian planning for the war in Palestine makes sense when seen through the lens of President Quwwatli's fear of 'Abdullah and the possibility that he would win British support for his Greater Syria plan.

For Egypt and Saudi Arabia, a greater worry even than the establishment of a small Jewish state on the Mediterranean coast was the fear that Jordan, allied with Israel, Iraq, and Turkey and backed by Great Britain would expand its borders. Such a powerful combination would act as a springboard for Hashemite ambitions in the region and would radically alter the balance of power in the Middle East. Egypt's primary goal was to rid itself of British influence. This ambition could not be realized if the Hashemite plans that would strengthen British influence in the region, were to succeed. King Faruq would be condemned in perpetuity to being subservient to Britain. For King 'Abdul 'Aziz Ibn Sa'ud, the prospect of having a more powerful Hashemite state to Arabia's north was equally objectionable. His kingdom's independence would be jeopardized by Hashemite ambitions to retake the Hijaz. It would force him to rely ever more heavily on the quixotic Arab League and on the protection of Great Britain and the United States.

Syria stood to lose the most from Hashemite expansion. Syria had no great power to protect it; once the French left Syria in 1946, Damascus was a political orphan. Proud though President Quwwatli was of winning Syria's independence from France without signing a humiliating military treaty (as Iraq, Jordan, and Egypt had with Britain), the price of true independence was high. Syria, vulnerable to its Hashemite neighbors because of its independent stand, was forced to cleave to the

Arab League for protection. Syria joined with Egypt and Saudi Arabia to form an anti-Hashemite bloc.

Quwwatli's determination to keep 'Abdullah at bay explains why he embraced the Arab League so warmly and why he insisted on transforming it from a purely political organization into a military alliance that could be deployed as an anti-Hashemite weapon. His fear of Hashemite designs in Palestine explains why he led the way in getting the *Jaysh al-Inqadh*, often translated as the Arab Liberation Army (ALA), up and running on Syrian soil; with the ALA he would be able to establish a claim to Palestine and block 'Abdullah's plan to absorb it. It explains why he pushed Egypt to commit its army to direct combat in Palestine. It also explains why he concurred with King Faruq in rejecting the Bernadotte plan during the summer of 1948. This peace proposal would have prevented total Arab defeat, limited the flight of the Palestinians from their homes, and severely limited the size of the Jewish state. However, it would have gratified 'Abdullah and the British by allowing Jordan to annex the non-Jewish parts of Palestine. The only conclusion one can draw from this information is that each stage of Syrian policy during the Palestine conflict was designed to protect Syrian independence and to thwart 'Abdullah's Greater Syria project. Neither the Jews nor the Palestinians were uppermost in Quwwatli's mind. Syria was his main concern, and his greatest wish was to preserve its independence, for which he had fought his entire life.

The disloyalty and incompetence of the Syrian army

President Quwwatli's obsession with the Hashemites and 'Abdullah's Greater Syria project can only be understood as a product of Syria's internal weaknesses. Had Quwwatli been more certain of his army's competence and loyalty, he would have had little to fear from 'Abdullah. Equally, had Quwwatli enjoyed greater control over the Syrian parliament or had the Syrian people been less divided, he could have ignored the challenge from 'Abdullah.

The army that President Quwwatli inherited from the Mandate was neither disciplined nor loyal. Unable to reform it and unable to trust it, Quwwatli kept it small and divided in order to protect his government from uprisings or military coups. Built by the French, the Syrian army was originally designed to fight Syrian nationalists. Many in its ranks had been recruited during the Mandate from Syria's minority and rural communities because they were the least likely to hold strong nationalist loyalties.[6] Consequently Syria's Sunni nationalist leaders feared it. In 1946, President Quwwatli confessed to one adviser that "ninety percent" of the army officers who had been left by the French had no "nationalist spirit." Though he reassured the troops at independence that they were "sons of this country" and that the nation was "proud of them and had forgotten the past", Quwwatli insisted that his advisers "not trust them."[7] At first, President Quwwatli entertained the idea of forming an additional military body to be named the "Republican Guard" of loyal recruits to protect him and his government.[8] After concluding that such a plan would not work, he decided it was wiser to tear down the "French" army and to build a new force of loyal nationalists from scratch. This was a large undertaking and required the cooperation of a loyal and well-trained cadre of military leaders, which Quwwatli did not have.

Once the French had left Syria in 1946, Quwwatli appointed a forceful and long-time ally, Nabih al-'Azma, to head the Ministry of Defense. No sooner did 'Azma begin to dismiss officers and implement his reforms, however, than a firestorm of protest broke out within the officer ranks. It quickly spread to the parliament, where the opposition took up the cause of the outraged officers and sought to bring down the government.[9] In an attempt to quell discontent, Quwwatli dismissed 'Azma only months after his appointment and halted his reforms. One disaffected Druze officer later recalled how Quwwatli cut the size of the army and lost whatever good will the officers had toward him and his government, writing:

The army had 30,000 effective fighters under the French, but it was slashed to roughly 6,000. It became a dwarf. Only one rule governed the process of dismissal: a policy of opportunism, personal interest, and individual survival. That was the first and greatest reason for the discontent which began to spread and multiply in the ranks of the army against the politicians, who were called "the men of the first rank:" Shukri al-Quwwatli [president], Jamil Mardam [prime minister], Ahmad Sharabati [minister of defense after 'Azma's dismissal], Sabri al-'Asali [minister of the interior], and other specimens of the "human race."[10]

Quwwatli made other attempts to reorganize and equip his army. He beseeched the Americans to send a team of military experts to take charge of rebuilding the army and of equipping and arming it, but without success.[11] He then approached Switzerland and Sweden with requests for a military mission and was again turned down.[12] In early 1947, the US Minister in Damascus reported that Syrian officials continued to ask him about a military mission because the government remained "dissatisfied with the present state of its army, coupled with . . . uneasiness over the irredentist aspirations of King 'Abdullah."[13]

President Quwwatli has often been accused of making no effort to supply his army with weapons, ammunition, and training. This is not entirely true. He did try, but only in the context of a larger training mission. While the army lacked a competent and loyal command structure, Quwwatli refused to entrust it with large quantities of arms. Khalid al-'Azm, Syria's ambassador to France from 1947 through 1948 until he was recalled to replace Jamil Mardam as prime minister in December 1948, insists that it would have been possible to purchase arms from "the Great Powers or from others such as Switzerland and Belgium during the years 1945, 1946, and the beginning of 1947," i.e. before the Western powers imposed their arms embargo on Palestine and the Arab states. Rather than build the Syrian army, 'Azm states, President Quwwatli "contented [himself] with giving ringing speeches and taking cheap popular positions while the army remained without arms or ammunition, without training or organization, and without a unified command of loyal officers."[14]

President Quwwatli had abandoned all hope of producing an effective or loyal army by the first months of 1947. Fearing a coup, he sought to paralyze the army by keeping it badly equipped, badly trained, and divided. He posted the most troublesome elements far from the capital and retained the most incompetent and corrupt officers in the highest ranks in the hope that their avarice and bickering would forestall attempts to organize a coup. When the new minister of defense, Ahmad al-Sharabati, asked the president for permission to dismiss both the chief of staff and his second in command, the one because he was corrupt and ineffective and the other because he loathed the first and frequently contravened orders, Quwwatli refused. "They are better than the others", he insisted to Sharabati.[15] With this command, Quwwatli acknowledged his inability to solve his military problem. He could neither destroy nor reform the army. He feared building it up and yet he did not dare tear it down. Despairing of a solution, he left the army wounded, angry, and distrustful.

To make matters worse, large numbers of Syria's top army officers made contact with King 'Abdullah and his agents in Syria.[16] Much has been written about how junior officers in the Syrian army were influenced by the radical leftist parties, such as the Ba'th, Socialist, and Communist Parties, which were beginning to play a role in Syrian politics at the time.[17] While this is undoubtedly true, none of these parties was an important force in Syrian politics before 1948. Combined, they had been able to get only one deputy elected to parliament in the elections of 1947: Akram al-Hawrani, the leader of the Arab Socialist Party. Though the radical left parties might fish in the troubled waters of the junior officer ranks, they had little appeal for the senior officers in the army. Most senior officers were concerned primarily with securing their positions and were not easily seduced by Marxist rhetoric or romantic nationalism. They looked to King 'Abdullah for support and a plan to end what many viewed as the criminal neglect of Syria's military needs.

Quwwatli's worst fear was that his officers would act as a fifth column for King 'Abdullah. Both the British and US diplomatic archives are riddled with coup warnings during the period. So are Syrian political memoirs and diaries.[18] Hardly a month went by in 1947 without a coup plot coming to light and warnings of imminent trouble being sounded. Most plot warnings were related to King 'Abdullah and what the British called the "Monarchist Movement" in Syria. Syrian officers were reporting that "50 percent to 75 percent of Syria's military forces would support a military putsch and the formation of a Greater Syria."[19] In February 1947, 'Abdullah "held discussions with representatives of his Syrian supporters, at which the feasibility of a joint coup was discussed."[20] Shortly after, 'Abdullah's Syrian supporters began to approach British representatives in Syria to win British approval for their plans. The British Consul in Aleppo reported one such meeting as follows:

Tawfik Bey Gharib, at one time Director of Police at Aleppo and now the leader of the Greater Syria Monarchist Movement in North Syria called upon me on 14th May, 1947 . . . [He] is no inexperienced politician . . . I can only regard as very dangerous his views with regard to the inevitability of a Coup d'Etat . . .

Tawfik Bey gave it as his opinion that the Jebel Druse, Alaouites, the Tribes, the country districts of Aleppo such as Idlib, Kafert Harim, Harim and a number of notables such as Mustafa Bey Barmada and Haj Fateh Marashli were solidly in favour of the Monarchist Movement. Regarding the army in the North, although the rank and file were divided, he had the support of a number of influential officers mentioning Captains Sami Hannoui [leader of Syria's second *coup d'etat*] and Alam ed Din [head of Tribal Control]. A number of other officers he considered were secretly in sympathy but afraid of losing their jobs if they declared themselves at this stage . . .

A monarchist uprising was inescapable sooner or later and he thought that twenty-four hours would suffice to deal with the pro-Republicans' armed resistance.[21]

Such plans for insurrection were common during the early years of Syria's independence. President Quwwatli was well informed about most of them. He built up a large network of spies to keep track of the monarchist movement in Syria and its military sympathizers. Captain Hubba, chief of the Syrian Deuxieme Bureau, "thought any trouble [in Syria] would be British-sponsored", and accordingly dispatched his agents to meet with 'Abdullah and determine which officers were negotiating with him.[22] His agents reported that many of the leading officers were in cahoots with the Jordanian king, including the chief of staff, his second in command, and Colonel Husni al-Za'im, who would later go on to replace General 'Atfi as chief of staff and ultimately overthrow Quwwatli in March 1949.[23] When Quwwatli personally confronted these officers on the subject of their plotting with 'Abdullah in 1947, he was assured that they had met the monarch or his agents as loyal Syrians in order to obtain information. Though they promised they would make no future contact with 'Abdullah, President Quwwatli could never be certain of their loyalty and was haunted by fears of Hashemite conspiracies. As one confidant of the president wrote in his diary:

> Everyone in the know is aware of how suspicions have overtaken the presidential palace to the extent that the President of the Republic has employed an army of spies who paint a picture of the world for him which only further exacerbates his anxieties and delusions. He trembles at the mention of Transjordan, its army and its King. He imagines that 'Abdullah has a secret party here . . .[24]

The monarchist movement acted as a lightning rod for the widespread discontent in the military. Among the broader Syrian population, King 'Abdullah's relentless propaganda campaign, carried out through the local press, acted like a steady rain, nourishing the seeds of divisiveness and distrust which were so plentifully strewn across Syrian soil.

The separatist tendencies of the Druze

At the top of Quwwatli's long list of internal opponents were the Druze, whom he feared would act as the advance guard for 'Abdullah's invasion of Syria. During the last half of 1947 the Druze rose in revolt against Damascus, and their leaders turned to King 'Abdullah and the British for help. The Druze Mountains were strategically situated in the south-eastern corner of Syria on the Jordanian border and close to Palestine. Under the French, the Druze had enjoyed a wide measure of autonomy, a privilege that President Quwwatli insisted had to end. At independence, the integration of the Jabal Druze into the rest of Syria became a crucial test of Quwwatli's ability to unite and centralize Syria. Defense Minister Sharabati admitted that the greatest "trouble point" in Syria was the Jabal Druze.[25] In the 1947 parliamentary elections, Atrash candidates won a sweeping victory in the Jabal Druze but President Quwwatli annulled the regional results to keep the Atrash from ruling. Furthermore, he slashed government subsidies to the region and, worst of all, he tried to stir up civil war among the Druze tribes by subsidizing and arming opponents of the Atrash, a number of lesser tribes that called themselves "the Populars." Unable to use the military to centralize the Druze region, Quwwatli resorted to his usual tactic of trying to divide his opponents.

Quwwatli's Druze strategy was a terrible failure. The Atrash chieftains proved to be more powerful and popular than he realized. They routed the Populars in the closing months of 1947, cut all phone and telegraph lines to Damascus and blocked road connections to the Jabal. What is more, they threatened to keep army vehicles from moving to the Palestine front and promised to assist the British in Palestine in exchange for British support against Damascus. They asked King 'Abdullah to annex the Druze region to Jordan and urged him to march on Damascus to carry forward his Greater Syrian plan.[26] As Syria began to head into war in Palestine at the beginning of 1948, Quwwatli was forced to back down on his Druze policy just as he had backed down earlier in his policy to reform the army. His attempts to patch up relations with the Atrashes during 1948 did not mollify the Druze leaders. They remained embittered and as determined as ever to bring down the president. To this end, they were prepared to act as the beachhead for 'Abdullah's strike on Damascus.

Jordan Encircles Syria

'Adil Arslan, one of the president's inner circle of advisors who represented Syria at the UN during 1948 and who sought to become minister of defense during the war, catalogs the vicissitudes of the President's "obsession" with 'Abdullah in his diary:

The fear of a Greater Syria under the rule of 'Abdullah has become an obsession in the Syrian government . . . The internal situation in Syria is so weak that it strengthens the hopes of the monarchists in convincing Britain of 'Abdullah's view that taking the throne in Syria would be easy . . . Shukri [al-Quwwatli] knows that the Arab tribes are without exception with the Amir, that the Jabal Druze, thanks to the plentiful gifts and titles conferred by the Amir on the Atrash and their likes resolutely opposes him, that the Alawites are enemies of his government, not to mention half the inhabitants of the cities and towns. Therefore, if the British were inclined to turn their back on him, his government would not hold out against a revolution for even a day.[27]

Throughout the war, Quwwatli feared that King 'Abdullah would implement his Greater Syria plan with the help of the Druze and possibly with the encouragement of his military officers. It is fair to say that he feared Jordan more than Israel. King 'Abdullah sounded out the Druze in both Syria and Lebanon about unifying their regions and giving them a large measure of autonomy within a Greater Syria in exchange for their support in helping to create it.[28] 'Adil Arslan was horrified that Quwwatli was concerned about the Jordanian danger more than that from Israel. In July 1948, he wrote in his diary:

Our brother Shukri has been terrified of Greater Syria for a long time. He was always anxious and slept fitfully because he was plagued by nightmares of the Jordanian army sweeping down on Damascus . . . But when the Palestine war came and underscored the Arab need for the Jordanian army and made clear the merits of that army, then suddenly, our friend [Quwwatli] encouraged Hajj Amin al-Husayni to declare the existence of his state in Jerusalem and began to eliminate every Syrian from the field of battle who . . . spoke highly of 'Abdallah's army. Now, on being informed that his policy in Palestine will lead 'Abdallah to make a move in the Jabal Druze, his nightmares have returned.[29]

Arslan, like many Syrians, believed this anti-Hashemite attitude was shortsighted and self-interested. He did not think King 'Abdullah was as bad as did Quwwatli. In May 1948 he wrote:

Shukri Bayk's view of the Palestine problem is wrong because 'Abdullah does not just want to expand his kingdom, whether it is to the East or North. If he can save Jerusalem with his army and participate in destroying Tel Aviv then let him have Palestine . . . The honor of the Arab nation is greater than that of thrones and presidencies.[30]

Arslan realized that Syria was incapable of defending Palestine alone. In his diaries he repeatedly laments Syria's weakness and berates the president for doing nothing to strengthen the army. One typical entry written in September 1947 reads:

Poor Palestine, no matter what I say about defending it my heart remains a seething volcano because I cannot convince anyone of importance in my country or in the rest of the Arab countries that it needs anything more than words . . . Because we have a small and ill-equipped army, we cannot stand up to the Zionist forces if they should suddenly decide to launch a strike at Damascus. We would be reduced to gathering together the bedouin tribes to fight against them.[31]

Arslan believed that because Jordan's army was the only instrument capable of saving Palestine, Syria should defer to King 'Abdullah. Quwwatli believed the opposite. To him, Syria's independence was more important than Palestine, and 'Abdullah was its greatest threat.

Shukri al-Quwwatli had good reason to fear 'Abdullah's Greater Syria plan. Not only was Syria weak, but Jordan's army was the best in the region. Commanded by British officers, the Jordanian Arab Legion was well trained and reliable. The prime minister of Egypt, Nuqrashi Pasha, acknowledged that the Jordanian army was superior to either the Egyptian or Syrian army when he proposed in October 1947 that the Arab League buy the Arab Legion from Jordan to serve as the guardian of Palestine.[32] Just as worrisome to Quwwatli was that Jordan had encircled Syria with a series of alliances. 'Abdullah had signed treaties with both Turkey and Iraq in 1947. From Turkey, 'Abdullah sought support for his Greater Syria plan in exchange for renouncing all Arab claims to the province of Alexandretta, which Turkey had annexed from Syria in 1939. In April, 'Abdullah announced a treaty of "Brotherhood and Alliance" with Iraq. The two Hashemite kingdoms had long sought to form a federation. 'Abdullah was determined to pursue close co-operation between the Hashemite monarchies to ensure the success of his Greater Syria plan. As one American official explained, King 'Abdullah's "vision and goal was a reunited Syria in federation with Iraq." It would be built "on the unity of the Hashemite House and the strong fundamental oneness of national aspirations."[33] Iraq also signed a formal treaty with Turkey. The flurry of Hashemite treaties concluded in 1947 worried President Quwwatli, who saw in them a sinister design on his country. He was not alone in his fears. US Secretary of State George Marshal also suspected that "the treaties reflected high policy moves away from the Arab League by the two Hashemite rulers with or without British approval."[34] The American secretary of state also worried that the Hashemites intended to push forward with the Greater Syria plan.

To Quwwatli, the question of Britain's policy toward the Greater Syria plan was of ultimate importance. He believed that "'Abdullah was the sheep and Britain the shepherd" on matters of high policy. Though Quwwatli badgered British officials on the Greater Syria question, insisting that they denounce it clearly and completely, the British refused to allay Syrian concerns. Instead, they intoned that "Her Majesty's Government's attitude was one of strict neutrality" and that the matter was "exclusively of concern to the peoples and states of the area." These platitudinous formulas only "encouraged 'Abdullah to advocate Greater Syria," Secretary of State Marshall observed.[35] Another factor that suggested that 'Abdullah might be the vehicle Britain would choose to reassert its influence in the Levant was that both Iraq and Egypt had refused to renew their military treaties with Britain, due to public outcry against them. Only Jordan had willingly and eagerly embraced its defense agreements with London.

Syria's alliance with Saudi Arabia and Egypt

Syria's policy toward the Palestine conflict grew directly out of its policy to contain Jordan. In August 1947, Quwwatli launched his attempt to form a military alliance between Syria, Saudi Arabia, and Egypt. The direct catalyst to Quwwatli's drive to form an anti-Hashemite military alliance was a shift in ʿAbdullah's Greater Syria campaign. After pro-Greater Syria candidates put in a lackluster showing in Syria's parliamentary elections, held during the summer of 1947, King ʿAbdullah decided to step up direct intervention into Syria's internal politics. On 4 August, he broadcast an announcement calling for the establishment of "a constituent assembly to decide on measures for the unification of Greater Syria and Iraq."[36] To underline the urgency of his request, ʿAbdullah sent the president of his cabinet to deliver a letter personally to Quwwatli, demanding the establishment of a constituent assembly. A similar letter was dispatched to every Syrian parliamentarian.

ʿAbdullah's actions posed a direct threat to Syria. Quwwatli hastily dispatched his personal secretary and soon-to-be foreign minister, Muhsin al-Barazi, to Saudi Arabia and Egypt to win the support of both countries' monarchs for an anti-Hashemite alliance. Barazi delivered a letter from Quwwatli to King ʿAbd al-ʿAziz Ibn Saʿud asking for a concerted response to ʿAbdullah. Syria would announce that Jordan was a part of Syria and should be absorbed into it as a republic and free from any alliance with a foreign power. Quwwatli asked King ʿAbd al-ʿAziz to make the same announcement on the radio. He also wanted the Saudis to push the tribes of Jordan to revolt. For this purpose, he asked the Saudis to move their troops to the Jordanian border and to announce, along with Syria, that Maʿan and ʿAqaba were Saudi territory, so that they could agitate for their immediate return.[37] The Saudi king agreed to make an announcement on Greater Syria that would be coordinated with Syria's. Furthermore, he stated that all the Jordanian tribes needed to get them moving was money. On the issue of Maʿan and ʿAqaba, however, he claimed that the dispute was being mediated by Britain, adding that the British were Saudi Arabia's friends. He let it be known that he was not prepared to ruin his relations with Britain for the sake of Syria. When pressed by Barazi, ʿAbd al-ʿAziz admitted that he concurred with Quwwatli that the British were behind ʿAbdullah's stepped-up Greater Syria agitation. He explained that he believed "the British wanted revenge" for the Egyptian refusal to sign a treaty with them. In his view, every time Egypt refused to cooperate with Britain, ʿAbdullah and the Hashemites would begin to press their Greater Syria plans, which the Saudis and the Syrians believed were linked to the general British policy in the region. The Saudi monarch insisted that ʿAbdullah's plan was in reality a Zionist-imperialist plot and that this should be exposed in their joint anti-Hashemite propaganda campaign.[38] When asked whether he believed that King ʿAbdullah could actually use the Arab Legion to take Syria and whether he could depend on Glubb Pasha, his British commander, to act on his orders and not Britain's,

King ʿAbd al-ʿAziz refused to answer. Instead he asked Barazi about Syria's internal problems and in particular about whether they could control the Druze. He advised the Syrian government to pay money to the Atrash leaders as they had done in the past in order to keep them compliant. Over the several days of discussion, the Saudis frequently returned to the issue of Syria's internal problems, indicating to Barazi that Syria would have to get its own house in order before it could ask its allies to take risks.

At the end of his talks Barazi declared that Quwwatli wanted to sign a military treaty of mutual defense with Saudi Arabia if the king would agree. ʿAbd al-ʿAziz demurred, saying such a treaty was premature. First, the Egyptians had to sign their agreement with the British, and second, this agreement would have to be negotiated through the Arab League and not as an independent arrangement. "I do not want to give an excuse to our enemies to leave the League," ʿAbd al-ʿAziz declared. When Barazi insisted that the alliance was not directed against the League, but was merely to serve to counter the Iraqi–Jordanian treaty and to demonstrate the unity of purpose between Arabia and Syria, the Saudi monarch replied, "the understanding between us is stronger than any treaty." Furthermore, he explained, Egypt would be angered if it was not included. But if Egypt were included, Britain would believe the alliance to be directed against it so long as the Egyptian problem remained unresolved. Thus Barazi was stymied. ʿAbd al-ʿAziz would not jeopardize his relations with the British for Syria by signing an anti-Hashemite treaty. He suggested to Barazi that he first approach King Faruq with the idea of a treaty.

Barazi traveled to Egypt, where he met with King Faruq on 25 August 1947. Barazi recorded his conversations in Egypt in great detail.[39] As during his conversation with King ʿAbd al-ʿAziz, little mention was made of the Zionists or of the Palestinian problem in his discussions with King Faruq. The conversation revolved entirely around the intentions of King ʿAbdullah and the British and what the other Arab states could do to stop their expansionist plans. Like Ibn Saʿud, king Faruq refused to agree to a military alliance with Syria even though Barazi did his utmost to convince Faruq that ʿAbdullah was willing and able to use force against Syria and would go to any lengths to accomplish his expansionist goals. He reported to Faruq that King ʿAbd al-ʿAziz shared Syria's concern about ʿAbdullah and that he "spent many sleepless nights because of the problem." The Saudi King, he said, "considered the entrance of the Sharifs into Syria a direct threat to his country . . . because they would then turn and attack him."[40] Despite Barazi's entreaties that Faruq sign a military alliance with Syria and

Saudi Arabia, the king explained that he was in the midst of delicate negotiations with the British and could not afford to provoke them at the time. A formal treaty was "premature", he stated. Instead, Syria, Saudi Arabia, Egypt, and Lebanon should work out an "oral" agreement about a political alliance at the next League meeting scheduled to be held in Beirut in October.[41] Faruq agreed with Barazi that "King 'Abdullah, 'Abd al-Ilah and Nuri al-Sa'id were willing instruments carrying out Britain's aims in the Egyptian question, in Palestine, and in the Greater Syria question." He also was convinced that 'Abdullah was working with the Zionists, the Arabs' greatest enemies. Because of this treachery, Faruq insisted, the most important step for Syria to take was to "expose in its public announcements the Zionist-imperialist aspect to 'Abdullah's plans."[42]

That President Quwwatli's Palestine policy was motivated by fear of 'Abdullah was made perfectly clear during Muhsin al-Barazi's second trip to Arabia and Egypt at the beginning of January 1948. Quwwatli hoped that the increased danger in Palestine would secure the success of Barazi's mission to get an anti-Hashemite military treaty signed in January where he had failed in September. Quwwatli also wanted Barazi to persuade both kings to fulfil their Arab League commitments to provide arms and monetary support for the Arab Liberation Army.[43] To Quwwatli's dismay, both Saudi Arabia and Egypt had neglected to fulfil their obligation to meet their commitments to send money and arms to the ALA. Barazi was dispatched to get their help.

To mollify the Saudi king, Barazi began his entreaties by declaring that Shukri al-Quwwatli was the symbol of friendship to the Saudi family. He continued,

Shukri [al-Quwwatli] is the symbol of opposition to the Hashemites and their ambitions. He is the sole guarantor of the stability of the republican order now standing in Syria and he is its protector against the conspiracies of King 'Abdullah and the Hashemites. If he were to fall from his place, God forbid, Syria would face the most mortal danger from the Anglo-Hashemite plots. No one but he can stand in the face of them.[44]

Barazi insisted that 'Abdullah's Greater Syria scheme was "closer than ever to realization if the partition plan should be carried out, because Jordan would get the Arab part." Once that was successful, there would be no stopping 'Abdullah and the British from closing in on Syria. King 'Abd al-'Aziz's son, Prince Sa'ud responded to Barazi's warnings after the king had retired without committing his country to a clear plan of action by explaining, "that is precisely what prompted me to insist on our fulfilling our duty to help Palestine. His Highness the Amir was hesitant, fearing that if we sent aid and arms 'Abdullah might be provoked into carrying out his plans."[45]

Prince Sa'ud reassured Barazi that the time had now come for Arabia, Syria, and Egypt to form a military alliance and that his brother, Prince Faysal, would travel to Egypt to pave the way for an alliance with King Faruq.[46] The Saudis also massed a number of troops on the Jordanian border to make sure their message to 'Abdullah was clear. For his part, King Faruq agreed that "Egypt, the Kingdom of Saudi Arabia, Syria and Lebanon would form a mutual defense bloc" and that he "would warn King 'Abdullah not to sign any form of treaty with the British that would damage his position." On hearing this news, Barazi explained that he could finally relax and rest assured that Syria no longer had to fear the English and Iraqis, who had just agreed to a new treaty.[47] The Anglo-Iraqi treaty, though announced, went unratified in 1948 due to large-scale demonstrations that erupted in Baghdad causing the government to fall.

By the end of January 1948, the Hashemite bloc and the "triangle alliance," as the bloc composed of Egypt, Saudi Arabia, and Syria has been called, took formal shape.[48] The passage of the partition plan was the catalyst for the formalization of these alliances. Syria acted as a whip, driving Egypt and Saudi Arabia to commit themselves to opposing the partition of Palestine. 'Abdullah's plan to avoid war and annex to Jordan the Arab portion of Palestine, where his troops were stationed under British auspices, forced Quwwatli to take the lead in opposing partition because it was a direct threat to Syrian independence. Arab historians have argued that Syria assumed this leading role because of its special heritage as the birthplace and heart of Arab nationalism.[49] This is no doubt true. Parties on both the left and right in Syria led frequent demonstrations demanding war and increased action from Quwwatli and the government. In the spring of 1948, they organized independent units of volunteers, which they sent into Palestine. As Muhsin al-Barazi told an American diplomat in April 1948, the "public's desire for war is irresistible."[50] Quwwatli could ignore public opinion only at his peril. It is easy to forget that Syria was a working democracy at the time and that its parliament, like the public, vociferously demanded that the government go to war in Palestine to keep it Arab.

Only one deputy in Syria's parliament, Farzat Mamlouk, spoke out against going to war in Palestine. He would later spend years in prison for his pro-Iraqi and British sympathies. In his unpublished memoirs Mamlouk describes the mood in the parliament on 27 April 1948, when the proposal to go to war was first debated. Outside the parliament crowds of demonstrators had gathered to chant in favor of war. Mamlouk writes:

Their cries and chants had a profound effect on the deliberations of the chamber, particularly as the deputies were divided into three groups. The first group was composed of those deputies whose nationalist feelings were inflamed just as were the voices of the demonstrators we could hear outside. The second group was composed of "the followers," those who automatically followed whatever the others did in all matters – and how were they going to vote . . .? The last group included the experienced and judicious deputies who were unable to oppose the government on such a weighty matter for fear of the voices they could hear resounding outside. Because of this, debate was restricted to the first group. They proclaimed their views in passionate and fiery speeches without any regard for the evil toward which they were driving the country.

I did not belong to any of these three groups, thank the Lord, because of my conviction that we were completely unprepared to save Palestine. I wanted to save Palestine in deed, not in word – not with slogans, speeches, and demonstrations. This conviction of mine was based on a careful study of the facts which I had collected from my brothers, the volunteers in the Liberation Army and from my friends among the army officers . . .[51]

Farzat Mamlouk was the lone voice of caution in the Syrian parliament. He explained why Syria should delay going to war until its military was prepared and until it had improved relations with its Arab neighbors and Great Britain. He described how weak the Arab position was and how unprepared the Syrian army was, and concluded as follows:

We and the other Arab countries should wait for another round and another occasion when we will be prepared to save beloved Palestine. Otherwise our true condition will be exposed, and the consequences will be terrible.

If we must go to war in compliance with the decision of the Arab Political Committee, then I propose that we must come to an understanding with Britain about entering into the war because the most powerful Arab armies on which we must rely in this war – and they are Egypt, Iraq, and Jordan – are subject to British orders and views. In addition we must settle our affairs with our neighbor Turkey in order to exploit its Islamism and benefit from its well known international influence and power. If we fail to do this, the war will bring only disaster and great evil to the Arab people of Palestine and to all the Arab countries.[52]

No sooner had Mamlouk delivered these words than the voices of the tribal *shaykhs* rang out in unison: "We agree with the words of Farzat." Then a deathly silence descended on the room; this silence was broken only when the vice-president of the chamber, on a sign from the prime minister, announced that the meeting was adjourned until the next day. Prime Minister Mardam took Mamlouk aside as he was leaving the building and insisted on a unanimous vote for war the next day. "If you only knew, my brother, the incredible lengths to which Shukri Bayk and I have had to go in order to convince the Arab countries to enter this war, you wouldn't oppose my request," the prime minister explained; "the public good demands it."[53]

The unanimous vote to send Syria's army into Palestine leaves no doubt that public opinion played an important part in convincing Quwwatli to go to war, but he did little to try to moderate it or educate the public to the realities of Syria's weakness and lack of preparation. All the same, the many memoirs and diaries that have now been published leave no doubt that Quwwatli's main goal in insisting that the Arab League intercede in Palestine was to protect Syria against 'Abdullah's Greater Syria plan.

Syria and the Arab Liberation Army

Syria had several reasons for building the Army of Liberation. President Quwwatli knew that the Syrian Army was not prepared for a major war, and that it was much safer for Syria to try to influence the situation in Palestine by building up a force to be paid for and armed by all the Arab League countries. Egypt was to pay for 42 percent of the costs, Syria and Lebanon 23 percent, Saudi Arabia 20 percent, and Iraq the remaining 15 percent. This would save Syria from exposing its own troops to defeat, which would have left the country exposed to attack from 'Abdullah and possibly Jewish forces. If the volunteer army were defeated, the loss would be born by the Arab League in general and the Palestinians in particular. Also, the ALA could be sent to fight in Palestine well before the British officially withdrew from their mandate on 15 May 1948 without forcing Syria officially to open hostilities against Britain. If the Arab countries failed to commit their armies to fight in Palestine, a possibility which seemed likely as Egypt agreed to participate only four days before the war began on 15 May 1948, the Syrian government would still be active. It would retain leverage in Palestine and be able to tell the Syrian public that it had done more than the other Arab countries to help the Palestinians. Most importantly, however, the ALA was to be used as an instrument to nip 'Abdullah's Greater Syria plan in the bud and to keep him from expanding his state over half of Palestine.

The evolution of President Quwwatli's military objectives in Palestine is recorded in the diaries of Taha al-Hashimi. Hashimi was an Iraqi pan-Arab nationalist and long-time intimate of Quwwatli who was appointed inspector general of the ALA and placed in charge of recruitment and training of the troops at the Qatana headquarters. His office was in the Syrian Ministry of Defense and he met daily with Syria's political and military leaders. Hashimi records that in October 1947, shortly after the

UN Special Committee on Palestine recommended partition as a solution and after Syria had failed to win either Saudi Arabia or Egypt over to the idea of an anti-Hashemite military alliance, Quwwatli explained:

The Greater Syria plan will start from the Arab part of Palestine. Because of this I have ordered the Syrian army to move to the Syrian–Palestinian border. The force which has taken up position there is 2,500 men. Also Lebanon will send 1000 men to its border. As soon as the forces of Iraq and Jordan enter Palestine, we will enter and take al-Nasira and the North.[54]

Quwwatli's strategy in Palestine was always designed to prevent ʿAbdullah's advance in the region and not to thwart the Jewish forces.

The president never doubted that he would need more than the Syrian army to defend his borders. "The real problem is to reform the Syrian army and to solve the problem of its leadership," he admitted in September of 1947.[55] Quwwatli's failure to reform the Syrian army influenced his decisions throughout the war. Until the army could be strengthened, he hoped to keep it out of the fighting. In its stead he would build up the Arab Liberation Army. "It is imperative that we restrict our efforts to the popular movement in Palestine," Quwwatli concluded. "We must strengthen it and organize its affairs as quickly as possible."[56] Prime Minister Jamil Mardam gave a lengthier explanation for why the Syrian army could not be sent into Palestine and why a volunteer army was needed.

Because [the Arab governments are undependable], I have decided . . . on the necessity of strengthening Palestine with arms and men and organizing their affairs and appointing a leader to take charge of their matters. The popular movement in Palestine is responsible for saving the situation, with the help of the Arab governments. This is because I doubt in the unity of the Arab armies and their ability to fight together . . . If the Arab armies, not least of all the Syrian army, are hit with an overwhelming surprise attack by the Jewish Haganah, it would lead to such a loss of reputation that the Arab governments would never be able to recover. The best thing is to leave the work to the Palestinians and to supply them with the help of the Arab governments. Ensuring an effective leadership in Palestine is of paramount importance and needs to be done with the greatest of haste. If the movement is destined to failure, God forbid, then it will be the people of Palestine who fail and not the Arab governments and their armies. So long as the position of the Kings and Amirs is one of caution and plots, this is the only sound policy.[57]

From the start of the conflict, Syria's leaders planned for defeat and sought to contain the damage to which their scanty resources and preparations would subject them. The ALA was meant to forestall the worst consequences of defeat and to protect Syria from the failure of the Arab governments to devise a common plan of battle or set of objectives in Palestine. In particular, President Quwwatli hoped the ALA could be used to block 'Abdullah's Greater Syria plan.

Fawzi al-Qawuqji, the commander in chief of the ALA in Palestine, explains in his memoirs how Quwwatli sought to use the ALA as a shield against 'Abdullah's ambitions and how inter-Arab rivalries had made any cooperation in Palestine impossible. He wrote:

> Perhaps King 'Abdullah was determined to realize his Greater Syria Project by means of Palestine. This possibility more than any other troubled the Syrian Government. And as for Iraq, which would send its army to the field of battle in Palestine by passing through Transjordan, how might it possibly act? Would it aid Jordan in the realization of the project? And as for Abd al Aziz bin Saud . . . he had to be prepared to act when the real intentions [of King 'Abdullah] became clear.
>
> His Excellency President al-Quwwatli one day asked me, "What are the steps that must and can be taken to prevent the occurrence of this grave danger?" I answered that the Army of Liberation in Palestine can prevent that because it will prevent a war between the Arab states. It will enable you to take the precautions that you consider necessary without those precautions influencing the course of the war between us and between the Jews in Palestine. So the president immediately gave the order to send a division of the Syrian army to the Palestinian–Jordanian border, where it remained frozen in place.[58]

Quwwatli's moment of truth

The Arab Liberation Army was hastily assembled. The volunteers came from a broad variety of backgrounds. By the end of January 1948, some 3,800 *mujahids* were receiving rudimentary training at the army base in Qatana and many had already slipped over the frontier into Palestine. Their numbers included 1,100 Iraqis, 700 Palestinians, 100 Egyptians, 40 Jordanians, 40 Yugoslavs, and 1,800 Syrians; many were from the region's ethnic and religious minorities.[59] All had come without arms or training. Most of the officer corps was Syrian, drawn from army volunteers. The Arab League stated that the Liberation Army was to have 16,000 men, but this number was never achieved. It is doubtful that the number of effective soldiers fighting under Qawuqji ever exceeded 5,000; they probably numbered considerably fewer. In mid-April, General Safwat claimed that he had no more than 3,000 volunteers under his command in Palestine.[60] The first units of fighters began to cross the Syrian border into Palestine at the end of January 1948.

By March, Fawzi al-Qawuqji had established his headquarters at Jaba near Nablus and sought to extend his control over northern Palestine and Samaria. It is no coincidence that the vast majority of the ALA units were stationed in the north and in Arab districts that 'Abdullah planned to annex.[61] As Doran explains, "with his headquarters in the northern West Bank, al-Qawuqji stood watch, as it were, against the incorporation of the area into the Jordanian kingdom."[62] Only a few hundred ALA troops were sent to regions, such as Haifa, Jerusalem, or Jaffa-Tel Aviv, which witnessed the most intense fighting, had the densest concentration of Palestinians, and needed help the most. This meant that local militias with little training, minimal command, or almost no ability to coordinate their resistance did most of the fighting and were quickly beaten by Zionist forces.

April was the decisive month of fighting. Beginning with Operation Nachshon, in which the Haganah cleared Palestinian villages on both sides of the Jaffa–Jerusalem road in order to assure access to Jerusalem for Jewish forces, and ending with the fall of Haifa on 22 April, the Arab community in Palestine began to collapse. Quwwatli refused to give the ALA orders to help the ailing cities, which fell under the jurisdiction of commanders who were not subject to his authority. He also refused to sacrifice Syrian arms, ammunition, and artillery which the militias in Palestine all demanded.

On 5 April, 'Abd al-Qadir al-Husayni, the leader of the Palestinian irregulars, the *Jihad Muqaddas*, who were defending the Jerusalem region, came to Damascus to get help. He begged Quwwatli and the members of the Military Committee in charge of the ALA for weapons, artillery, and support. He was refused any assistance because 'Abd al-Qadir was under the command of Hajj Amin al-Husayni, the *mufti* of Jerusalem and head of the Higher Arab Executive, which refused to recognize the Arab League's and Quwwatli's authority over Palestine. As 'Abd al-Qadir stormed out of the meeting to make his way back to the fighting at Qastel, where he would be killed within days, he screamed in a rage at Quwwatli and the Committee: "You're all traitors, and history will record that you lost Palestine."[63] For Quwwatli, retaining control of northern Palestine and protecting Syria's frontier was more important than coming to the defense of Jerusalem. One leading Palestinian officer, who fought with the *mufti*'s forces, concludes that, "the Arab Liberation Army's mission was to wreck the organized resistance of the *Jihad Muqaddas* (the *mufti*'s forces) in which the young men of Palestine enlisted."[64]

Throughout the month of April, Quwwatli and the Syrian command were beset with pleas for help from beleaguered fighters in Palestine who had run out of ammunition and were being routed by Zionist forces. For Quwwatli, the moment of truth came at the end of April, when Syrian officers, in particular Adib Shishakli, who commanded the ALA forces

in the Safad region, requested immediate assistance and supplies from
the Syrian army itself. Quwwatli had to decide whether to reduce the
strength of the Syrian army, or, even worse, to commit the army to
action in order to rescue the position of the ALA in Palestine. He
telegraphed for assistance from Lebanon, Egypt, and Saudi Arabia, but
they could spare nothing. A Syrian envoy to Jordan returned from
Amman with the news that Glubb Pasha insisted that Syria send its
army into Palestine to assist the ALA and that it contribute ammunition
and artillery. For his part, ʿAbdullah answered in riddles, saying "what
will be will be" and "for everything there is a time," and the like.[65] Later
the same day, General Ismaʿil Safwat, the commanding officer of the
Military Committee overseeing the ALA, returned from Amman with
the news that ʿAbdullah wanted to be named commander-in-chief of all
the Arab forces. Taha al-Hashimi records that at this point President
Quwwatli, under intense pressure from the demands of the ALA, King
ʿAbdullah, and his crumbling domestic position, flew into a rage.
Hashimi writes:

The gist of what he said was that King ʿAbdullah wanted to play games and that
the English were goading him on in order to exploit the situation to impose a
treaty on Syria. Our independence is a thorn in their side and they want our
army to be first into battle so that it will be destroyed. When it is, they will
pretend to come to our aid and for that they will exact the price of our
enslavement. The British are preparing the road for ʿAbdullah to spread his
influence across Palestine and Syria. They cannot stand to see Syria independent and, thus, only want us to send our army in to destroy it. Independence has
cost us too much. Never, never will I sacrifice our army which is the only thing
protecting us from ʿAbdullah's influence, etc. That is the snare that I want to
avoid falling into at all costs. I hold the honor of my country very dear. I
sacrificed everything I had in order to win its independence. Syria alone is the
heart and brain of Arabism. Syria is independent and proud of its independence.
We have made a great effort to help Palestine. But I do not want to gamble away
my army if it is the only thing protecting Syria from these games and
conspiracies. If King ʿAbdullah wants to send in his army, let him send it in. I
welcome him. But if he wants Syria to bear the brunt of the Palestinian problem
alone, well that will never happen.[66]

Throughout the spring and summer of 1948 President Quwwatli was
primarily concerned with preventing any serious engagement with
Zionist forces lest Syrian defenses be destroyed and the way left open for
King ʿAbdullah to carry out his plan to conquer Syria.

The inspector general of the ALA, Taha al-Hashimi, records one early
conversation over Syria's larger military plan which makes clear that
Syrian and ALA leaders planned for limited objectives in Palestine.
During the last days of December 1947 as the first ALA troops were

preparing to enter Palestine, General Isma'il Safwat, the commanding officer of the Arab League Military Committee, asked Prime Minister Mardam (also chairman of the Palestine Committee of the Arab League) what the mission of the ALA was: "Was it expected to destroy Zionism in Palestine or just hold Arab positions for some political goal?" Mardam responded that all the ALA had to do was hold on to some northern positions. President Quwwatli, who was prone to dramatic mood shifts and bouts of depression during the war, flew into a rage and contradicted his prime minister. "He said the goal was to destroy the Zionist threat altogether as the governments had been saying, otherwise they would be subject to the mockery and dissatisfaction of the people." Hashimi explains that this was the first that any of Quwwatli's military and political leaders had heard of "this new plan of political objectives"; the group sat dumbfounded, waiting for someone to break the uneasy silence and for the president to regain his composure.[67]

Syria never planned to do more in Palestine than to capture a few northern towns. This was not because the Arab League failed to ask for more.[68] Rather, Syria did not have the military strength to play a significant military role in Palestine. Its political leaders did not trust their officers; they did not believe the other Arab countries would undertake their share of fighting; and, perhaps most importantly, they feared Jordanian plans for a takeover.

The Syrian army in the Palestine War

The Syrian army played a very limited role in the Palestine War. President Quwwatli did not develop a plan to conquer Palestine and he was well aware of his army's limitations. The small number of troops that he deployed at the Palestinian border speaks for his limited goals. In May 1948, just before Syria sent its troops into Palestine, British intelligence estimated that Syria had no more than 4,500 men available to fight in Palestine.[69] Glubb Pasha estimated the number of Syrian troops in Palestine did not exceed 3,000; the CIA estimated that Syria had only 1,000 men deployed in Palestine by late June and another 1,500 men near the border in Syria for a "total of 2,500 effective men."[70] Quwwatli pursued a cautious policy in Palestine.

Syria tasted the first bitter fruits of defeat during its initial thrust into Palestine six days after the beginning of official hostilities on 15 May. Its forces were repulsed at the village of Samakh and the *kibbutzim* Degania A and B in the border region just south of Lake Tiberias. Three hundred Syrian soldiers were killed or wounded, largely by Israeli machine-gunners.[71] In the Syrian press and parliament the reaction to this defeat was immediate. No one hesitated to point the finger at the government and its failure to arm or prepare the military adequately. In response President Quwwatli dismissed both the chief of staff, General 'Atfi, and Defense Minister Ahmad Sharabati. Prime Minister Mardam took over the duties of the Ministry of Defense and Quwwatli elevated Colonel Husni al-Za'im, the head of the Gendarmerie, to become chief of staff.

Despite Syria's initial loss, its forces were able to occupy a thin strip of Palestinian land during the first two months of the war. When the 1923 border of Palestine was drawn by the British, it was demarcated not with Palestine's defense but its water in mind. The boundary was drawn so that all of Lake Tiberias, including a 10-meter wide strip of beach along its northeastern shore, would stay inside Palestine. From Lake Tiberias north to Lake Hula the boundary was drawn between 50 and 400 meters east of the Jordan River, keeping that stream entirely within Palestine. Palestine also received a thin salient of land stretching east between the Syrian and Jordanian border along the Yarmouk River, the Jordan's largest tributary, out to the town of al-Hamma – today's Hamat-Gader. All of this territory east of the Jordan River and Lake Tiberias was indefensible and easily taken by Syrian troops. The Syrian army also managed to cross the river just south of Lake Hula to occupy Kibbutz Mishmar Hayarden and defend it against several Israeli counter-attacks.[72] Syrian forces also established a foothold in the extreme northeastern corner of Palestine, just east of the Jewish settlement of Dan. Thus Syria occupied three distinct enclaves within Palestine/Israel in the northern, central, and southern regions of the 1923 border. In all, these three enclaves as well as the thin strip stretching along the eastern perimeter of the Jordan and Tiberias added up to 66.5 square kilometers of land. It became a part of the demilitarized zone following the 1949 armistice.[73] Other than its two small operations to grab villages across the Jordan River, the Syrian army remained largely inactive during the 1948 war.

The ALA remained in the Galilee until November 1948, when it was driven into Lebanon by Jewish forces that were moved up from the south. The Syrian government persisted in denying assistance to the ALA during the summer of 1948, effectively "condemning them to death," in the words of 'Adil Arslan.[74] Taha al-Hashimi spent much of his energy during the late summer and fall of 1948 trying to dismiss Fawzi al-Qawuqji as commander of the ALA. Qawuqji and many of his officers lost faith in the Arab leaders when they refused to send him arms or deploy their armies to help him. Disaffected, Qawuqji began to operate on his own account and by August 1948 refused to obey orders from Syrian leaders or Taha al-Hashimi. According to Hashimi, Qawuqji began to plot with Syrian and Lebanese officers belonging to Antun Sa'ada's Syrian Social-Nationalist Party among others and with pro-Hashemite officers and King 'Abdullah to overthrow the government in Damascus.[75] Evidently, Qawuqji planned to overthrow the Lebanese government first, then take Syria, and ultimately unite with Jordan and Iraq. As Hashimi explained: "In this way he believes that the movement will result in the unification of the Arab countries and the establishment of a republic. Then he will attack the Jews and push them out of Palestine."[76] The Arab Liberation Army became a great nuisance to President Quwwatli by the end of the war. Furthermore, Qawuqji's plotting reanimated the president's fear of a Greater Syria plan and the disloyalty of his officers.

Conclusion

The Syrian government's overarching goal during the 1948 War was to keep King 'Abdullah from carrying out his plan to unite Greater Syria. President Quwwatli was more concerned with protecting his country from possible Jordanian conquest than he was with assisting the Palestinians or fighting the Zionists. In many respects, it is helpful to view the struggle in Palestine as an inter-Arab conflict, which the Israeli forces ably exploited to conquer Palestine. Though the Arab armies did not openly fight each other, their actions were mutually destructive because they refused to cooperate and willfully stood by as Zionist forces destroyed one Palestinian militia and Arab army after the next. The mutual enmity and distrust of the two Arab blocs – the Hashemite bloc and the Egyptian, Saudi, and Syrian bloc – not to mention the Palestinian forces under the command of Hajj Amin al-Husayni, was greater than their desire to keep Palestine from the Jews. The Arab governments each pursued their own national interests and so were unable to formulate a common plan of battle against the Zionists.

Syria's military policy during the 1948 war was a product of its own political and military weakness. Fearing domestic unrest if it did nothing, and military defeat and possible conquest if it entered the fighting in earnest, Syria contented itself with grabbing a few small towns on the Palestine side of the border to establish a negotiating position and to stand guard against King 'Abdullah's grandiose Greater Syria plan. Because President Quwwatli believed that a peaceful partition of Palestine between Israel and Jordan would bolster King 'Abdullah's power and assist his plan to build Greater Syria, he pursued a policy of war and rejected any peace plan or solution that benefited

Jordan. This explains why Syria was first into the war and last out. Shukri al-Quwwatli believed that in order to stop Jordanian aggrandizement, Syria and the other Arab states had to take control of the Palestine situation by commandeering the Palestinian resistance movement as well as by advocating the entrance of the Arab armies into combat in Palestine. As Fawzi al-Qawuqji wrote, President Quwwatli feared that "King 'Abdullah was determined to realize his Greater Syria Project by means of Palestine. This possibility more than any other troubled the Syrian Government . . . Only after this, very far after this, came the problem of Palestine itself."[77]

Notes

For an elaboration of the arguments made in this chapter, see Joshua Landis and Michael Doran, eds, *The Arab–Israeli War of 1948: Inter-Arab Rivalry and the Making of a Regional State System* (Princeton NJ, forthcoming).

1 The most noted of these works is Avi Shlaim's *Collusion across the Jordan: King Abdullah, the Zionist Movement, and the Partition of Palestine* (Oxford and New York, 1988).

2 Avi Shlaim, "The Debate About 1948," *IJMES* 27 (1995) 287–304.

3 Thomas Mayer, "Arab Unity of Action and the Palestine Question, 1945–48," *Middle East Studies* 22 (1986) 331–49; and his, "Egypt's 1948 Invasion of Palestine," *Middle East Studies* 22 (1986) 20–35.

4 Works that investigate the war from the perspective of Arab actors and share some of the conclusions presented here are: Michael Doran, *Pan-Arabism before Nasser: Egyptian Power Politics and the Palestine Question* (New York, 1999); and Zvi Elpeleg, *The Grand Mufti* (Tel Aviv, 1989). Also see Zvi Elpeleg, "Why Was "Independent Palestine" Never Created in 1948?" *The Jerusalem Quarterly* 50 (1989) 3–22; and Moshe Ma'oz, *Syria and Israel: From War to Peacemaking* (New York, 1995).

5 The growing number of diaries, memoirs, and memoranda written by Arab statesmen of the 1948 period that have now been published make infrequent mention of the threat posed by Israel. Their pages are filled with the jockeying of the Arab states.

6 N. E. Bou-Nacklie, "Les Troupes Spéciales: Religious and Ethnic Recruitment, 1916–1946," *IJMES* 25 (1993) 647.

7 Taha al-Hashimi, *Mudhakkirat Taha al-Hashimi* [The Diaries of Taha al-Hashimi], ed. Khaldun Sati'a al-Husri, vol. II, (Beirut, 1978), p. 101. I would like to thank Michael Doran for bringing this invaluable memoir to my attention.

8 *Ibid.*, p. 102.

9 Khayriyya al-Qasimiyya, *Ra'il al-'arabi al-awal: hayat wa awraq Nabih wa 'Adil al-'Azma* [The First Arab Vanguard: The Lives and Papers of Nabih and 'Adil al-'Azma] (London, 1991), p. 118. Nabih al-'Azma was the defense minister who was dismissed. Further detail on this episode can be found in Farzat Mamlouk, "Asa'a li-l-jaysh [The Mistreatment of the

Army]," unpublished ms, p. 17. I would like to thank Ahmad Mamlouk who gave me access to his father's memoirs and personal papers, which contained this article about the causes of the Za'im coup in March 1949. Farzat Mamlouk was a deputy in parliament throughout this period and a friend of Husni al-Za'im.

10 Fadl Allah Abu Mansur, *A'asir dimashq* [Damascus Storms] (Beirut, 1959), pp. 38–39.

11 America realized that "it might find itself in an embarrassing if not impossible position if the United States should become involved in the Palestine question in a manner displeasing to Syria." Thus, US officials informed President Quwwatli that there were "several rather serious obstacles in the way of furnishing an American military mission," and suggested that he petition Sweden for a military mission. USNA, Acheson, Mathews, and Henderson "Requested American Military Mission to Syria" (8 May 1946), 890D.20 Missions/ 5–846. Also see: USNA, Loy Henderson to Mr. Mathews, "Memorandum: Request for American Military Mission to Syria and Lebanon" (21 December 1945), 890D.20 Mission/ 12–2145; Moose (Damascus) to secretary of state (8 May 1947), 890D.20 Mission/ 5–847; and USNA, George Marshal (secretary of state) to American Legation (Damascus) (14 May 1947), 890.20 Missions/ 5–847.

12 For a full discussion of Syria's attempts to get military assistance before 1948 see Joshua Landis, "Nationalism and the Politics of Za'ama: the Collapse of Republican Syria, 1945–1949" (Ph.D. dissertation, Princeton University, 1997), pp. 227–36.

13 USNA, James Moose (Damascus) to secretary of state (8 May 1947), 890D.20 Mission/ 5–847.

14 Khalid al-'Azm, *Mudhakkirat Khalid al-'Azm* [Memoirs of Khalid al-'Azm] 3 vols. (Beirut, 1972), vol. I, p. 384. 'Azm was sent to France in May 1947 when Jamil Mardam became prime minister. He spent most of his time trying to buy arms from private companies. The first shipment of French arms arrived in Syria during the last month of 1948, after which France became Syria's major arms supplier right up to the Soviet deal brokered by 'Azm in 1956. 'Azm explains that in 1947 two French Jewish cabinet ministers managed to foil every arms purchase he negotiated with French companies during the war. Nevertheless, he maintains that he could have bought arms during his first months in Paris, if only Jamil Mardam had facilitated his efforts (pp. 343–47).

15 Hashimi, *Mudhakkirat*, p. 156.

16 PRO, Kirkbride (Amman) to Howe (14 August 1946), FO 371/ 52902/ E9175, reports that "three envoys of the high command of the Syrian Army . . . were awaiting an opportunity of seeing Glubb in connection with the idea of forming a Greater Syria"; Vaughan-Russell (Aleppo) to Scrivener (19 May 1947), FO 371/ 62125. USNA (Suitland) RG 84/ Box 16/ 1947: 120.7–800, contains many telegrams, from Moose (Damascus) to the secretary of state during March and April 1947, claiming the possibility that an "attempt will be made within a month, more or less, to overthrow present Syrian Government . . . Insurgent movement centered in Syrian Army [12 March 1947]."

17 Patrick Seale, *The Struggle for Syria: A Study of Post-War Arab Politics, 1945–1958* (London, 1965), p. 45. Also see: Colonel Muhammad Safa, *Asrar al-inqilabat fi suriya: tashih li-za'im mu'ali Akram al-Hawrani* [The Secrets of the Syrian Coups: A Correction to the Eminent Leader Akram al-Hawrani] (n.p., n.d.), pp. 52–55.

18 For a full description of the plotting see Landis, "Nationalism and the Politics," pp. 222–44.

19 PRO, "The Greater Syria Movement" (10 January 1948), FO 371/ 61497/ E9137, p. 13; Vaughan-Russell (Aleppo) to Scrivener (19 May 1947), FO 371/ 62125; USNA (Suitland) Moose (Damascus) to secretary of state (15 March 1947), RG 84/ Box 16/ 1947: 120.7–800.

20 PRO, "The Greater Syria Movement" (10 January 1948), FO 371/ 61497/ E9137.

21 PRO, Vaughan-Russell (Aleppo) to Damascus, "Conversation with Tawfik Bey Gharib, leader of the Greater Syria Monarchist movement in North Syria" (19 May 1947) FO371/62125.

22 USNA (Suitland) James Moose (Damascus) to secretary of state (15 March 1947), RG-84, Box 16, 1947, 120.7–800.

23 This story is related by Munir al-Rayyis, who was a close friend of Defense Minister Sharabati. Munir al-Rayyis, *al-Kitab al-dhahabi li'l-thawrat al-wataniyya* [The Golden Book of National Revolts] (Beirut, 1977), pp. 426–430. The essentials of this story are corroborated by Ahmad al-Laham, general secretary of the Ministry of Defense, who claimed that Chief of Staff 'Atfi met personally with 'Abdallah and was the chief organizer of sedition among the top officers; cf. Hashimi, *II.* p. 151.

24 'Adil Arslan, *Mudhakkirat al-'Amir 'Adil Arslan: al-mustadrak 1948* [The Diaries of 'Adil Arslan: The Emendation of 1948], ed. Yussif Ibish (Beirut, 1994), entry of 29 May 1948, p. 115. Hashimi, *Mudhakkirat*, entry of 12 December 1947, p. 189.

25 USNA (Suitland) James Moose (Damascus) to secretary of state (15 March 1947), RG-84, Box 16, 1947, 120.7–800.

26 For a full account of Quwwatli's Jabal Druze problems see Joshua Landis, "Shishakli and the Druzes: Integration and Intransigence," in T. Philipp & B. Schäbler, eds., *The Syrian Land: Processes of Integration and Fragmentation in Bilad al-Sham from the 18th to the 20th Century* (Stuttgart, 1998) pp. 369–395; and chapter 2 of Landis, "Nationalism and the Politics."

27 'Adil Arslan, *Mudhakkirat al-Amir 'Adil Arslan* [The Diaries of *Amir* 'Adil Arslan], ed. Yusif Ibish, vol. II (Beirut, 1983), pp. 578, 661. Ibish published Arslan's diaries in two installments. Three volumes were published in the early 1980s. They excluded all entries for the year 1948, which were published in 1994 because they covered the war in Palestine and were presumably too politically sensitive to publish earlier.

28 Ilan Pappé, "Sir Alec Kirkbride and the Making of Greater Transjordan," *Asian and African Studies*, 23 (1989) p. 49.

29 Arslan, *Mudhakkirat 1948*, pp. 121–22.

30 *Ibid.*, pp. 109–10.

31 Arslan, *Mudhakkirat*, vol. II, entry of 10 September 1947, pp. 800–1.

32 Doran, *Pan-Arabism*, pp. 113–16.

33 *FRUS, 1947, vol.* 5 (Washington DC, 1971) Ambassador Wadsworth (Baghdad) to secretary of state (12 June 1947) fn. p. 749.

34 *Ibid.*, Secretary of State Marshall to Embassy in Iraq (12 June 1947), pp. 748–49.

35 *Ibid.*, Secretary of State Marshall to Legation in Saudi Arabia (26 July 1947), p. 752.

36 Muhsin al-Barazi, *Mudhakkirat Muhsin al-Barazi, 1947–1949* [Memoirs of Muhsin al-Barazi], ed. Khayriyya Qasimiyya, ed. (Beirut, 1994) p. 15.

37 *Ibid.*, pp. 18–19.

38 *Ibid.*, p. 21.

39 *Ibid.*, pp. 44–53.

40 *Ibid.*, p. 46.

41 *Ibid.*, pp. 52–53.

42 *Ibid.*, p. 48.

43 Thomas Mayer, 'Arab Unity of Action," p. 341.

44 Barazi, *Mudhakkirat*, p. 63.

45 *Ibid.*, pp. 65–66. 'Abd al-'Aziz was angry with Quwwatli during this meeting because the Syrian parliament refused to pass a bill allowing for the construction of a US pipeline to carry Saudi oil through Syria. Quwwatli had openly scolded the Saudi king for continuing to do business with the US. The king told Barazi that he did not appreciate being lectured to about nationalism by Quwwatli, especially when Quwwatli was pleading for Saudi help against 'Abdullah. The job of reassuring the Syrians that Saudi Arabia would assist them was left to the Princes Sa'ud and Faysal.

46 *Ibid.*, p. 67.

47 *Ibid.*, p. 70.

48 See Doran, *Pan-Arabism*, p. 6.

49 See, for instance, the introduction by Khayriyya al-Qasimiyya to the Barazi memoirs.

50 USNA, Memminger (Damascus) to secretary of state, "Damascus Demonstrators Demand Syrian Army Intervention in Palestine," (27 April 1948) 890D.00/4–2748.

51 Farzat Mamlouk, *"al-Irtijal fi inqadh filastin"* [The Lack of Preparation in Saving Palestine], unpublished ms., n.d., p. 19. In 1957 Farzat Mamlouk, along with Hasan al-Atrash, 'Adnan al-'Atasi, and many other pro-Hashemite Syrian politicians, was tried and found guilty of treason for conspiring with Iraq to overthrow the pro-Egyptian Syrian government and unify the two countries in 1957. He fled to Lebanon, where he remained until the early 1960s, when he returned to Syria. Following the 1966 coup he was imprisoned in Palmyra, where he remained for several years before being placed under house arrest in Duma, where he spent the last fifteen years of his life writing his memoirs.

52 *Ibid.*, p. 21.

53 *Ibid.*, p. 21.

54 Hashimi, *Mudhakkirat*, pp. 155.

55 *Ibid.*, entry of 22 September 1947, p. 150.

56 *Ibid.*, entry of 23 November 1947, p. 171.

57 *Ibid.*, entry of 15 November 1947, p. 167.

58 Fawzi al-Qawuqji, *Filastin fi mudhakkirat Fawzi al-Qawuqji* [Palestine in the Memoirs of Fawzi al-Qawuqji] vol. II, Khayriyya Qasimiyya, ed. (Beirut, 1975), pp. 135–36. I thank Michael Doran for bringing this passage to my attention.

59 Arslan, *Mudhakkirat 1948*, p. 111. Arslan claims the majority were Druze, Circassian and Ismaili. Over a thousand Assyrians led by their king also volunteered, having traveled down from the Jazira.

60 Haim Levenberg, *The Military Preparations of the Arab Community of Palestine, 1945–1948* (London, 1993), p. 232.

61 *Ibid.*, p. 200.

62 Doran, *Pan-Arabism*, p. 120.

63 Bahjat Abu Gharbiyya, *Fi khidam al-nidal al-'arabi al-filastini: mudhakkirat al-munadil Bahjat Abu Gharbiyya,1916–49* [In the Service of the Arab-Palestinian Struggle: The memoirs of the Freedom Fighter Bahjat Abu Gharbiyya] (Beirut, 1993), as quoted in "Selected Documents on the 1948 Palestine War," annotated by Walid Khalidi in *Journal of Palestine Studies* 27/ 3 (1998) p. 75.

64 Muhammad Fa'iz al-Qasri, *Harb filastin, 'am 1948* [The Palestine War of 1948], vol. II (Damascus, 1962), p. 258.

65 Hashimi, *Mudhakkirat*, entry of 25 April 1948, p. 215.

66 *Ibid.*, p. 217.

67 Hashimi, *Mudhakkirat* entry of 27 December 1947, p. 183.

68 Here the documentary evidence would contradict Ilan Pappé's conclusion that Syria was willing to send a larger force and was prevented only by the Arab League military committee's failure to ask Syria to contribute more troops. *The Making of the Arab–Israeli Conflict, 1947–1951* (London, 1992), p. 106.

69 *FRUS, 1948*, vol. V, part 2, Tuck (ambassador in Egypt) to secretary of state (14 May 1948), p. 991.

70 John Bagot Glubb, *A Soldier with the Arabs* (London, 1957), p. 94; *FRUS, 1948*, vol. V, part 2, "Report by the Central Intelligence Agency", Washington (27 July 1948), p. 1244.

71 Arslan, *Mudhakkirat 1948*, entry of 23 May 1948, p. 111.

72 Ma'oz, *Syria and Israel*, p. 19.

73 Frederic C. Hof, "The Line of June 4, 1967," *Middle East Insight* (September 1999).

74 Arslan, *Mudhakkirat 1948*, entry of 23 May 1948, p. 111.

75 Hashimi, *Mudhakkirat*, p. 234. For further confirmation that Qawuqji was planning a coup see Hani al-Hindi, *Jaysh al-inqadh* (Beirut, 1974) p. 112.

76 *Ibid.*, entry of 21 November 1948, p. 246.

77 Qawuqji, *Filastin*, vol. II, p. 136.

9   Afterword: the consequences of 1948*

Edward W. Said

I might as well begin with my own experience of 1948, and what it meant for many of the people around me. I talk about this at some length in my memoir *Out of Place*.[1] My own immediate family was spared the worst ravages of the catastrophe: we had a house and my father a business in Cairo, so even though we were in Palestine during most of 1947 when we left in December of that year, the wrenching, cataclysmic quality of the collective experience (when 780,000 Palestinians, literally two-thirds of the country's population were driven out by Zionist troops and design) was not one we had to go through. I was 12 at the time so had only a somewhat attenuated and certainly no more than a semi-conscious awareness of what was happening; only this narrow awareness was available to me, but I do distinctly recall some things with special lucidity. One was that every member of my family, on both sides, became a refugee during the period; no one remained in our Palestine, that is, that part of the territory (controlled by the British Mandate) that did not include the West Bank which was annexed to Jordan. Therefore, those of my relatives who lived in Jaffa, Safad, Haifa, and West Jerusalem were suddenly made homeless, in many instances penniless, disoriented, and scarred forever. I saw most of them again after the fall of Palestine but all were greatly reduced in circumstances, their faces stark with worry, ill-health, despair. My extended family lost all its property and residences, and like so many Palestinians of the time bore the travail not so much as a political but as a natural tragedy. This etched itself on my memory with lasting results, mostly because of the faces which I had once remembered as content and at ease, but which were now lined with the cares of exile and homelessness. Many families and individuals had their lives broken, their spirits drained, their composure destroyed forever in the context of seemingly unending, serial dislocation: this was and still is for me of the greatest poignancy. One of my uncles went from Palestine to Alexandria to Cairo to Baghdad to Beirut and now in his 80s lives, a sad, silent man, in Seattle. Neither he nor his immediate family ever fully recovered. This is emblematic of the larger story of loss and dispossession, which continues today.

The second thing I recall was that for the one person in my family who somehow managed to pull herself together in the aftermath of the *nakba*, my paternal aunt, a middle-aged widow with some financial means, Palestine meant service to the unfortunate refugees, many thousands of whom ended up penniless, jobless, destitute, and disoriented in Egypt. She devoted her life to them in the face of government obduracy and sadistic indifference. From her I learned that whereas everyone was willing to pay lip service to the cause, only a very few people were willing to do anything about it. As a Palestinian, therefore, she took it as her lifelong duty to set about helping the refugees – getting their children into schools, cajoling doctors and pharmacists into giving them treatment and medicine, finding the men jobs, and above all, being there for them, a willing, sympathetic and above all selfless presence. Without administrative or financial assistance of any kind, she remains an exemplary figure for me from my early adolescence, a person against whom my own terribly modest efforts are always measured and, alas, always found wanting. The job for us in my lifetime was to be literally unending, and because it derived from a human tragedy so profound, so extraordinary in saturating both the formal as well as the informal life of its people down to the smallest detail, it has been and will continue to need to be recalled, testified to, remedied. For Palestinians, a vast collective feeling of injustice continues to hang over our lives with undiminished weight. If there has been one thing, one particular delinquency committed by the present group of Palestinian leaders for me, it is their supernally gifted power of forgetting: when one of them was asked recently what he felt about Ariel Sharon's accession to Israel's Foreign Ministry, given that he was responsible for the shedding of so much Palestinian blood, this leader said blithely, we are prepared to forget history – and this is a sentiment I neither can share nor, I hasten to add, easily forgive.

One needs to recall by comparison Moshe Dayan's statement in 1969:

We came to this country which was already populated by Arabs, and we are establishing a Hebrew, that is a Jewish state here. In considerable areas of the country [*the total area was about 6 percent – EWS*] we bought the lands from the Arabs. Jewish villages were built in the place of Arab villages, and I do not even know the names of these Arab villages, and I do not blame you, because these geography books no longer exist; not only do the books not exist, the Arab villages are not there either. Nahalal [Dayan's own village] arose in the place of Mahalul, Gevat in the place of Jibta, [Kibbutz] Sarid in the place of Haneifs and Kefar Yehoshua in the place of Tel Shaman. There is not one place built in this country that did not have a former Arab population.[2]

What also strikes me about these early Palestinian reactions is how largely unpolitical they were. For twenty years after 1948 Palestinians were immersed in the problems of everyday life with little time left over for organizing, analyzing, and planning, although there were some attempts to infiltrate Israel, try some military action, write and agitate. With the exception of the kind of work produced in Mohammed Hassanein Haykal's *Ahram* Strategic Institute, Israel to most Arabs and even to Palestinians was a cipher, its language unknown, its society unexplored, its people and the history of their movement largely confined to slogans, catch-all phrases, negation. We saw and experienced its behavior towards us but it took us a long while to understand what we saw or what we experienced.

The overall tendency throughout the Arab world was to think of military solutions to that scarcely imaginable country, with the result that a vast militarization overtook every society almost without exception in the Arab world; coups succeeded each other more or less unceasingly and, worse yet, every advance in the military idea brought an equal and opposite diminution in social, political, and economic democracy. Looking back on it now, the rise to hegemony of Arab nationalism allowed for very little in the way of democratic civil institutions, mainly because the language and concepts of that nationalism itself devoted little attention to the role of democracy in the evolution of those societies. Until now, the presence of a putative danger to the Arab world has engendered a permanent deferral of such things as an open press, or unpoliticized universities, or freedoms to research, travel in, and explore new realms of knowledge. No massive investment was ever made in the quality of education, despite largely successful attempts on the part of the Nasser government in Egypt as well as other Arab governments to lower the rate of illiteracy. It was thought that, given the perpetual state of emergency caused by Israel, such matters, which could only be the result of long-range planning and reflection, were luxuries that were ill-afforded. Instead, arms procurement on a huge scale took the place of genuine human development with negative results that we live with until today. Thirty percent of the world's arms were still bought by Arab countries in 1998–99. Along with the militarization went the wholesale persecution of communities, preeminently but not exclusively the Jewish ones, whose presence in our midst for generations was suddenly thought to be dangerous. I know that there was an active Zionist role in stimulating unrest between the Jews of Iraq, Egypt, and elsewhere on the one hand, and the governments of those Arab countries were scarcely democratic, on the other, but it seems to me to be incontestable that there was a xenophobic enthusiasm officially

decreeing that these and other designated "alien" communities had to
be extracted by force from our midst. Nor was this all. In the name of
military security in countries like Egypt there was a bloody minded,
imponderably wasteful campaign against dissenters, mostly on the left,
but independent-minded people too whose vocation as critics and
skilled men and women was brutally terminated in prisons, by fatal
torture and summary executions. As one looks back at these things in
the context of 1948, it is the immense panorama of waste and cruelty
that stands out as the immediate result of the war itself.

Along with that went a scandalously poor treatment of the refugees
themselves. It is still the case, for example, that the 40,000–50,000
Palestinian refugees resident in Egypt must report to a local police
station every month; vocational, educational, and social opportunities
for them are curtailed, and the general sense of not belonging adheres to
them despite their Arab nationality and language. In Lebanon the
situation is direr still. Almost 400,000 Palestinian refugees have had to
endure not only the massacres of Sabra, Shatila, Tell el Zaatar, Dbaye,
and elsewhere, but have remained confined in hideous quarantine for
almost two generations. They have no legal right to work in at least sixty
occupations, they are not adequately covered by medical insurance, they
cannot travel and return, they are objects of suspicion and dislike. In
part – and I shall return to this later – they have inherited the mantle of
opprobrium draped around them by the PLO's presence (and since
1982 its unlamented absence) there, and thus they remain in the eyes of
many ordinary Lebanese a sort of house enemy to be warded off and/or
punished from time to time. A similar situation in kind, if not in degree,
exists in Syria. As for Jordan, though it was (to its credit) the only
country where Palestinians were given naturalized status, a visible fault
line exists between the disadvantaged majority of that very large
community and the Jordanian establishment for reasons that scarcely
need to be spelled out here. I might add, however, that for most of these
situations where Palestinian refugees exist in large groups within one or
another Arab country – all of them as a direct consequence of 1948 – no
simple, much less elegant or just, solution exists in the foreseeable
future. It is also worth asking why it is that a destiny of confinement and
isolation has been imposed on a people who quite naturally flocked to
neighboring countries when driven out of theirs, countries which
everyone thought would welcome and sustain them. More or less the
opposite took place: no welcome was given them (except in Jordan) –
another unpleasant consequence of the original dispossession in 1948.

This now brings me to a specially significant point, namely the
emergence since 1948 in both Israel and the Arab countries of a new

rhetoric and political culture. For the Arabs this was heralded in such landmark books as Constantine Zurayk's *Ma'nat al-Nakba*,[3] the idea that because of 1948 an entirely unprecedented situation had arisen for which, again, an unprecedented state of alertness and revival was to be necessary. What I find more interesting than the emergence of a new political rhetoric or discourse – with all its formulas, prohibitions, circumlocutions, euphemisms, and sometimes empty blasts – is its total water-tightness (to coin a phrase) with regard to its opposite number. Perhaps it is true to say that this occlusion of the other has its origin in the *irreconcilability of Zionist conquest* with *Palestinian dispossession*, but the developments out of that fundamental antinomy led to a separation between the two on the official level that was never absolutely real even though on a popular level there was a great deal of enthusiasm for it. Thus we now know that Nasser, whose rhetoric was next to none in implacability and determination, was in contact with Israel through various intermediaries, as was Sadat, and of course Mubarak. This was even more true of Jordan's rulers, somewhat less so (but nevertheless the case) with Syria. I am not advancing a simple value judgment here since such disparities between rhetoric and reality are common enough in all politics. But what I am suggesting is that a sort of orthodoxy of hypocrisy developed inside the Arab and Israeli camps that in effect fueled and capitalized the worst aspect of each society. The tendency towards orthodoxy, uncritical repetition of received ideas, fear of innovation, one or more types of double-speak, etc. has had an extremely rich life.

I mean, in the Arab case, that the rhetorical and military hostility toward Israel led to more, not less ignorance about it, and ultimately to the disastrous politico-military performances of the 1960s and 1970s. The cult of the army which implied that there were only military solutions to political problems was so prevalent that it overshadowed the axiom that successful military action had to derive from a motivated, bravely led, and politically integrated and educated force, and this could only issue from a citizens' society. Such a desideratum was never the case in the Arab world, and was rarely practised or articulated. In addition, a nationalist culture was consolidated that encouraged rather than mitigated Arab isolation from the rest of the modern world. Israel was soon perceived not only as a Jewish but as a Western state, and as such was completely rejected even as a suitable intellectual pursuit for those who were interested in finding out about the enemy.

From that premise a number of horrendous mistakes flowed. Among those was the proposition that Israel was not a real society but a makeshift quasi-state; its citizens were there only long enough to be scared into leaving; Israel was a total chimera, a "presumed" or "alleged" entity, not a real state. Propaganda to this effect was crude, uninformed, ineffective. The rhetorical and cultural conflict – a real one – was displaced from the field so to speak to the world stage, and there too with the exception of the Third World, we were routed. We never mastered the art of putting our case against Israel in human terms, no narrative was fashioned, no statistics were marshalled and employed, no spokespersons trained and refined in their work emerged. We never learned to speak one, as opposed to several contradictory languages. Consider the very early days before and after the 1948 debacle when people like Musa al-Alami, Charles Issawi, Walid Khalidi, Albert Hourani, and others like them undertook a campaign to inform the Western world, which is where Israel's main support derived from, about the Palestinian case. Now contrast those early efforts, which were soon dissipated by infighting and jealousy, with the official rhetoric of the Arab League or of any one or combination of Arab countries. These were (and alas continue to be) primitive, badly organized and diffused, insufficiently thought through. In short, embarrassingly clumsy, especially since the human content itself, the Palestinian tragedy, was so potent, and the Zionist argument and plan *vis-à-vis* the Palestinians so outrageous. By impressive contrast, the Israeli system of information was for the most part successful, professional, and in the West, more or less all-conquering. It was buttressed in parts of the world like Africa and Asia with the export of agricultural, technological, and academic expertise, something the Arabs never really got into. That what the Israelis put out was a tissue of ideological half-truths is less important than that as a confection it served the purpose of promoting a cause, an image, and an idea about Israel that both shut out the Arabs and in many ways disgraced them.

Looking back on it now, the rhetorical conflict that derived from and was a consequence of 1948 was amplified well beyond anything like it anywhere else in the world. For part of the time it took on some of the vehemence and prominence of the Cold War which framed it for almost thirty years. What was strange about it is that like the events of 1948 themselves there was no real Palestinian representation at all until 1967, and the subsequent prominence of the PLO. Until then we were simply known as the Arab refugees who fled because their leaders told them to. Even after the research of Erskine Childers and Walid Khalidi utterly disputed the validity of those claims and proved the existence of Plan Dalet thirty-eight years ago, we were not to be believed.[4] Worse yet, those Palestinians who remained in Israel after 1948 acquired a singularly solitary status as Israeli Arabs, shunned by other Arabs, treated by Israeli Jews under a whip by the military administration and, until 1966, by stringent emergency laws applied and assigned to them as non-Jews. The queerness of this rhetorical conflict in comparison say, with the war between American and Japanese propagandists during World War Two as chronicled by John Dower[5] is that Israeli misinformation, like the Zionist movement itself, allowed no room for an indigenous opponent, someone on the ground whose land, society, and history were simply taken from him/her. We were largely invisible, except occasionally as *fedayin* and terrorists or as part of the menacing Arab hordes who wanted to throttle the young Jewish state, as the expression had it.

One of the most unfortunate aspects of this state of affairs is that even the word "peace" acquired a sinister, uncomfortable meaning for the Arabs, at just the time that Israeli publicists used it at every opportunity. We want peace with the Arabs, they would say, and, sure enough, the echo went around that Israel fervently desired peace, while the Arabs – ferocious, vengeful, gratuitously bent on violence – did not. In fact, what was at issue between Israelis and Palestinians was never peace but the possibility for Palestinians of restitution of property, nationhood, identity – all of them blotted out by the new Jewish state. Moreover, it appeared to Palestinians that peace with Israel was a form of exterminism that left us without political existence: it meant accepting as definitive and unappealable the events of 1948, the loss of our society and homeland. So, even more alienated from Israel and everything it stood for, the whole idea of separation between the two peoples acquired a life of its own, though it meant different things for each. Israelis wanted it in order to live in a purely Jewish state, freed from its non-Jewish residents both in memory and in actuality. Palestinians wanted it as a method for getting back to their originary existence as the Arab possessors of Palestine. The logic of separation has operated since 1948 as a persistent motif and has now reached its apogee and its logical conclusion in the hopelessly skewed and unworkable Oslo accords. At only the very rarest of moments did either Palestinians or Israelis try to think their histories and cultures – inextricably linked for better or for worse – together, contrapuntally, in symbiotic, rather than mutually exclusive terms. The sheer distortion in views both of history and of the future that has resulted is breathtaking and requires some example and analysis here.

I don't think that anyone can honestly disagree that since 1948 the Palestinians have been the victims, Israelis the victors. No matter how much one tries to dress up or prettify this rather bleak formulation, its truth shines through the murk just the same. The general argument from Israel and its supporters has been that the Palestinians brought it on themselves: why did they leave? Why did the Arabs declare war? Why did they not accept the 1947 plan of partition? And so on and on. None of this, it should be clear, justifies Israel's subsequent official behavior both toward itself and its Palestinian victims, where a hard cruelty, a dehumanizing attitude, and an almost sadistic severity in putting down the Palestinians has prevailed over all the years. The frequently expressed Israeli and general Jewish feeling, that Israel is in serious peril and that Jews will always be targets of anti-Semitic opportunity, that is buttressed by appeals to the Holocaust, to centuries of Christian anti-Semitism, and to Jewish exile, is a potent and in many ways justifiable sentiment. I have gone on record as saying that *it is* justified for Jews – even for American Jews whose experiences have been nowhere near as traumatic as their European counterparts – to feel the agonies of the Holocaust as their own, even unto the present, but I keep asking myself whether the use of that feeling to keep Palestinians in more or less permanent submission can repeatedly be justified on those grounds alone? And are the official and intemperate (to say the least) harangues about Israeli security justified, given what a miserable lot has been the Palestinians'? Are the huge numbers of soldiers, the obsessive, excessive, measures about terrorism, the endless fencing in, the interrogations, the legal justification of torture for twelve years, the nuclear, biological, and chemical options, the discriminations against Israeli Palestinians, the fear and contempt, the bellicosity – one could go on and on – are all these things not a sort of massive distortion in perception and mode of life, all of them premised on and fueled by the extreme separatist, not to say xenophobic sentiment that Israel must be, must remain at all costs an endangered, isolated, unloved Jewish state? Doesn't one have the impression that the language and discourse of Israel – there are exceptions, of course – generally signify a refusal to engage with the common regional history except on these extreme separatist terms?

Here is Adorno discussing distortions of language in the dominated and the dominating:

The language of the dominant turns against the masters, who misuse it to command, by seeking to command them, and refuses to serve their interests. The language of the subjected, on the other hand, domination alone has stamped, so robbing them further of the justice promised by the unmutilated, autonomous word to all those free enough to pronounce it without rancor. Proletarian language is dictated by hunger. The poor chew words to fill their bellies. From the objective spirit of language they expect the sustenance refused them by society; those whose mouths are full of words have nothing else between their teeth. So they take revenge on language. Being forbidden to love it, they maim the body of language, and so repeat in impotent strength the disfigurement inflicted on them.[6]

The compelling quality of this passage is the imagery of distortion inflicted on language, repeated, reproduced, turning inward, unable to provide sustenance. And so it seems to me has been the interplay since 1948 between the official discourses of Zionism and Palestinian nationalism, the former dominating but in the process twisting language to serve an endless series of misrepresentations which does not serve their interests (Israel is *more* insecure today, less accepted by Arabs, more disliked and resented), the latter using language as a compensatory medium for the unfulfillment of a desperate political self-realization. For years after 1948 the Palestinians are an absence, a desired and willed nonentity in Israeli discourse, on whom various images of absence have been heaped – the nomad, the terrorist, the fellah, the Arab, the fanatic, and so forth. For Palestinians their official discourse has been full of the affirmation of presence, yet a presence mostly dialectically annulled in the terms of power politics and hence affirmed in a language like that of Darwish's poem *Sajjil Ana 'Arabi*[7] – "I am here, take note of me'– or in the ludicrous trappings including honor guard and bagpipes of a head of state allowed himself by Yasir Arafat. Over time it is the distortions that are increased, not the amount of reality in the language.

This is a difficult point to try to express, so let me give it another formulation. The modern history of the struggle for Palestinian self-determination can be regarded as an attempt to set right the distortions in life and language inscribed so traumatically as a consequence of 1948. There has never been any shortage of Palestinian resistance, and while it is true that there have been some advances here and there in Palestinian struggle – the intifada and the invigorations provided by the PLO before 1991 being two of the most notable – the general movement either has been much slower than that of Zionism, or it has been regressive. Where the struggle over land has been concerned there has been a net loss, as Israel through belligerent as well as pacific means has asserted its actual hold on more and more of Palestinian land. I speak here of course of sovereignty, military power, actual settlement. I contrast that with what I shall call Palestinian symptoms of response, such as the multiple rhetorical attempts to assert the existence of a Palestinian state, to bargain with Israel over conditions of Israeli (and not Palestinian) security, and the general untidiness, sloppiness, and carelessness – absence of preparations, maps, files, facts, and figures among Palestinian negotiators in the Oslo process – that have characterized what can only be called a lack of ultimate seriousness in dealing with the real, as opposed to the rhetorical, conditions of dispossession. These, as I said earlier, multiply the distortions stemming from the original condition of loss and dispossession: rather than rectifications they offer additional dislocations and the reproduction of distortions whose widening effects extend the whole range, from war, to increasing numbers of refugees, more property abandoned and taken, more frustration, more anger, more humiliation, and so on. From all this derives the force of Rosemary Sayigh's startlingly appropriate, and even shattering phrase, "too many enemies"[8] – the poignancy is that Palestinians, by a further dialectical transformation, have even become their own enemies through unsuccessful and self-inflicted violence.

For Israel and its supporters – especially its Western liberal supporters – none of this has mattered very much, even though the encomia to Israel and/or a generalized embarrassed silence when Israel has indulged itself in ways normally not permitted any other country have been unrelenting. One of the main consequences of 1948 is an ironic one: as the effects of that highly productive dispossession have increased, so too the tendency has been to overlook their source, to concentrate on pragmatic, realistic, tactical responses to "the problem" in the present. The present peace process is unthinkable without an amnesiac official abandonment, which I deplore, by the Palestinian leaders of what happened to them in 1948 and thereafter. And yet they could not be in the position they are in without that entirely concrete and minutely, intensely lived experience of loss and dispossession for which 1948 is both origin and enduring symbol. So there is an eerie dynamic by which the reliving of our mistakes and disasters comes forward collectively without the force or the lessons or even the recollection of our past. We are perpetually at the starting point, looking for a solution now, even as that "now" itself bears all the marks of our historical diminishment and human suffering.

In both the Israeli and Palestinian cases there is, I think, a constitutive break between the individual and the whole, which is quite striking, especially in so far as the whole is, as Adorno once put it, the false. Zeev Sternhell has shown in his historical analysis of Israel's founding narratives that an idea of the collective overriding every instance of the particular was at the very heart of what he calls Israel's nationalist socialism.[9] The Zionist enterprise he says was one of conquest and redemption of something referred to almost mystically as "the land." Humanly the result was a total subordination of the individual to a corporate self, presumed to be the new Jewish body, a sort of super-collective whole in which the constituent parts were insignificant compared to that whole. Many of the institutions of the state, specially the Histadrut and the land agency, overrode anything that might smack of individualism, or of individual agency since what was always of the utmost importance was the presumed good of the whole. Thus, according to Ben-Gurion, nationhood mattered more than anything else: consequently, frugality of lifestyle, self-sacrifice, pioneer values were the essence of the Israeli mission. Sternhell traces out with more detail than anyone I know what sorts of complications and contradictions were entailed by this vision – how, for example, Histadrut leaders and military men got higher pay than the laborers who were, in the going phrase, conquering the wasteland, even though an ideology of complete egalitarianism (often referred to abroad as "socialism') prevailed. Yet this did not evolve once Israel became an independent state. "The pioneering ideology, with its central principles – the conquest of land, the reformation of the individual, and self-realization – was not an ideology of social change; it was not an ideology that could establish a secular, liberal state and put an end to the war with the Arabs."[10] Nor, it must be added, could it develop a notion of citizenship since it was meant to inform a state of the Jewish people, not of its individual citizens. The project of Zionism therefore was not only this entirely new modern state but, as Sternhell puts it, the very negation of the diaspora.

It would be extremely difficult to find within the parallel Arab dominant ideology or practice of the period after 1948 – whether we look in the annals of Ba'thism, Nasserism, or general Arab nationalism – anything like a concerned attention paid to the notion of citizenship. Quite the contrary, there was if anything a mirror image of Zionist corporatism except that most of the ethnic and religious exclusivity of Jewish nationalism is not there. In its basic form Arab nationalism is inclusive and pluralistic generally, though like Zionism there is a quasi-messianic, quasi-apocalyptic air about the descriptions in its major texts (of Nasserism and Ba'thism) of revival, the new Arab individual, the emergence and birth of the new polity, etc. As I noted earlier, even in the emphasis on Arab unity in Nasserism one feels that a core of human individualism and agency is missing, just as in practice it is simply not part of the national program in a time of emergency. Now the Arab security state already well described by scholars, political scientists, sociologists, and intellectuals, is a nasty or sorry thing in its aggregate, repressive, and monopolistic in its notions of state power, coercive when it comes to issues of collective well-being. But, once again, thunderingly silent on the whole matter of what being a citizen, and what citizenship itself, entails beyond serving the motherland and being willing to sacrifice for the greater good. On the issue of national minorities there are some scraps of thought here and there, but nothing in practice, given the fantastic mosaic of identities, sects, and ethnicities in the Arab world. Most of the scholarly, scientific literature that I have read on the Arab world – the best and most recent of which is critical and highly advanced – speaks about clientelism, bureaucracies, patriarchal hierarchies, notables, and so on, but spends depressingly little time talking about *muwatana* (citizenship) as a key to the sociopolitical and economic morass of recession and de-development that is now taking place. Certainly, accountability is left out of the critical picture more or less totally.

I am not the only one to have said, though, that one of the brightest consequences of 1948 is the emergence of new critical voices, here and there, in the Israeli and Arab worlds (including diasporas) whose vision is both critical and integrative. By that I mean such schools as the Israeli "new historians," their Arab counterparts and, among many of the younger area studies specialists in the West, those whose work is openly revisionist and politically engaged. Perhaps it is now possible to speak of a new cycle opening up in which the dialectic of separation and separatism has reached a sort of point of exhaustion, and a new process might be beginning, glimpsed here and there within the anguished repertoire of communitarianism which by now every reflecting Arab and every Jew somehow feels as the home of last resort. It is of course true and even a truism that the system of states in the region has done what it can do as a consequence of 1948, that is, provide what purports to be a sort of homogenized political space for like people, for Syrians, Jordanians, Israelis, Egyptians and so on. Palestinians have and continue to aspire to a similar consolidation of self-hood with geography, some unity of the nation, now dispersed, with its home territory. Yet the problem of the Other remains, for Zionism, for Palestinian nationalism, for Arab and/or Islamic nationalism. There is, to put it simply, an irreducible, heterogenous presence always to be taken account of which, since and because of 1948, has become intractable, unwishable away, *there*.

How then to look to the future? How to see it, and how to work towards it, if all the schemes either of separatism or exterminism, or of going back either to the Old Testament or the Golden Age of Islam or to the pre-1948 period, simply will not do, will not work? What I want to propose is an attempt to flesh out the emergence of a political and intellectual strategy based on just peace and just coexistence based on equality. This strategy is based on a full consciousness of what 1948 was for Palestinians and for Israelis, the point being that no bowdlerization of the past, no diminishment of its effects can possibly serve any sort of decent future. I want to suggest here the need for a new kind of grouping, one that provides a critique of ideological narratives as well as a form that is compatible with real citizenship and a real democratic politics.

1. We need to think about two histories not separated ideologically, but together, contrapuntally. Neither Palestinian nor Israeli history at this point is a thing in itself, without the other. In so doing we will necessarily come up against the basic irreconcilability between the Zionist claim and Palestinian dispossession. The injustice done to the Palestinians is essential to these two histories, as is also the effect of Western anti-Semitism and the Holocaust.

2. The construction of what Raymond Williams termed an emergent composite identity based on that shared or common history, irreconcilabilities, antinomies and all. What we will then have is an overlapping and necessarily unresolved consciousness of Palestine/Israel through its history, not despite it.

3. A demand for rights and institutions of common citizenship, not of ethnic or religious exclusivity, with its culmination in a unitary state, as well as rethinking the Law of Return and Palestinian return together. Citizenship should be based on the just solidarities of coexistence and the gradual dissolving of ethnic lines.

4. The crucial role of education with special emphasis on Other. This is an extremely long-term project in which the diaspora/exilic and research communities must play a central role. There are now at least two or perhaps more warring research paradigms: to its credit this series of interventions acknowledges the transitional state of research on Israel/Palestine, its precarious, rapidly evolving, and yet fragmentary and uneven character.

Ideally of course the goal is to achieve consensus by scholars and activist intellectuals that a new, synthetic paradigm might slowly emerge which would re-orient the combative and divisive energies we've all had to contend with into more productive and collaborative channels. This cannot occur, I believe, without some basic agreement, a compact or entente whose outlines would have to include regarding the Other's history as valid but incomplete as usually presented, and second, admitting that despite the antinomy these histories can only continue to flow together, not apart, within a broader framework based on the notion of equality for all. This of course is a secular, and by no means a religious, goal and I believe it needs to start life by virtue of entirely secular, not religious or exclusivist, needs. Secularization requires demystification, it requires courage, it requires an irrevocably critical attitude towards self, society, and other. But it also requires a narrative of emancipation and enlightenment for all, not just for one's own community.

For those who challenge all this and call it utopian or unrealistic, my answer is a simple one: show me what else is available today. Show me a scheme for separation that isn't based on abridged memory, continued injustice, unmitigated conflict, apartheid. There just isn't one, hence the value of what I've tried to outline here.

Notes

1 Edward W. Said, *Out of Place* (London, 1999).
2 *Haaretz* [Tel Aviv daily newspaper], 4 April 1969.
3 Constantine Zurayk, *Ma'nat al-Nakba* [The Meaning of the Catastrophe] (Beirut, 1948).
4 Erskine Childers, "The Other Exodus," *The Spectator* (12 May 1961); Walid Khalidi, "Plan Dalet: Master Plan for the Conquest of Palestine," *Middle East Forum* (November 1961), reprinted and extended in *Journal of Palestine Studies* 18 (1988) 4–37.
5 John Dower, *War Without Mercy: Race and Power in the Pacific War* (London, 1986).
6 Theodor Adorno, *Minima Moralia* (New York and London, 1989), p. 102.
7 Mahmoud Darwish, *Poems from Palestine* (Eugene OR, n.d.).
8 Rosemary Sayigh, *Too Many Enemies* (London, 1994).
9 Zeev Sternhell, *The Founding Myths of Israel* (Princeton NJ, 1998).
10 *Ibid.*, p. 46.

Bibliography

'Abd al-Mun'im, Muhammad Faysal, *Asrar 1948* [Secrets of 1948] (Cairo, 1968).

'Abd al-Nasir, Gamal *Falsafat al-thawra* [The Philosophy of the Revolution] (Cairo, n.d.).

Filastin: min aqwal al-ra'is Gamal 'Abd al-Nasir [Palestine: Words of President Gamal 'Abd al-Nasir] (Cairo: n.d.).

Mudhakkirat 'Abd al-Nasir 'an harb filastin 'am 1948 ['Abd al-Nasir's Memoirs of the 1948 Palestine War] (Paris, n.d.).

'Abd al-Satar, Ibrahim, *Karithat al-'arab fi filastin* [The Arab Disaster in Palestine] (n.p., n.d.).

Abdullah, King of Jordan, *My Memoirs Completed: "Al-Takmilah"* (London, 1978).

Abu Gharbiyya, Bahjat, *Fi khidam al-nidal al-'arabi al-filastini: mudhakkirat al-munadil Bahjat Abu Gharbiyya,1916–49* [In the Service of the Arab–Palestinian Struggle: The Memoirs of the Freedom Fighter Bahjat Abu Gharbiyya] (Beirut, 1993).

Abu Lughod, Ibrahim, ed., *The Transformation of Palestine* (Evanston IL, 1971).

Abu Mansur, Fadl Allah, *A'asir dimashq* [Damascus Storms] (Beirut, 1959).

Abu Nuwar, Ma'an, *Fi sabil al-quds* [On the Road to Jerusalem] (Amman, 1968).

Adorno, Theodor, *Minima Moralia* (New York and London, 1989).

Ahmad, Fawzi, *'Abd al-Salam Muhammad 'Arif* (Baghdad, 1989).

'Alami, Musa al-, *Ibrat filastin* [Lessons from Palestine] (Beirut, 1949).

'Ali, Falih Khalid, *Al-Harb al-'arabiyya al-isra'iliyya, 1948–1949, wa ta'sis isra'il* [The Arab–Israeli War, 1948–1949, and the Establishment of Israel] (Beirut, 1982).

'Allush, Naji, *Al-Muqawama al-'arabiyya fi filastin* [The Arab Resistance in Palestine] (Beirut, 1968).

Anon., *Al-'Amaliyat al-harbiyya bi filastin 'am 1948* [Military Operations in Palestine, 1948] (Cairo, 1961).

'Aqqad, Salah al-, *Qadiyyat filastin: al-marhala al-harija, 1945–1956* [The Palestine Question: The Difficult Phase] (Cairo, 1968)

'Arif, 'Arif al-, *Al-Nakba* [The Catastrophe], 5 vols. (Beirut, 1956–61).

Arslan, 'Adil, *Mudhakkirat al-amir 'Adil Arslan: al-mustadrak 1948* [The Diaries of 'Adil Arslan: the Emendation of 1948], ed. Yussif Ibish, 3 vols. (Beirut, 1994).

'Azm, Khalid al-, *Mudhakkirat Khalid al-'Azm* [Memoirs of Khalid al-'Azm] (Beirut, 1972).

Badri, Hasan al-, *Al-Harb fi ard al-salam: al-jawla al-'arabiyya al-isra'iliyya, 1947–1949* [War in the Land of Peace: The First Arab–Israeli Round, 1947–1949] (Beirut, 1976).

Al-Ta'awun al-'askari al-'arabi [Arab Military Cooperation] (Riyad, 1982).

Bakhit, Muhammad Adnan al-, Hind Abu al-Sha'ir, and Nawfan Raja al-Suwariyya, eds., *Al-Watha'iq al-hashimiyya: awraq 'Abdullah bin al-Husayn* [The Hashemite Documents: The Papers of 'Abdullah bin al-Husayn], vol. v, *Palestine 1948* (Amman, 1995).

Barazi, Muhsin al-, *Mudhakkirat Muhsin al-Barazi, 1947–1949* [Memoirs of Muhsin al-Barazi], Khayriyya Qasimiyya, ed. (Beirut, 1994).

Bar-Joseph, Uri, *The Best of Enemies: Israel and Transjordan in the War of 1948* (London, 1987).

Bashir, Sulayman, *Judhur al-wisaya al-urduniyya* [The Roots of the Jordanian Trusteeship] (Jerusalem, 1980).

Batatu, Hanna, *The Old Social Classes and the Revolutionary Movements of Iraq* (Princeton NJ, 1982).

Bauer, Yehuda, *History of the Holocaust* (New York, 1982).

Ben-Gurion, David, *Yoman ha-milhama* [War Diary: The War of Independence, 1948–1949], 3 vols., Gershon Rivlin and Elhanan Orren, eds. (Tel Aviv, 1982).

Rebirth and Destiny of Israel (New York, 1954).

Benjamin of Tudela, *Sefer hamassa'ot* [The Itinerary], ed., M. N. Adler (London, 1907).

Ben Tzvi, Itzhak, "The Druze Community in Israel," *Israel Exploration Journal* 4/2 (1954) 65–76.

Bernadotte, Folke, *To Jerusalem*, tr. Joan Bulman (London, 1951).

Blanc, Haim, "Druze Particularism: Modern aspects of an Old Problem," *Middle Eastern Affairs* 3/11 (1952) 315–21.

Bou-Nacklie, N. E., "Les Troupes Spéciales: Religious and Ethnic Recruitment, 1916–1946," *IJMES* 25 (1993) 645–60.

Budayri, Hind Amin al-, *Ard filastin: bayna maza'im al-sihyuniyya wa haqa'iq al-tarikh* [The Land of Palestine: Between the Claims of Zionism and the Facts of History] (Cairo, 1998).

Burke III, Edmund, ed., *Struggle and Survival in the Modern Middle East* (Berkeley CA, 1993).

Collins, Larry and Dominique Lapierre, *O Jerusalem* (New York, 1972).

Dabbagh, Mustafa Murad, *Biladuna filastin* [Palestine, Our Country], 10 vols. (Beirut, 1965–76).

Danin, Robert, "The Rise and Fall of Arms Control in the Middle East, 1947–1955: Great Power Consultation, Coordination, and Competition" (D.Phil. thesis, University of Oxford, 1999).

Darwaza, Muhammad 'Izzat, *al-Qadiyya al-filastiniyya fi mukhtalaf marahiliha* [The Palestine Question in All its Facets] (Beirut, 1959).

Doran, Michael, *Pan-Arabism before Nasser: Egyptian Power Politics and the Palestine Question* (New York, 1999).

Doumani, Beshara, *Rediscovering Palestine: The Merchants and Peasants of Jabal Nablus, 1700–1900* (Berkeley CA, 1995).

Dower, John, *War Without Mercy: Race and Power in the Pacific War* (London, 1986).

Dunkelman, Ben, *Dual Allegiance: An Autobiography* (New York, 1976).

Eisenberg, Laura, *My Enemy's Enemy: Lebanon in the Early Zionist Imagination, 1900–1948* (Detroit MI, 1994).

Elliot, Matthew, *"Independent Iraq": The Monarchy and British Influence, 1941–1958* (London, 1996).

Elpeleg, Zvi, *The Grand Mufti* (Tel Aviv, 1989).

  The Grand Mufti: Hajj Amin al-Hussaini, Founder of the Palestinian National Movement (London, 1993).

  "Why Was 'Independent Palestine' Never Created in 1948?" *The Jerusalem Quarterly* 50 (1989) 3–22.

Eppel, Michael, *The Palestine Conflict in the History of Modern Iraq* (London, 1984).

Epstein, Eliahu, "The Druse people – Druse community in Palestine – Traditional friendship to the Jews," *Palestine Near East and Economic Magazine* 29 (1939) 162–67.

Eshel, Tzadok, *Hativat Carmeli beMilhemet haKomemiut* [*The Carmeli Brigade in the War of Independence*] (Tel Aviv, 1973).

Falah, Salman, "A History of the Druse Settlements in Palestine during the Ottoman Period," in Moshe Maoz (ed.), *Studies on Palestine during the Ottoman Period* (Jerusalem, 1975), pp. 31–48.

Faraj, Raja Sa'id, *Duruz filastin fi fatrat al-intidab al-britani* [*The Druze of Palestine in the Period of the British Mandate*] (Daliyat al-Karmil, 1991).

Finkelstein, Norman, *Image and Reality of the Israel–Palestine Conflict* (London, 1995).

  "Myths, Old and New," *Journal of Palestine Studies* 21/1 (1991) 66–89.

Firro, Kais, *A History of the Druzes* (Leiden, 1992).

  The Druzes in the Jewish State (Leiden, 1999).

Flapan, Simha, *The Birth of Israel: Myths and Realities* (New York, 1987).

Gat, Moshe, *The Jewish Exodus from Iraq, 1948–1951* (London, 1996).

Gelber, Yoav, "Druze and Jews in the War of 1948," *Middle Eastern Studies* 31 (1995) 446–60.

  Jewish–Transjordanian Relations, 1921–1948 (London, 1997).

Ghuri, Amin al-, *Al-Mu'amara al-kubra wa ightiyal filastin* [The Great Conspiracy and the Assassination of Palestine] (Cairo, 1955).

Glubb, John Bagot, *A Soldier with the Arabs* (London, 1957).

Green, Steven, *Taking Sides: America's Secret Relations with a Militant Israel* (New York, 1984).

Haim, Sylvia G., ed., *Arab Nationalism: An Anthology* (Berkeley CA, 1962).

Harkabi, Yehoshafat, *Arab Attitudes to Israel* (Jerusalem, 1972).

Hasani, 'Abd al-Razzaq al-, *Tarikh al-wizarat al-'iraqiyya* [History of the Iraqi Cabinets] (Beirut, 1982).

Hashimi, Taha al-, *Mudhakkirat Taha al-Hashimi* [The Diaries of Taha al-Hashimi], Khaldun Sati'a al-Husri, ed. (Beirut, 1978).

Haykal, Muhammad Hasanayn, *Al-Mufawadat al-siriyya bayna al-'arab wa isra'il* [Secret Negotiations between the Arabs and Israel] (Cairo, 1996).

Al-ʿUrush waʾl-juyush: kadhalik infajara al-siraʿa fi filastin [Thrones and Armies: Thus Erupted the Struggle in Palestine] (Cairo, 1998).

Heikal, Muhammed Hussein, *Mudhakkirat fiʾl-siyasa al-misriyya* [Memoirs in Egyptian Politics] (Cairo, 1978).

Hindi, Hani al-, *Jaysh al-inqadh* [The Liberation Army] (Beirut, 1974).

Hitti, Philip K., *The Origins of the Druze People and Religion, with Extracts from the Sacred Writings* (New York, 1928).

Hobsbawm, E. J., *Nations and Nationalism since 1780: Programme, Myth, Reality* (Cambridge, 1990).

Hobsbawm, Eric and Terence Ranger, eds., *The Invention of Tradition* (Cambridge, 1984).

Hof, Frederic C., "The Line of June 4, 1967," *Middle East Insight* (September 1999).

Hourani, Albert, "Ottoman Reform and the Politics of Notables," in W. Polk and R. Chambers, eds., *Beginnings of Modernization in the Middle East: The Nineteenth Century* (Chicago IL, 1968), pp. 41–68.

Hurewitz, J. C., ed., *The Middle East and North Africa in World Politics: A Documentary Record*, 2 vols. (New Haven CT, 1975–79).

Husayni, Muhammad Amin al-, *Haqaʾiq ʿan qadiyyat filastin* [Facts about the Palestine Question] (Cairo, 1956).

Ilan, Amitzur, *The Origins of the Arab–Israeli Arms Race: Arms, Embargo, Military Power and Decision in the 1948 Palestine War* (Basingstoke, 1996).

Iraq, Government of, *Taqrir lajnat al-tahqiq al-niyabiyya fi qadiyyat filastin* [Report of the Parliamentary Committee of Enquiry into the Palestine Question] (Baghdad, 1949).

Israel, State of, *Political and Diplomatic Documents, December 1947–May 1948* (Jerusalem, 1979).

Jubury, Salih Saʾib al-, *Mihnat filastin wa asraruha al-siyasiyya waʾl-ʿaskariyya* [The Palestine Disaster and its Political and Military Secrets] (Beirut, 1970).

Kanafani, Ghassan, *Thawrat 1936–39 fi filastin: khalfiyyat wa tafasil wa tahlil* [The Revolt of 1936–39 in Palestine: Background, Details and Analysis] (Beirut, 1974).

Karsh, Ephraim, *Fabricating Israeli History: The "New Historians"* (London, 1997).

Kayyali, A. W., *Palestine: A Modern History* (London, 1978).

Kedourie, Elie, *Arabic Political Memoirs and Other Studies* (London, 1974).

"The Break Between Muslims and Jews in Iraq," in M. R. Cohen and A. R. Udovitch, eds., *Jews Among Arabs: Contacts and Boundaries* (Princeton NJ, 1989), pp. 21–63.

Khalaf, Issa, *Politics in Palestine: Arab Factionalism and Social Disintegration, 1939–1948* (Albany NY, 1991).

Khalidi, Rashid, *Palestinian Identity: The Construction of Modern National Consciousness* (New York, 1997).

Khalidi, Walid al-, ed., *All That Remains: The Palestinian Villages Occupied and Depopulated by Israel in 1948* (Washington DC, 1992).

Dayr Yasin (Beirut, 1998).

From Haven to Conquest: Readings in Zionism and the Palestine Problem Until 1948 (Beirut, 1971).

Khamsun ʿaman ʿala harb 1948, ula al-hurub al-sihyuniyya al-ʿarabiyya [Fifty Years since the 1948 War, the First of the Arab–Zionist wars] (Beirut, 1998).

Khamsun ʿaman ʿala taqsim filastin, 1947–1997 [Fifty Years Since the Partition of Palestine] (Beirut, 1998).

"Plan Dalet: Master Plan for the Conquest of Palestine," *Journal of Palestine Studies* 18/1 (1988) 4–37.

"Selected Documents on the 1948 Palestine War," *Journal of Palestine Studies* 27/3 (1998) 60–105.

Al-Sihyuniyya fi miʾat ʿam, 1897–1997 [A Century of Zionism] (Beirut, 1998).

Khuri, Yusif, *Al-Mashariʿ al-wuhdawiyya al-arabiyya, 1913–1989* [The Arab Nationalist Projects] (Beirut, 1988).

Kilani, Haytham al-, *Al-Istratijiyat al-ʿaskariyya liʾl-hurub al-ʿarabiyya al-israʾiliyya, 1948–1988* [Military Strategies of the Arab–Israeli Wars, 1948–1988] (Beirut, 1999).

Kirk, George, *The Middle East, 1945–1950* (London, 1954).

Kohlberg, Etan, "Some Imami-Shiʿi views on Taqiyya," *Journal of the American Oriental Society*, 95 (1975) 395–402.

Koren, David, *Kesher Neʾeman* [Steadfast Alliance] (Tel Aviv, 1991).

Kubba, Muhammad Mahdi, *Mudhakkirati* [My Memoirs] (Beirut, 1965).

Kurzman, Dan, *Genesis 1948: The First Arab–Israeli War* (London, 1972).

Landis, Joshua, "Nationalism and the Politics of Zaʿama: The Collapse of Republican Syria, 1945–1949" (Ph.D. dissertation, Princeton University, 1997).

"Shishakli and the Druzes: Integration and Intransigence," in T. Philipp and B. Schäbler, eds., *The Syrian Land: Processes of Integration and Fragmentation in Bilad al-Sham from the 18th to the 20th Century* (Stuttgart, 1998), pp. 369–95.

Layish, Aharon, "Taqiyya among the Druzes," *Asian and African Studies* 19/13 (1985) 245–281.

Lesch, Ann Mosely, *Arab Politics in Palestine, 1917–1939: The Frustration of a Nationalist Movement* (Ithaca NY, 1979).

Levenberg, Haim, *The Military Preparations of the Arab Community of Palestine, 1945–1948* (London, 1993).

Lockman, Zachary, *Comrades and Enemies: Arab and Jewish Workers in Palestine, 1906–1948* (Berkeley CA, 1996).

Lorch, Netanel, "A Comparative History of the Arab–Israeli Conflict," *Revue Internationale d'Histoire Militaire* 42 (1979) 148–62.

Lustick, Ian, "Israeli History: Who is Fabricating What?" in *Survival* 39 (1997) 156–66.

McCarthy, Justin, *The Population of Palestine: Population Statistics of the Late Ottoman Period and the Mandate* (New York, 1990).

McDowall, David, *A Modern History of the Kurds* (London, 1996).

Madi, Munib al- and Sulayman Musa, *Tarikh al-urdunn fiʾl-qarn al-ʿishrin* [The History of Jordan in the Twentieth Century] (Amman, 1959).

Majali, Hazzaʿ al-, *Mudhakkirati* [My Memoirs] (Amman, 1960).

Maʿoz, Moshe, *Syria and Israel: From War to Peacemaking* (New York, 1995).

Marlowe, John, *Rebellion in Palestine* (London, 1946).

Masalha, Nur, "A Critique of Benny Morris," *Journal of Palestine Studies* 21/1 (1991) 90–97.

Expulsion of the Palestinians: the Concept of "Transfer" in Zionist Political Thought, 1882–1948 (Washington DC, 1992).

Mattar, Philip, *The Mufti of Jerusalem: al-Hajj Amin al-Husayni and the Palestinian National Movement* (New York, 1988).

Matthews, Weldon, "The Arab Istiqlal Party in Palestine, 1927–1934" (Ph.D. dissertation, University of Chicago, 1998).

Mayer, Thomas, "Arab Unity of Action and the Palestine Question, 1945–48," *Middle East Studies* 22 (1986) 331–49.

"Egypt's 1948 Invasion of Palestine," *Middle East Studies* 22 (1986) 20–35.

Meir, Golda, *My Life* (London, 1975).

Morris, Benny, *1948 and After: Israel and the Palestinians* (Oxford, 1994).

"A New look at Central Zionist Documents," *Alpayim* 12 (1996) 93–103.

"Operation Hiram Revisited: A Correction," *Journal of Palestine Studies* 28/2 (1999) 68–76.

"Refabricating 1948," *Journal of Palestine Studies* 27/2 (Winter 1998).

"Response to Finkelstein and Masalha," *Journal of Palestine Studies*, 21/1 (1991) 98–114.

The Birth of the Palestinian Refugee Problem, 1947–1949 (Cambridge, 1988).

Musa, Sulayman, *Ayyam la tunsa* [Unforgettable Days] (Amman, 1982, 2nd ed. 1997).

Mustafa, Hasan, *Al-Taʿawun al-ʿaskari al-ʿarabi* [Arab Military Cooperation] (Beirut, 1964).

Nashashibi, Nasser Eddin, *Jerusalem's Other Voice: Ragheb Nashashibi and Moderation in Palestinian Politics, 1920–1948* (Exeter, 1990).

Nathan, Robert, Oscar Gass, and Daniel Creamer, *Palestine: Problem and Promise, An Economic Study* (Washington DC, 1946).

Nazzal, Nafez, *The Palestinian Exodus from the Galilee, 1948* (Beirut, 1978).

Nevo, Joseph, *King ʿAbdullah and Palestine: A Territorial Ambition* (London, 1996).

O'Ballance, Edgar, *The Arab–Israeli War, 1948* (London, 1956).

Palestine Liberation Organisation Research Office, *Awraq hukumat ʿumum filastin* [Documents of the All-Palestine Government] (Beirut, n.d.).

Palumbo, Michael, *The Palestinian Catastrophe* (London, 1987).

Pappé, Ilan, *Britain and the Arab–Israeli Conflict, 1948–51* (London, 1988).

The Making of the Arab–Israeli Conflict, 1947–1951 (London, 1992).

"Sir Alec Kirkbride and the Making of Greater Transjordan," *Asian and African Studies* 23 (1989) 43–70.

Parsons, Laila, *The Druze between Palestine and Israel, 1947–1949* (London, 2000).

"The Druze, the Jews and the Creation of a Shared History," Ron Nettler and Suha Taji-Farouki, eds., *Muslim-Jewish Encounters: Intellectual Traditions and Modern Politics* (London, 1998), pp. 131–48.

"The Palestinian Druze in the 1947–49 Arab–Israeli War" *Israel Studies* 2/1 (1997) 72–93.

Qasimiyya, Khayriyya al-, *Raʿil al-ʿarabi al-awal: hayat wa awraq Nabih wa ʿAdil al-ʿAzma* [The First Arab Vanguard: The Lives and Papers of Nabih and ʿAdil al-ʿAzma] (London, 1991).

Qasri, Muhammad Fa'iz al-, *Harb filastin, 'am 1948* [The Palestine War of 1948], vol. II (Damascus, 1962, and Cairo, 1971).

Qawuqji, Fawzi al-, *Filastin fi mudhakkirat Fawzi al-Qawuqji* [Palestine in the Memoirs of Fawzi al-Qawuqji] vol. II, ed. Khayriyya Qasimiyya (Beirut, 1975).

Rayyis, Munir al-, *Al-Kitab al-dhahabi li'l-thawrat al-wataniyya* [The Golden Book of National Revolts] (Beirut, 1977).

Reiter, Yitzhak, *Islamic Endowments in Jerusalem under British Mandate* (London, 1996).

Roubicek, Marcel, *Echo of the Bugle: Extinct Military and Constabulary Forces in Palestine and Transjordan, 1915–1967* (Jerusalem, 1974).

Rusan, Mamduh al-, *Ma'arik bab al-wad* [The Battles of Bab al-Wad] (Amman, n.d.).

  'Iraq wa qadaya al-sharq al-'arabi al-qawmiyya [Iraq and the Nationalist Causes of the Arab East] (Beirut, 1979).

Safa, Muhammad, *Asrar al-inqilabat fi suriya: tashih li-za'im mu'ali Akram al-Hawrani* [The Secrets of the Syrian Coups: A Correction to the Eminent Leader Akram al-Hawrani] (n.p., n.d.).

Said, Edward W., *Out of Place* (London and New York, 1999).

Sa'id, Khalil, *Tarikh al-jaysh al-'iraqi fi filastin 1948–1949* [History of the Iraqi Army in Palestine 1948–1949] (Baghdad, 1969).

Salibi, Kamal, *A Modern History of Jordan* (London, 1993).

Sayigh, Anis, *Al-Hashimiyun wa qadiyya filastin* [The Hashemites and the Palestine Problem] (Beirut, 1966).

Sayigh, Rosemary, *Too Many Enemies* (London, 1994).

Sayigh, Yezid, *Armed Struggle and the Search for State: The Palestinian National Movement, 1949–1993* (Oxford, 1997).

Schectman, Joseph, *The Mufti and the Fuhrer: The Rise and Fall of Haj Amin el-Husseini* (New York, 1965).

Schleifer, S. Abdullah, "The Life and Thought of 'Izz-id-Din al-Qassam," *The Islamic Quarterly* 22 (1979) 61–81.

Schulze, Kirsten E., *Israel's Covert Diplomacy in Lebanon* (London, 1998).

Seale, Patrick, *The Struggle for Syria: A Study of Post-War Arab Politics, 1945–1958* (London, 1965, new edn London, 1986).

Segev, Tom, *1949: The First Israelis* (New York, 1986).

Seikaly, May, *Haifa: Transformation of an Arab Society, 1918–1939* (London, 1995).

Sela, Avraham, "Arab Historiography of the 1948 War: The Quest for Legitimacy," in Laurence J. Silberstein, ed., *New Perspectives on Israeli History: The Early Years of the State* (New York, 1991), pp. 124–154.

  "Transjordan, Israel and the 1948 War: Myth, Historiography and Reality," *Middle Eastern Studies* 28 (1992) 623–88.

Shahin, Hanna, *"Al-Muwajaha al-isra'iliyya al-'arabiyya al-ula, 1948, wa atharaha 'ala wadh al-sha'b al-filastini"* [The First Arab–Israeli Confrontation and its Impact on the Palestinian People] *Shu'un Filistiniyya* 109 (December 1980).

Shakib, Ibrahim, *Harb filastin, 1948, ru'iya masriyya* [The Palestine War, 1948: An Egyptian Perspective] (Cairo, 1986).

Shapira, Anita, "Politics and Collective Memory: The Debate over the 'New Historians' in Israel," *History and Memory* 7 (1995) 9–40.

Shara'a, Sadiq al-, *Hurubuna ma' isra'il, 1947–1973* [Our Wars with Israel] (Amman, 1997).

Sharett, Moshe, *Besha'ar ha-umot, 1946–1949* [At the Gate of the Nations, 1946–1949] (Tel Aviv, 1958).

Sharif, Kamil Isma'il al-, *Al-Ikhwan al-muslimun fi harb filastin* [The Muslim Brothers in the Palestine War] (Cairo, 1951).

Shlaim, Avi, *Collusion across the Jordan: King Abdullah, the Zionist Movement, and the Partition of Palestine* (Oxford and New York, 1988).

    The Politics of Partition (Oxford, 1998).

    "The Debate About 1948," *IJMES* 27 (1995) 287–304.

    "The Rise and Fall of the All-Palestine Government in Gaza," *Journal of Palestine Studies*, 20/1 (1990) 37–53.

Sivan, Emmanuel, *Mythes Politiques Arabes* (Paris, 1995).

Smith, Barbara, *The Roots of Separation in Palestine: British Economic Policy, 1920–1929* (Syracuse NY, 1995).

Sternhell, Zeev, *The Founding Myths of Israel: Nationalism, Socialism, and the Making of the Jewish State* (Princeton NJ, 1998).

Tadros, Noha, '*Min dhikrayat al-madi*, Souvenirs: Autobiographie et representation de soi. 'Issa al 'Issa (journaliste Palestinien 1878–1950)," (Ph.D. dissertation, Institut National des Langues et Civilisations Orientales, Paris, 1999).

Tall, 'Abdullah al-, *Karithat filastin* [The Catastrophe of Palestine] (Cairo, 1958, new edn 1959).

Tayi, Ahmed Faraj, *Safahat matwiya 'an filastin* [Forgotten Pages on Palestine] (Cairo, 1967).

Teveth, Shabtai, "Charging Israel with Original Sin," *Commentary* (September, 1989).

Tsur, Jacob, *Zionism: The Saga of a National Liberation Movement* (New York, 1977).

Weizmann, Chaim, *Trial and Error: The Autobiography of Chaim Weizmann* (London, 1949).

Wilson, Mary, *King 'Abdullah, Britain and the Making of Jordan* (Cambridge, 1987).

Windawi, Mouayad Ibrahim K. al-, "Anglo-Iraqi Relations 1945–1958" (Ph.D. dissertation, University of Reading, 1989).

Yazbak, Mahmoud, *Haifa in the Late Ottoman Period, 1864–1914: A Muslim Town in Transition* (Leiden, 1998).

Zu'aytir, Akram, *Al-Haraka al-wataniyya al-filistiniyya, 1935–1939: yawmiyyat Akram Zu'aytir* [The Palestinian National Movement, 1935–1939: The Diaries of Akram Zu'aytir] (Beirut, 1980).

Zurayk, Constantine, *Ma'nat al-nakba* [The Meaning of the Catastrophe] (Beirut, 1948).

    The Meaning of the Disaster, R. Bayley Winder, tr. (Beirut, 1956).

Index

Cambridge Middle East Studies 15